THE

MERMAID

SERIES

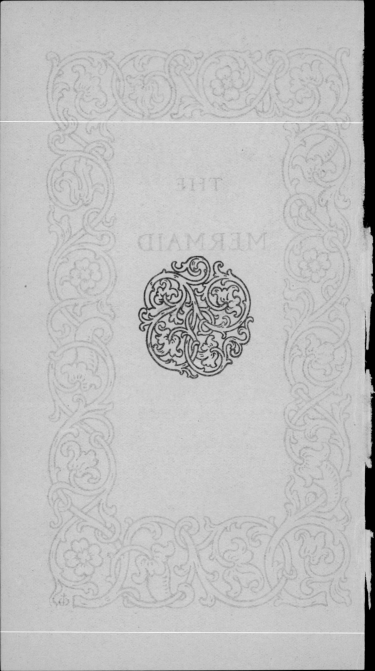

GEORGE CHAPMAN

THE MERMAID SERIES

Literal Reproductions of the Old Text, with etched Frontispieces.

Other Volumes in Preparation

Conscium Evasi diem.

George Chapman.

GEORGE CHAPMAN

1559- 1634

EDITED, WITH AN INTRODUCTION AND NOTES

BY

WILLIAM LYON PHELPS

M.A. (*Harvard*), *Ph.D.* (*Yale*)

INSTRUCTOR IN ENGLISH LITERATURE AT YALE COLLEGE

"I lie and dream of your full Mermaid wine."—*Beaumont*

LONDON
T. FISHER UNWIN

NEW YORK
CHARLES SCRIBNER'S SONS

> " What things have we seen
> Done at the Mermaid ! heard words that have been
> So nimble, and so full of subtle flame,
> As if that every one from whence they came
> Had meant to put his whole wit in a jest,
> And had resolved to live a fool the rest
> Of his dull life."
>
> *Master Francis Beaumont to Ben Jonson.*

> " Souls of Poets dead and gone,
> What Elysium have ye known,
> Happy field or mossy cavern,
> Choicer than the Mermaid Tavern ? "
>
> *Keats.*

PREFATORY NOTE

HE text of this edition has been carefully taken from the literal reprint of Chapman's plays, published by John Pearson in 1873. The spelling has been modernised, and the punctuation altered to fit the sense ; here I have been helped by R. H. Shepherd's edition, though I have often found it advisable to differ from that. I have had to insert many stage directions, to account for the presence and absence of characters ; and for three plays I have had to make lists of the *dramatis personæ.*

It was not altogether easy to select "best plays" of Chapman for publication, but I finally decided on *All Fools* as his best comedy, the D'Ambois plays as most characteristic, and the Byron series as the best examples of "that full and heightened style" which Webster admired. It is hoped that this edition of Chapman, containing the only comfortably readable text, will be found useful not merely in University courses, but for general purposes.

W. L. P.

YALE COLLEGE, NEW HAVEN, U.S.A.,
June 19, 1895.

CONTENTS

GEORGE CHAPMAN

THE life of Chapman includes practically that whole period of literature known as the Elizabethan drama. He was born before *Gorboduc* and *Gammer Gurton's Needle*; when *Tamburlaine* appeared, he was nearly thirty; he survived Shakspere, Beaumont, Middleton, and Fletcher; every important play of the age was acted during his lifetime. He thus had the opportunity to watch the rise, fruition, and decay of what has been justly called the greatest part of the greatest period of the greatest literature of the world; a tremendous superlative that will be questioned only by those who have not read the material it describes.

Although 1557 is often given as the year of Chapman's birth, we learn, with presumable accuracy, from the circular inscription on his portrait, that he was born in 1559. His birthplace was, in all probability, Hitchin, a town in the northern part of Hertfordshire, thirty - four miles from London. His education was obtained at Oxford, and all indications point to his having also been a student at Cambridge. At Oxford he made something of a reputation as a classical scholar ; and our respect for him is not diminished when we are told that he had a contempt for logic and philosophy. The method of teaching metaphysics at that time was almost sure to arouse repugnance, if not rebellion, in any mind endowed with originality or common sense. So Chapman, who is certainly the most metaphysical of all Elizabethan dramatists, must have cultivated that part of his nature with little help from the University curriculum.

From his graduation to the year 1594, we know nothing of his life ; we can only conjecture. But it is probable that he spent some time in Continental travel ; possibly in France and Italy almost certainly in Germany, if the familiarity with that tongue displayed in *Alphonsus* is at all significant. In 1594 he published *The Shadow of Night*, " containing two poetical hymns."

It is impossible to ascertain at what exact time he joined the London playwright group, and became a professional writer for the stage. It was probably about 1595 or 1596, for in 1598 he had an established reputation. In that year he is mentioned among the well-known dramatists, in the famous enumeration of Francis Meres. His first extant comedy, *The Blind Beggar of Alexandria*, was produced on February 12, 1596. From every point of view, it is absolutely worthless. In 1599 was published his next comedy, *An Humorous Day's Mirth*, which unfortunately shows scarcely any improvement on the other.

The work on which Chapman's fame principally depends is, of course, his translation of Homer. The first portion of this appeared in 1598 : *Seaven Bookes of the Iliades of Homer, Prince of Poets. Translated according to the Greeke in judgement of his best Commentaries.* In translating he used the fourteen syllabled rime, which more nearly expresses the Greek hexameter than any other English measure. In 1611 the complete translation of the *Iliad* was published, and by 1615 the whole of the *Odyssey*, which was written in the heroic couplet. Although many critics have judged Chapman's Homer to be the finest English translation ever made, it may more properly be ranked as an original work—a great Elizabethan classic. It has not only immortalised Chapman, but it must stand as one of the noblest monuments of the golden age of English literature.

In 1605 two remarkable plays appeared ; Chapman's comic masterpiece, *All Fools*, and the spirited comedy *Eastward Ho*, composed by Chapman, Marston, and Ben Jonson. The three men must have been expert judges of each other's literary faults ; for their joint production is singularly free from their individual defects. The play is not marred by Jonson's customary verbosity and pedantry, nor by Marston's disgusting vulgarity, nor by Chapman's obscurity and formlessness. Some remarks in it deemed uncomplimentary to King James caused Chapman and Marston to be sent to prison ; whither Jonson, with that touch of *noblesse* hat makes us forget all his faults, volun-

tarily accompanied them. All three were shortly
released.

The play *All Fools* has been identified with *The
World Runs on Wheels*, which Chapman wrote in
1599, and which was acted the same year. The
name was changed to *All Fools but the Fool*, and
then to *All Fools*. The influence of Ben Jonson is
discernible in two ways ; in the complete cynicism
which pervades the play, and in the characters,
many of whom are simply humour-studies. But—
a rare thing in Chapman—we find a real plot ;
artificial, over-subtle, too ingenious, perhaps, but
steadily moving forward to a climax. The play
abounds in excellent scenes ; and the fun lies fully
as much in the situations as in the characters ; a
skilful combination of two forms of comedy. It
impresses one as particularly well adapted for the
stage ; but it would require a constellation of actors,
since nearly every character has more than one
good chance.

The Gentleman Usher (1606) has been extrava-
gantly praised by some of Chapman's admirers.
It is an entirely different class of work from *All
Fools ;* that was a realistic satire, this is a romantic
poem. But although it contains some beautiful
scenes—such as the betrothal of Vincentio and
Margaret—it lacks almost every qualification of
a good play. In construction it is slipshod and
slovenly ; the plot is worthless ; and the improba-
bilities do not seem to be presented with any
attempt at verisimilitude. Then the characterisation is poor—vague in the extreme ; the person-

ages are all shadowy and unreal, so common a fault in Chapman's comedies; it is impossible to grasp or to retain them.

The same year (1606) another comedy, *Monsieur D'Olive*, appeared. This play opens surprisingly well; the first scenes and speeches have the true Elizabethan ring; they are full of life and spirit. But just as the reader's expectations have been raised to a high pitch, the play weakens, wanders aimlessly awhile, and then loses itself in a dreary Sahara of verbosity.

The year 1607 brings us to the first of Chapman's remarkable group of French tragedies— *Bussy D'Ambois*. Here is an instance of the Elizabethan drama figuring in one of its most important capacities, the nearest analogy to which is the modern newspaper. Chapman selected material that was practically contemporary, arranged it in dramatic form, and presented it to the English groundlings and gallery goddesses. As to the reasons which led him to use this material, we are wholly in the dark; but his dramatic methods in using it are still more difficult to understand. The ordinary motive in arranging foreign matter for the delectation of the pit is clear enough; it was to inflame patriotic feeling, by exhibiting French and Spanish Roman Catholics in most unenviable situations.[1] But Chapman apparently had no such purpose; to be sure he introduces some flattering speeches concerning England and Elizabeth; but, wonderful

[1] As, for example, Middleton's *Game at Chess*.

to relate, the Duke of Guise, whose name to an
English Protestant was symbolical of everything
particularly fiendish, is represented as something of
a hero ; and such a portrayal, to a demonstrative
audience which had no difficulty in remembering St Bartholomew's Day, is sufficiently remarkable.   There is not only no attempt to make
political capital, but there is almost too obvious a
scorn of public opinion.   Furthermore, no pains
are taken to insure historical accuracy; in the
Byron plays, we find, as we expect to find, the
greatest of all French kings, Henry of Navarre,
represented as exactly a model of what a sovereign
should be ; but we are no less surprised in the
D'Ambois series to find his wretched predecessor,
Henry III., almost equally admirable.   Taken
together, these four plays are unique in English
literature.

Chapman drew his material mainly from De
Thou ; [1] but in the D'Ambois plays he uses him
very little, whereas in the Byron series he follows
him fairly closely.   The two D'Ambois plays are
entirely separate and distinct.   The first, published
in 1607, contains, as almost every critic has had
occasion to remark, the best and the worst of
Chapman's work.   The hero is after the school of
Tamburlaine ; a bold, glorious braggart, quick-
witted, loud-mouthed (Modesty was not an Eliza-

[1] *Historiæ sui temporis*, by Jacque-Auguste De Thou (Thuanus) ;
the standard edition is in 14 vols., London, 1733. The French
translation, *Histoire Universelle*, is in 16 vols., London, 1734, with
a remarkably copious analytical index, by the aid of which one can
easily compare any scene in Chapman with its original.

bethan virtue), sword always loose in scabbard
and whose love choices sublimely overlooked the
ordinary obstacle of a husband. In love and war,
is alike invincible; and is finally overcome only
treachery.

mall wonder is it, that with a play containing
much gold and so much dross, critics have
d widely in their estimation of its worth,
ding as its faults and virtues have been
most in their minds.[1] Dryden, and after
undred years of criticism Dryden is still
listening to, gives no uncertain sound; in
lication to *The Spanish Friar* (1681), he
have sometimes wondered, in the reading,
become of those glaring colours which
ne in *Bussy D'Ambois* upon the th
I had taken up what I supposed a
, I found I had been cozened with a
hing but a cold, dull mass, which
longer than it was shooting; a
ssed up in gigantic words,
oseness of expression

o burn a *D'Ambois* annually to the memory of Jonson."[1] It is important to remember that these are the words, not only of a truly great critic, but of a man who had seen and judged the play from a seat in the theatre. Skilfully acted before a crowded and enthusiastic house, Dryden had joined heartily in the applause; then, taking up the work in cold blood, and finding it full of fustian and bombast, he felt that he had been deceived under false pretences; for his language in

s quotation is ... that of a man who thinks he has been imposed up , and is determined t give vent to his righteous wrath. His expressio "glittered no longer than it was shooting," evident means that Bussy was more effective on the sta the closet. That a man like Dryd should find such a tragedy better to see than read, is to our stage notions almost incompreh sible; but his impressions furnish additional pr of the real stage effectiveness of many Elizabe plays that could not draw to d *The Revenge of Bus* has little family resemblance to his brother. Bussy is like Tamburlaine, but Clermont suggests Hamlet. He resembles the melancholy Dane not only in his powers of reflection, and in his innate good breeding, but in his constant postponement of revenge.

The D'Ambois plays belong distinctly to the Tragedy of Blood, and in a dim way foreshadow the decay of the drama. The repeated stabbing and torture of Tamyra before the eyes of the audience, the letter written in her blood, the gloomy vault and the presence of ghosts of murdered men, together with all the conventional machinery of the melodrama, are the regular features of that curious development of Blood Tragedies, which began with *The Spanish Tragedy* and *Titus Andronicus*, which affected Shakspere, Marlowe, Middleton, Ford, Tourneur, which reached a grand climax in Webster, and which survives to-day in cheap sensational theatres. For as truly as the Elizabethan drama descended from the Mysteries, so truly does our present melodrama come from the noisy Tragedy of Blood.

Chapman's tragedies indicate the decay of the drama in their search for the horrible, in their public display of physical anguish, and in their free use of ghosts. The introduction of the supernatural element greatly mars these two plays; for instead of giving colour and atmosphere, as in *Macbeth*, it is here too evidently superfluous. Ghosts are causelessly dragged in, and form not an integral, but wholly an incidental, feature; their

entrances and exits are so clumsily managed, that
they not only utterly fail to impress us with
horror, but make it difficult for us to swallow a
guffaw.[1]

Although the D'Ambois plays are most distinctly the characteristic works of their author, and
are most essential to a thorough understanding of
him, the two Byron dramas are by many considered Chapman's masterpieces of tragedy. In
sustained power, they are certainly superior to the
D'Ambois pair; for although, as is so often the
case in Chapman, action and movement play a
subordinate part to poetry and declamation, there
is more of the steadily good and less of the absolutely bad than in any other of his dramatic
works. There are, perhaps, fewer magnificent
outbursts; but there is distinctly less rubbish.
These two plays are not by any means separate,
like the D'Ambois dramas; they make one tragedy
in ten acts, without a break in the thought. More-
over, they are much more nearly contemporary
than the chronicles of D'Ambois; the Duke Biron
was executed in 1602, and Chapman's two plays,
although published in 1608, were written about
1605. The friendship of King Henry for his
proud favourite forms one of the most interesting
episodes in history; from a bare narrative of the
facts, up to the detailed account given by De Thou,

---

[1] Observe the stage direction in *The Revenge*, act v., scene i.
"Music, and the Ghost of Bussy enters, leading the Ghosts of the
Guise, Monsieur, Cardinal Guise, and Chatillon; they dance about
the dead body, and exeunt."

any one may see for himself how admirable a subject it is for dramatic treatment. Unfortunately, Chapman has missed most of his opportunities; that wonderful instinct for dramatic situation, which led Webster to construct from a coarse narrative the splendid tragedy of *The Duchess of Malfi*, seems sadly lacking in Chapman. But the character of Byron he has fully grasped, and has given us in him one of the most striking figures of the Elizabethan drama. With a nature originally noble, but gradually tainted with pride and conceit, skilfully worked on by smiling pickthanks and base newsmongers, his better qualities perceptibly pass into eclipse, and the man's darkened soul stands forth with a certain Satanic grandeur. His magnificent speech after the interview with the magician is a noble succession of mighty lines, ending with a strong climax, in which we may plainly see through the Duke's mask the glowing eyes of Chapman himself.

> "Give me a spirit that on this life's rough sea
> Loves t'have his sails fill'd with a lusty wind,
> Even till his sail-yards tremble, his masks crack,
> And his rapt ship run on her side so low
> That she drinks water, and her keel plows air.
> There is no danger to a man that knows
> What life and death is ; there's not any law
> Exceeds his knowledge ; neither is it lawful
> That he should stoop to any other law.
> He goes before them, and commands them all,
> That to himself is a law rational."

The final death-scene in the *Tragedy* is another, fortunate example of how the clouds and mists that commonly envelop the soul of our great poet break away, and give him complete liberty of expression. The Duke, finally confronted with the actual presence of death, feels his wonted bravado forsaking him; he alternates between piteous supplication and reckless defiance, his soul torn with conflicting passions. There is but one scene similar to this which surpasses it, and that is the agonising cry of Browning's Guido as the executioners descend the stair.

> "Life is all!
> I was just stark mad,—let the madman live
> Pressed by as many chains as you please pile!
> Don't open! Hold me from them! I am yours,
> I am the Granduke's—no, I am the Pope's!
> Abate,—Cardinal,—Christ,—Maria,—God, . . .
> Pompilia, will you let them murder me?"

But Byron, unlike Guido, after writhing in agony, and vainly casting about for help or delay, finally succumbs in these splendid lines, in which in the last moment the strength of bitterness overcomes the horror of death.

> "And so farewell for ever. Nevermore
> Shall any hope of my revival see me.
> Such is the endless exile of dead men.
> Summer succeeds the spring; autumn the summer;
> The frosts of winter, the fall'n leaves of autumn;
> All these and all fruits in them yearly fade,
> And every year return; but cursed man
> Shall never more renew his vanish'd face.
>
> Strike, strike, O strike; fly, fly, commanding soul
> And on thy wings for this thy body's breath,
> Bear the eternal victory of death."

In 1611 Chapman returned to comedy in *May*

Day, a play of no value. If he had not written *The Blind Beggar of Alexandria* and *An Humorous Day's Mirth*, we might class this as the worst of his productions. *The Widow's Tears* (1612) is far superior, but still not a real success. It has some genuine force, some dramatic situations, and some powerful speeches; but the interest is not well sustained. Furthermore, it is flavoured by a combination of coarseness and cynicism, which leaves a most disagreeable impression.

From 1613 to 1631 we hear nothing of Chapman's writing for the stage; in Jonson's life there is a similar, but not so lengthy, dramatic hiatus. Chapman was busied with other matters, and apparently let the stage alone. In 1631, however, he published *The Tragedy of Cæsar and Pompey*, to which he prefixed an interesting dedication, whence we learn that the play had never been acted. Chapman evidently thought this a superior literary performance; but it adds scarcely any lustre to his name. The character that seems chiefly to have interested him is Cato, into whose mouth is put many reflective dissertations. There are some finely poetical lines, which Lamb included in his *Specimens*.

Twenty years after Chapman's death, two additional tragedies of his first saw the light. These are *Alphonsus, Emperor of Germany*, and *Revenge for Honour*, both published in 1654. The first is interesting for the knowledge of the German language and customs which it shows; some have accounted for this on the hypothesis that he was

assisted by a German writer, but it seems more
probable that Chapman had obtained the necessary
knowledge by travel in Germany.[1] *Revenge for
Honour* is clearly superior to *Alphonsus ;* and by
the number of feminine endings, it has been
generally assigned to a late period in Chapman's
life. It is sufficiently sanguinary to claim a place
in the Tragedy of Blood.

Three plays, partly written by Chapman, may
be included in a complete list of his dramatic
works; the excellent comedy of *Eastward Ho*,
already discussed; *The Ball* (1639), by Chapman
and Shirley, a comedy in no way remarkable; and
one more French tragedy, *Philip Chabot, Admiral
of France* (1639), also written by the same two
authors. The impossibility, in spite of confident
guesses, of discovering what parts were written by
Chapman and what by Shirley, make a discussion
of the merits of these plays unnecessary, in so
short a space as we have at our command.

Just one masque by Chapman is extant. *The
Memorable Maske of the two Honorable Houses or
Inns of Court ; the Middle Temple and Lyncolns
Inne.* This was performed at Whitehall, in February 1614. It was given in the most lavish and
magnificent style. Chapman must have written
other pieces that are now lost, in order to justify
Jonson's egotistical compliment, that "next himself, only Fletcher and Chapman could make a
masque."

---

[1] See Karl Elze's edition of this play for a thorough discussion
both of its merits and of the questions it suggests.

On May 12, 1634, Chapman died, and was buried in St. Giles's churchyard. A monument was erected over his grave by the famous architect Inigo Jones, which still remains standing. The personal character of Chapman seems to have been highly respectable; and he numbered among his friends some of the most prominent men of the day.

Chapman's fame as a translator of Homer has unduly exalted his merits as a dramatist; he is to-day one of the best-known names in the Elizabethan drama, but an unbiassed study of his work for the stage will show that as a dramatist he has been vastly over-rated.[1] Compare the relative importance of the names of Chapman and Dekker; but is there a single play of the former that we would exchange for *The Honest Whore* or *The Shoemaker's Holiday*? Dekker has suffered from neglect; Chapman has more reputation than his plays will justify. Far be it from one who assumes as a labour of love the task of editing Chapman, to decry his virtues or to be wilfully blind to the inspiration of his splendid verse; but in judging him as a dramatist, we must judge him by those qualities essential to successful dramatic work. In epic, in narrative, in descriptive poetry, he is all and more than we could wish; but only one of his plays, *All Fools*, is well constructed, and many of them are indescribably poor. His form-

---

[1] Presumptuous as it may sound, I cannot help feeling that Mr Swinburne, Professor Ward, and Mr Lowell have all greatly over-rated Chapman.

lessness and weakness as a playwright have never
been sufficiently estimated; and the infinite
verbosity of his plays has caused much needless
suffering to patient readers.

In a review of Chapman's fourteen extant
dramas—seven comedies and seven tragedies—the
quality that seems most prominent is his subtlety
of thought. In psychological analysis of character
he is weak; but his strength in philosophical
reflection is so evident, even to himself, that he
can seldom resist a temptation to this indulgence.
A comparison of Marlowe's famous apostrophe to
beauty, beginning

> "If all the pens that ever poets held," [1]

with Chapman's treatment of the same subject, is
certainly suggestive.

> " And what is beauty? A mere quintessence,
>   Whose life is not in being, but in seeming ;
>   And therefore is not to all eyes the same,
>   But like a cozening picture, which one way
>   Shows like a crow, another like a swan." [2]

Aspiration is the key-note in Marlowe; in
Chapman it is Reflection. And although his genius
for meditation often gives us splendid passages, as
in *The Revenge of Bussy D'Ambois* and in *Cæsar
and Pompey*, it must be confessed that it is as
much a defect in his dramas as was Jonson's
pedantry. We should remember in reading
Chapman that he did not begin to write for the

---

[1] *Tamburlaine*, act v., scene i.
[2] *All Fools*, act i., scene i.

stage until he was nearly forty years old ; by that
time the hey-day of the imagination is past; we
naturally look, not for spontaneous bursts of
glorious poetry, but for more sober thought. The
fire of youth, which illumines all Marlowe's dramas,
is absent from Chapman's. Furthermore, next to
Jonson, he was the most learned of all Elizabethan
dramatists ; and while his pedantry is by no means
so obtrusive as Jonson's, he undoubtedly had much
more learning than was sufficient for the composition of a good play. His dramas all show an utter
lack of spontaneity ; the glory of Marlowe, the
freshness of Heywood, the joyousness of Dekker—
we search in vain for these qualities in Chapman.

In characterisation he is painfully weak. He
never loses himself in his characters, like Shakspere and Middleton ; he tries faithfully to do so,
but cannot succeed. The splendid speeches in his
tragedies have often no reference to the person
who speaks them ; they are all Chapman's own,
and distributed indifferently. In reading his
comedies, one always has to keep a finger on the
list of *dramatis personæ ;* the names mean nothing
to us, and we forget them with mournful swiftness.
Mr Lowell remarked that the coarseness of his
plays was a kind of wilful coarseness, not natural ;
the people do not talk like genuine low-lived
characters, as in the plays of Dekker, but rather
as Chapman thought they ought to talk. In the
passion of love Chapman is sometimes as bad as
Cowley ; he masters all the apparatus of passion,
carefully works himself into a frenzy, and talks

loudly; but we do not hear the language of the heart.

Although Chapman's tragedies must rank as literature much higher than his comedies, he was too self-conscious and too deliberate to fully succeed in tragic art. His statement in the dedication to *The Revenge of Bussy D'Ambois*, that "material instruction, elegant and sententious excitation to virtue, [1] and deflection from her contrary, being the soul, limbs and limits of an authentical tragedy," is sufficient to wreck any play that faithfully follows such doctrine. And with the exception of some notable scenes where Chapman burst his bonds of learning and self-conceit, and spoke out loud and bold, his tragedies often suggest premeditated fury. He feels that he ought to assume the grand style, and so, though not in the least excited himself, he makes his characters attitudinise and saw the air, while in this storm of declamation, passion is calmly sleeping. This is the chief reason why so many of Chapman's characters are not convincing.

But the great difficulty with Chapman's style is his obscurity. He is the only Elizabethan dramatist who is really obscure. Ben Jonson often requires the closest attention; but in the words of Schopenhauer, Chapman wrote lines "to which the mind in vain torments itself to attach any meaning." His obscurity is two-fold: he often needs Falstaff's brand of sherris-sack, which "ascends

---

[1] However much we admire Chapman's personality, is there not a touch of hypocritical cant here? How about the "sententious excitation to virtue" in *Revenge for Honour?* May we not condemn Chapman out of his own mouth?

me into the brain ; dries me there all the foolish and dull and crudy vapours which environ it ;" and, in the second place, besides his misty intellect, he unfortunately has some impediment in his speech, which makes articulation difficult, if not impossible. He is plainly tongue-tied ; many times he begins a passage grandly, and then unexpectedly gets into those "no thoroughfares" that wrought such trouble with Dickens's parliamentary orator. When the mighty spirit of Chapman—for he had a mighty spirit—does get the better of its environment, and finds its true voice, we are swept along resistless on the rushing torrent. At its worst, Chapman's thorny style leads us into a great wood ; at its best, it has a deep-sea quality, now a succession of rolling swells, and now infinitely calm, "too full for sound and foam." It is at such times that we fully understand Webster's acknowledgment of how much he had learned from "that full and heightened style of Master Chapman."

Chapman's intellectual kinship to Ben Jonson is sufficiently obvious. The two men stand somewhat apart from their fellows. Both were proud, contemptuous of public opinion, self-conscious, and somewhat burdened with a sense of their own importance ; both were scholars and theorists ; both satirists, lacking human sympathy ; both had strongly-marked personalities, highly respectable and not lovable. Jonson was Chapman's superior in stage-craft and in his lyrical gift ; but Jonson never reaches the "proud full sail" of Chapman's noblest verse. WM. LYON PHELPS.

ALL FOOLS

CHAPMAN'S play, *All Fools*, was acted in 1599, and published in 1605, memorable also as the year in which *Eastward Ho* appeared. The play was acted both at the Blackfriars Theatre and afterwards before King James. Although his best comedy, Chapman, in the dedication, calls it the "least allow'd birth" of his brain.

PROLOGUS

TO

MY LONG LOVED AND HONOURABLE FRIEND,

SIR THOMAS WALSINGHAM, KNIGHT.

HOULD I expose to every common eye,
    The least allow'd birth of my shaken brain;
    And not entitle it particularly
    To your acceptance, I were worse than vain.
    And though I am most loth to pass your sight
With any such like mark of vanity;
Being mark'd with age for aims of greater weight,
And drown'd in dark death-ushering melancholy,
Yet lest by others' stealth it be imprest,
    Without my passport, patch'd with others' wit,
Of two enforced ills I elect the least;
    And so desire your love will censure it;
Though my old fortune keep me still obscure,
The light shall still bewray [1] my old love sure.

               [1] Betray.

PROLOGUS

THE fortune of a Stage (like Fortune's self),
    Amazéth greatest judgments; and none
    knows
    The hidden causes of those strange effects,
That rise from this Hell, or fall from this Heaven:
Who can show cause why your wits, that in aim
At higher object, scorn to compose plays,
(Though we are sure they could, would they vouchsafe
    it,)
Should (without means to make) judge better far
Than those that make; and yet ye see they can.
For without your applause, wretched is he
That undertakes the Stage; and he's more blest,
That with your glorious favours can contest.

    Who can show cause why th' ancient Comic vein
Of Eupolis and Cratinus (now revived,
Subject to personal application)
Should be exploded by some bitter spleens?
Yet merely Comical and harmless jests
(Though ne'er so witty) be esteem'd but toys,
If void of th' other satyrism's sauce?

    Who can show cause why quick Venerian jests
Should sometimes ravish? sometimes fall far short
Of the just length and pleasure of your ears?
When our pure dames think them much less obscene,
Than those that win your panegyric spleen?
But our poor dooms,[1] alas! you know are nothing

               [1] Judgments.

To your inspired censure; ever we
Must needs submit; and there's the mystery.
   Great are the gifts given to united heads,
To gifts, attire, to fair attire, the stage
Helps much; for if our other audience see
You on the stage depart before we end; [1]
Our wits go with you all, and we are fools.
So Fortune governs in these stage events;
That merit bears least sway in most contents.
Auriculas Asini quis non habet?
How we shall then appear, we must refer
To magic of your dooms, that never err.

  [1] The gallants who sat on the stage sometimes noisily left the
theatre in the midst of a play, to show their condemnation of it.

DRAMATIS PERSONÆ

GOSTANZO,

MARC ANTONIO, } Knights.

VALERIO, son to Gostanzo.

FORTUNIO, elder son to Marc Antonio.

RINALDO, the younger.

DARIOTTO,

CLAUDIO, } Courtiers

CORNELIO, a start-up Gentleman.

CURIO, a Page.

KYTE, a Scrivener.

FRANCIS POCK, a Surgeon.

GAZETTA, wife to Cornelio.

BELLANORA, daughter to Gostanzo.

GRATIANA, stolen wife to Valerio.

ALL FOOLS

ACT THE FIRST

SCENE I

Enter RINALDO, FORTUNIO, VALERIO.

I. Can one self cause, in subjects so alike
As you two are, produce effect so unlike?
One like the Turtle[a] all in mournful
strains,
Wailing his fortunes. Th' other like the Lark
Mounting the sky in shrill and cheerful notes;
Chanting his joys aspired, and both for love?
In one, love raiseth by his violent heat
Moist vapours from the heart into the eyes,
From whence they drown his breast in daily showers:
In th' other, his divided power infuseth
Only a temperate and most kindly warmth,
That gives life to those fruits of wit and virtue,
Which the unkind hand of an uncivil father
Had almost nipp'd in the delightsome blossom.

---

[a] Turtledove.

37

Fo. O, brother, love rewards our services
With a most partial and injurious hand,
If you consider well our different fortunes :
Valerio loves, and joys the dame he loves ;
I love, and never can enjoy the sight
Of her I love ; so far from conquering
In my desires' assault, that I can come
To lay no battery to the fort I seek,
All passages to it so strongly kept,
By strait guard of her father.

    Ri. I dare swear,
If just desert in love measured reward,
Your fortune should exceed Valerio's far ;
For I am witness (being your bedfellow)
Both to the daily and the nightly service
You do unto the deity of love,
In vows, sighs, tears, and solitary watches.
He never serves him with such sacrifice,
Yet hath his bow and shafts at his command :
Love's service is much like our humorous lords,
Where minions carry more than servitors,
The bold and careless servant still obtains ;
The modest and respective nothing gains ;
You never see your love unless in dreams,
He, Hymen puts in whole possession.
What different stars reign'd when your loves were
    born,
He forced to wear the willow, you the horn ?
But, brother, are you not ashamed to make
Yourself a slave to the base lord of love,
Begot of fancy, and of beauty born ?
And what is beauty ? a mere quintessence,
Whose life is not in being, but in seeming ;
And therefore is not to all eyes the same,

But like a cozening picture, which one way
Shows like a crow, another like a swan;
And upon what ground is this beauty drawn?
Upon a woman, a most brittle creature,
And would to God (for my part) that were all.

Fo. But tell me, brother, did you never love?

Ri. You know I did, and was beloved again,
And that of such a dame as all men deem'd
Honour'd and made me happy in her favours:
Exceeding fair she was not; and yet fair
In that she never studied to be fairer
Than Nature made her; beauty cost her nothing,
Her virtues were so rare, they would have made
An Ethiop beautiful: at least so thought
By such as stood aloof, and did observe her
With credulous eyes; but what they were indeed
I'll spare to blaze,[1] because I loved her once,
Only I found her such, as for her sake,
I vow eternal wars against their whole sex,
Inconstant shuttlecocks, loving fools, and jesters;
Men rich in dirt, and titles sooner won
With the most vile than the most virtuous;
Found true to none: if one amongst whole hundreds
Chance to be chaste, she is so proud withal,
Wayward and rude, that one of unchaste life
Is oftentimes approved a worthier wife:
Undressed, sluttish, nasty to their husbands,
Spunged up, adorned, and painted to their lovers:
All day in ceaseless uproar with their households,
If all the night their husbands have not pleased them;
Like hounds, most kind, being beaten and abused
Like wolves, most cruel, being kindliest used.

Fo. Fie, thou profanest the deity of their sex.

[1] Publish.

Ri. Brother, I read that Egypt heretofore
Had Temples of the richest frame on earth ;
Much like this goodly edifice of women :
With alabaster pillars were those Temples
Upheld and beautified, and so are women,
Most curiously glazed, and so are women,
Cunningly painted too, and so are women,
In outside wondrous heavenly, so are women ;
But when a stranger view'd those fanes within,
Instead of gods and goddesses, he should find
A painted fowl, a fury, or a serpent ;
And such celestial inner parts have women.

Va. Rinaldo, the poor fox that lost his tail,
Persuaded others also to lose theirs :
Thyself, for one perhaps that for desert
Or some defect in thy attempts refused thee,
Revilest the whole sex, beauty, love, and all :
I tell thee Love is Nature's second sun,
Causing a spring of virtues where he shines ;
And as without the sun, the world's great eye,
All colours, beauties, both of Art and Nature,
Are given in vain to men, so without love
All beauties bred in women are in vain ;
All virtues born in men lie buried,
For love informs them as the sun doth colours,
And as the sun, reflecting his warm beams
Against the earth, begets all fruits and flowers ;
So love, fair shining in the inward man,
Brings forth in him the honourable fruits
Of valour, wit, virtue, and haughty thoughts,
Brave resolution, and divine discourse :
Oh, 'tis the Paradise, the heaven of earth ;
And didst thou know the comfort of two hearts,
In one delicious harmony united,

As to joy one joy, and think both one thought,
Live both one life, and therein double life;
To see their souls met at an interview
In their bright eyes, at parley in their lips,
Their language, kisses: and to observe the rest,
Touches, embraces, and each circumstance
Of all love's most unmatched ceremonies;
Thou wouldst abhor thy tongue for blasphemy.
Oh! who can comprehend how sweet love tastes
But he that hath been present at his feasts?

Ri. Are you in that vein too, Valerio?
'Twere fitter you should be about your charge,
How plow and cart goes forward; I have known
Your joys were all employ'd in husbandry,
Your study was how many loads of hay
A meadow of so many acres yielded,
How many oxen such a close would fat.
And is your rural service now converted
From Pan to Cupid? and from beasts to women?
Oh, if your father knew this, what a lecture
Of bitter castigation he would read you!

Va. My father? why, my father? does he think
To rob me of myself? I hope I know
I am a gentleman; though his covetous humour
And education hath transform'd me baily,[1]
And made me overseer of his pastures,
I'll be myself, in spite of husbandry.

Enter GRATIANA.

And see, bright heaven, here comes my husbandry.

[*Amplectitur eam.*

Here shall my cattle graze, here Nectar drink,
Here will I hedge and ditch, here hide my treasure:

[1] Bailiff.

O poor Fortunio, how wouldst thou triumph,
If thou enjoy'd'st this happiness with my sister!

Fo. I were in heaven if once 'twere come to that.

Ri. And methinks 'tis my heaven that I am past it.
And should the wretched Machiavellian,
The covetous knight, your father, see this sight,
Lusty Valerio?

Va. 'Sfoot, sir, if he should,
He shall perceive ere long my skill extends
To something more than sweaty husbandry.

Ri. I'll bear thee witness, thou canst skill of dice,
Cards, tennis, wenching, dancing, and what not?
And this is something more than husbandry:
Th'art known in ordinaries, and tobacco-shops,
Trusted in taverns and in vaulting-houses,
And this is something more than husbandry.
Yet all this while, thy father apprehends[1] thee
For the most tame and thrifty groom in Europe.

Fo. Well, he hath ventured on a marriage,
Would quite undo him, did his father know it.

Ri. Know it? Alas, sir, where can he bestow
This poor gentlewoman he hath made his wife,
But his inquisitive father will hear of it?
Who, like the dragon to th' Hesperian fruit,
Is to his haunts? 'Slight hence, the old knight
    comes.

Intrat GOSTANZO.   *Omnes aufugiunt.*

Go. Rinaldo.

Ri. Who's that calls? What, Sir Gostanzo?
How fares your knighthood, sir?

Go. Say, who was that
Shrunk at my entry here? was't not your brother?

---

[1] Takes.

Ri. He shrunk not, sir; his business call'd him
    hence.

Go. And was it not my son that went out with
    him?

Ri. I saw not him; I was in serious speech
About a secret business with my brother.

Go. Sure 'twas my son; what made he here? I
    sent him
About affairs to be dispatch'd in haste.

Ri. Well, sir, lest silence breed unjust suspect,
I'll tell a secret I am sworn to keep,
And crave your honoured assistance in it.

Go. What is't, Rinaldo?

Ri. This, sir; 'twas your son.

Go. And what young gentlewoman graced their
    company?

Ri. Thereon depends the secret I must utter;
That gentlewoman hath my brother married.

Go. Married?   What is she?

Ri. 'Faith, sir, a gentlewoman;
But her unnourishing dowry must be told [1]
Out of her beauty.

Go. Is it true, Rinaldo?
And does your father understand so much?

Ri. That was the motion, sir, I was entreating
Your son to make to him, because I know
He is well spoken, and may much prevail
In satisfying my father, who much loves him,
Both for his wisdom and his husbandry.

Go. Indeed, he's one can tell his tale, I tell you,
And for his husbandry—

Ri. Oh, sir, had you heard
What thrifty discipline he gave my brother,

---

[1] Counted.

For making choice without my father's knowledge,
And without riches, you would have admired him.

 Go. Nay, nay, I know him well ; but what was it?

 Ri. That in the choice of wives men must respect
The chief wife, riches, that in every course
A man's chief load-star should shine out of riches ;
Love nothing heartily in this world but riches ;
Cast off all friends, all studies, all delights,
All honesty, and religion for riches ;
And many such, which wisdom sure he learn'd
Of his experient father ; yet my brother
So soothes his rash affection, and presumes
So highly on my father's gentle nature,
That he's resolved to bring her home to him,
And like enough he will.

 Go. And like enough
Your silly [1] father too, will put it up ;
An honest knight, but much too much indulgent
To his presuming children.

 Ri. What a difference
Doth interpose itself 'twixt him and you,
Had your son used you thus ?

 Go. My son, alas !
I hope to bring him up in other fashion,
Follows my husbandry, sets early foot
Into the world ; he comes not at the city,
Nor knows the city arts.

 Ri. But dice and wenching.   [*Aversus.*

 Go. Acquaints himself with no delight but getting,
A perfect pattern of sobriety,
Temperance and husbandry, to all my household ;
And what s his company, I pray? not wenches.

 Ri. Wenches? I durst be sworn he never smelt

      [1] Simple.

A wench's breath yet ; but methinks 'twere fit
You sought him out a wife.

 Go. A wife, Rinaldo?

He dares not look a woman in the face.

 Ri. 'Sfoot, hold him to one ; your son such a
 sheep?

 Go. 'Tis strange in earnest.

 Ri. Well, sir, though for my thriftless brother's
 sake,

I little care how my wrong'd father takes it,
Yet for my father's quiet, if yourself
Would join hands with your wise and toward son,
I should deserve it some way.

 Go. Good Rinaldo,

I love you and your father, but this matter
Is not for me to deal in ; and 'tis needless.
You say your brother is resolved, presuming
Your father will allow it.

   Enter MARC ANTONIO.

 Ri. See, my father !

Since you are resolute not to move him, sir,
In any case conceal the secret, [*Abscondit se.*
By way of an atonement let me pray you will.

 Go. Upon mine honour.

 Ri. Thanks, sir.

 Ma. God save thee, honourable Knight Gostanzo.

 Go. Friend Marc Antonio ! welcome ; and I think
I have good news to welcome you withal.

 Ri. He cannot hold.

 Ma. What news, I pray you, sir?

 Go. You have a forward, valiant, eldest son ;
But wherein is his forwardness and valour?

 Ma. I know not wherein you intend him so.

Go. Forward before, valiant behind, his duty;
That he hath dared before your due consent
To take a wife.

Ma. A wife, sir? what is she?

Go. One that is rich enough: her hair pure amber;
Her forehead mother of pearl, her fair eyes
Two wealthy diamants; her lips, mines of rubies;
Her teeth are orient pearl, her neck pure ivory.

Ma. Jest not, good sir, in an affair so serious;
I love my son, and if his youth reward me
With his contempt of my consent in marriage,
'Tis to be fear'd that his presumption builds not
Of his good choice, that will bear out itself;
And being bad, the news is worse than bad.

Go. What call you bad? is it bad to be poor?

Ma. The world accounts it so; but if my son
Have in her birth and virtues [1] held his choice
Without disparagement, the fault is less.

Go. Sits the wind there? Blows there so calm a
gale
From a contemned and deserved anger?
Are you so easy to be disobey'd?

Ma. What should I do? If my enamour'd son
Have been so forward, I assure myself
He did it more to satisfy his love
Than to incense my hate, or to neglect me.

Go. A passing kind construction! suffer this,
You ope him doors to any villany;
He'll dare to sell, to pawn, run ever riot,
Despise your love in all, and laugh at you.
And that knight's competency you have gotten
With care and labour, he with lust and idleness
Will bring into the stipend of a beggar——

[1] Accomplishments.

All to maintain a wanton whirligig,
Worth nothing more than she brings on her back,
Yet all your wealth too little for that back.
By heaven, I pity your declining state,
For, be assured, your son hath set his foot
In the right pathway to consumption :
Up to the heart in love ; and for that love
Nothing can be too dear his love desires :
And how insatiate and unlimited
Is the ambition and the beggarly pride
Of a dame hoised from a beggar's state
To a state competent and plentiful,
You cannot be so simple not to know.

   Ma. I must confess the mischief : but, alas !
Where is in me the power of remedy ?

    Go. Where?   In your just displeasure : cast him
       off,
Receive him not ; let him endure the use
Of their enforced kindness that must trust him
For meat and money, for apparel, house,
And everything belongs to that estate,
Which he must learn with want of misery,
Since pleasure and a full estate hath blinded
His dissolute desires.

   Ma. What should I do ?
If I should banish him my house and sight,
What desperate resolution might it breed
To run into the wars, and there to live
In want of competency, and perhaps
Taste th' unrecoverable loss of his chief limbs,
Which while he hath in peace, at home with me,
May, with his spirit, ransom his estate
From any loss his marriage can procure.

    Go. Is't true ?   No, let him run into the war,

And lose what limbs he can : better one branch
Be lopp'd away, than all the whole tree should perish :
And for his wants, better young want than old.
You have a younger son at Padua—
I like his learning well—make him your heir,
And let your other walk : let him buy wit
At's own charge, not at's father's ; if you lose him,
You lose no more than that was lost before ;
If you recover him, you find a son.

Ma. I cannot part with him.

Go. If it be so,
And that your love to him be so extreme,
In needful dangers ever choose the least :
If he should be in mind to pass the seas,
Your son Rinaldo (who told me all this)
Will tell me that, and so we shall prevent it.
If by no stern course you will venture that,
Let him come home to me with his fair wife ;
And if you chance to see him, shake him up,
As if your wrath were hard to be reflected,
That he may fear hereafter to offend
In other dissolute courses. At my house,
With my advice, and my son's good example,
Who shall serve as a glass for him to see
His faults, and mend them to his precedent,
I make no doubt but of a dissolute son
And disobedient, to send him home
Both dutiful and thrifty.

Ma. O, Gostanzo !
Could you do this, you should preserve yourself
A perfect friend of me, and me a son.

Go. Remember you your part, and fear not mine :
Rate him, revile him, and renounce him too :
Speak, can you do't, man ?

Ma. I'll do all I can.   [*Exit* MARC.

Go. Alas! good man, how nature overweighs him!

RINALDO *comes forth.*

Ri. God save you, sir.

Go. Rinaldo, all the news
You told me as a secret, I perceive
Is passing common; for your father knows it;
The first thing he related was the marriage.

Ri. And was extremely moved?

Go. Beyond all measure:
But I did all I could to quench his fury:
Told him how easy 'twas for a young man
To run that amorous course: and though his choice
Were nothing rich, yet she was gently born,
Well qualified, and beautiful. But he still
Was quite relentless, and would needs renounce him.

Ri. My brother knows it well, and is resolved
To trail a pike in field, rather than bide
The more fear'd push of my vex'd father's fury.

Go. Indeed, that's one way: but are no more means
Left to his fine wits, than t'incense his father
With a more violent rage, and to redeem
A great offence with greater?

Ri. So I told him:
But to a desperate mind all breath is lost.

Go. Go to, let him be wise, and use his friends,
Amongst whom I'll be foremost, to his father:
Without this desperate error he intends
Join'd to the other; I'll not doubt to make him
Easy return into his father's favour;
So he submit himself, as duty binds him:
For fathers will be known to be themselves,

D

And often when their angers are not deep
Will paint an outward rage upon their looks.

Ri. All this I told him, sir ; but what says he?
" I know my father will not be reclaim'd,
He'll think that if he wink at this offence,
'Twill open doors to any villany.
I'll dare to sell, to pawn, and run all riot,
To laugh at all his patience, and consume
All he hath purchased to an honour'd purpose,
In maintenance of a wanton whirligig,
Worth nothing more than she wears on her back."

Go. The very words I used t'incense his father !
But, good Rinaldo, let him be advised :
How would his father grieve, should he be maim'd,
Or quite miscarry in the ruthless war?

Ri. I told him so ; but, " Better far," said he,
" One branch should utterly be lopp'd away,
Than the whole tree of all his race should perish ;
And for his wants, better young want than old."

Go. By heaven, the same words still I used to his
  father !
Why comes this about?   Well, good Rinaldo,
If he dare not endure his father's looks,
Let him and his fair wife come home to me,
Till I have qualified his father's passion.
He shall be kindly welcome, and be sure
Of all the intercession I can use.

Ri. I thank you, sir ; I'll try what I can do,
Although I fear me I shall strive in vain.

Go. Well, try him, try him.   [*Exit.*

Ri. Thanks, sir, so I will.
See, this old politic dissembling knight,
Now he perceives my father so affectionate,
And that my brother may hereafter live

By him and his, with equal use of either,
He will put on a face of hollow friendship.
But this will prove an excellent ground to sow
The seed of mirth amongst us ; I'll go seek
Valerio and my brother, and tell them
Such news of their affairs as they'll admire.[1]   [*Exit.*

Enter GAZETTA, BELLANORA, GRATIANA.

Ga. How happy are your fortunes above mine !
Both still being woo'd and courted ; still so feeding
On the delights of love, that still you find
An appetite to more ; where I am cloy'd,
And being bound to love-sports, care not for them.

Be. That is your fault, Gazetta ; we have loves,
And wish continual company with them
In honour'd marriage-rites, which you enjoy.
But seld' or never can we get a look
Of those we love.   Fortunio, my dear choice,
Dare not be known to love me, nor come near
My father's house ; where I as in a prison
Consume my lost days, and the tedious nights,
My father guarding me for one I hate.
And Gratiana here, my brother's love,
Joys him by so much stealth that vehement fear
Drinks up the sweetness of their stolen delights :
Where you enjoy a husband, and may freely
Perform all obsequies you desire to love.

Ga. Indeed I have a husband, and his love
Is more than I desire, being vainly jealous ;
Extremes, tho' contrary, have the like effects,
Extreme heat mortifies[2] like extreme cold ;
Extreme love breeds satiety as well
As extreme hatred ; and too violent rigour

---

[1] Wonder at.   [2] Kills.

Tempts chastity as much as too much licence;
There's no man's eye fix'd on me, but doth pierce
My husband's soul: If any ask my welfare,
He straight doubts treason practised to his bed:
Fancies but to himself all likelihoods
Of my wrong to him, and lays all on me
For certain truths; yet seeks he with his best
To put disguise on all his jealousy,
Fearing perhaps lest it may teach me that
Which otherwise I should not dream upon:
Yet lives he still abroad at great expense,
Turns merely [1] gallant from his farmer's state,
Uses all games and recreations;
Runs races with the gallants of the Court,
Feasts them at home, and entertains them costly,
And then upbraids me with their company.

Enter CORNELIO.

See, see, we shall be troubled with him now.

Co. Now, ladies, what plots have we now in hand?
They say, when only one dame is alone
She plots some mischief; but if three together,
They plot three hundred. Wife, the air is sharp,
Y'ad best to take the house, lest you take cold.

Ga. Alas! this time of year yields no such danger.

Co. Go in, I say; a friend of yours attends [2] you.

Ga. He is of your bringing, and may stay.

Co. Nay, stand not chopping logic; in, I pray.

Ga. Ye see, gentlewomen, what my happiness is,
These humours reign in marriage, humours, humours.

[*Exit, he followeth.*

Gr. Now by my sooth, I am no fortune-teller,
And would be loth to prove so; yet pronounce

---

[1] Absolutely.   [2] Waits for.

This at adventure,[1] that 'twere indecorum
This heifer should want horns.

  Be. Fie on this love !
I rather wish to want than purchase so.

  Gr. Indeed, such love is like a smoky fire
In a cold morning; though the fire be cheerful,
Yet is the smoke so sour and cumbersome,
'Twere better lose the fire than find the smoke:
Such an attendant then as smoke to fire,
Is jealousy to love; better want both
Than have both.

Enter VALERIO *and* FORTUNIO.

  Va. Come, Fortunio, now take hold
On this occasion, as myself on this:
One couple more would make a barley-break.[2]

  Fo. I fear, Valerio, we shall break too soon.
Your father's jealous spy-all will displease us.

  Va. Well, wench, the day will come his Argus eyes
Will shut, and thou shalt open: 'sfoot, I think
Dame Nature's memory begins to fail her;
If I write but my name in mercer's books,
I am as sure to have at six months' end,
A rascal at my elbow with his mace,
As I am sure my father's not far hence;
My father yet hath ought[3] Dame Nature debt,
These threescore years and ten, yet calls not on him;
But if she turn her debt-book over once,
And finding him her debtor, do but send
Her sergeant, John Death, to arrest his body,
Our souls shall rest, wench, then, and the free light

[1] Random.
[2] An old country game, played around grain stacks.
[3] Owed.

Shall triumph in our faces : where now night,
In imitation of my father's frowns,
Lowers at our meeting.

Enter RINALDO.

See where the scholar comes.

 Ri. Down on your knees, poor lovers, reverence
  learning.

 Fo. I pray thee, why, Rinaldo?

 Ri. Mark what cause

Flows from my depth of knowledge to your loves,
To make you kneel and bless me while you live.

 Va. I pray thee, good scholar, give us cause.

 Ri. Mark, then, erect your ears ; you know what
  horror

Would fly on your love from your father's frowns,
If he should know it.　And your sister here
(My brother's sweetheart) knows as well what rage
Would seize his powers for her, if he should know
My brother woo'd her, or that she loved him.
Is not this true? speak all.

 Omnes. All this is true.

 Ri. It is as true that now you meet by stealth,

In depth of midnight, kissing out at grates,
Climb over walls.　And all this I'll reform.

 Va. By logic?

 Ri. Well, sir, you shall have all means

To live in one house, eat and drink together,
Meet, and kiss your fills.

 Va. All this by learning?

 Ri. Ay, and your frowning father know all this.

 Va. Ay, marry, small learning may prove that.

 Ri. Nay, he shall know it, and desire it too,

Welcome my brother to him, and your wife,

Entreating both to come and dwell with him.
Is not this strange?

Fo. Ay, too strange to be true.

Ri. 'Tis in this head shall work it; therefore, hear:
Brother, this lady you must call your wife,
For I have told her sweetheart's father here
That she is your wife; and because my father,
(Who now believes it) must be quieted,
Before you see him, you must live awhile,
As husband to her, in his father's house.
Valerio, here's a simple mean for you
To lie at rack and manger with your wedlock,
And, brother, for yourself to meet as freely
With this your long-desired and barred love.

Fo. You make us wonder.

Ri. Peace; be ruled by me,
And you shall see to what a perfect shape
I'll bring this rude plot, which blind chance (the ape
Of council and advice) hath brought forth blind.
Valerio, can your heat of love forbear,
Before your father, and allow my brother
To use some kindness to your wife before him?

Va. Ay, before him, I do not greatly care,
Nor anywhere indeed; my sister here
Shall be my spy: if she will wrong herself,
And give her right to my wife, I am pleased.

Fo. My dearest life, I know, will never fear
Any such will or thought in all my powers.
When I court her, then, think I think 'tis thee;
When I embrace her, hold thee in mine arms:
Come, let us practise 'gainst [1] we see your father.

Va. Soft, sir; I hope you need not do it yet;
Let me take this time.

[1] Before.

Ri. Come, you must not touch her.

Va. No, not before my father.

Ri. No, nor now,
Because you are so soon to practise it,
For I must bring them to him presently.[1]
Take her, Fortunio ; go hence man and wife,
We will attend you rarely with fix'd faces.
Valerio, keep your countenance, and conceive
Your father in your forged sheepishness,
Who thinks thou darest not look upon a wench,
Nor know'st at which end to begin to kiss her.

[*Exeunt.*

[1] Immediately.

ACT THE SECOND

SCENE I

Gostanzo, Marc Antonio.

O. It is your own too simple lenity,
And doting indulgence shown to him
still, [1]
That thus hath taught your son to be no
son ;
As you have used him, therefore, so you have him :
Durst my son thus turn rebel to his duty,
Steal up a match unsuiting his estate,
Without all knowledge of a friend or father,
And, to make that good with a worse offence,
Adsolve [2] to run beyond sea to the wars ;
Durst my son serve me thus? Well, I have stay'd
him,
Though much against my disposition,
And this hour I have set for his repair
With his young mistress and concealed wife ;
And in my house, here, they shall sojourn both,
Till your black anger's storm be overblown.
Ma. My anger's storm? Ah, poor Fortunio,

[1] Always.   [2] Resolve.

57

One gentle word from thee would soon resolve
The storm of my rage to a shower of tears.

 Go. In that vein still? Well, Marc Antonio,
Our old acquaintance and long neighbourhood
Ties my affection to you, and the good
Of your whole house; in kind regard whereof
I have advised you, for your credit's sake,
And for the tender welfare of your son,
To frown on him a little; if you do not,
But at first parley take him to your favour,
I protest utterly to renounce all care
Of you and yours, and all your amities.
They say he's wretched that out of himself
Cannot draw counsel to his proper weal.
But he's thrice wretched that has neither counsel
Within himself, nor apprehension
Of counsel for his own good, from another.

 Ma. Well, I will arm myself against this weakness
The best I can. I long to see this Helen
That hath enchanted my young Paris thus,
And's like to set all our poor Troy on fire.

 Enter VALERIO *with a* Page. MARC *retires himself.*

 Go. Here comes my son. Withdraw, take up your
  stand;
You shall hear odds betwixt your son and mine.

 Va. Tell him I cannot do't; shall I be made
A foolish novice, my purse set a-broach [1]
By every cheating come-you-seven, [2] to lend
My money, and be laugh'd at? tell him plain
I profess husbandry, and will not play
The prodigal, like him, 'gainst my profession.

 Go. Here's a son.

   [1] Open.   [2] Gambler.

Ma. An admirable spark !

Page. Well, sir, I'll tell him so.   [*Exit* Page.

Va. 'Sfoot, let him lead
A better husband's life, and live not idly ;
Spending his time, his coin and self on wenches.

Go. Why, what's the matter, son ?

Va. Cry mercy, sir : why there comes messengers
From this and that brave gallant ; and such gallants
As I protest I saw but through a grate.

Go. And what's this message ?

Va. Faith, sir, he's disappointed
Of payments ; and disfurnish'd of means present ;
If I would do him the kind office therefore
To trust him but some seven-night with the keeping
Of forty crowns for me, he deeply swears,
As he's a gentleman, to discharge his trust ;
And that I shall eternally endear [1] him
To my wish'd service, he protests and contests.

Go. Good words, Valerio ; but thou art too wise
To be deceived by breath.   I'll turn thee loose,
To the most cunning cheater of them all.

Va. 'Sfoot ; he's not ashamed besides to charge me
With a late promise ; I must yield [2] indeed
I did (to shift him with some contentment)
Make such a frivall [3] promise.

Go. Ay, well done ;
Promises are no fetters ; with that tongue
Thy promise past, unpromise it again.
Wherefore has man a tongue of power to speak,
But to speak still to his own private purpose ?
Beasts utter but one sound ; but men have change
Of speech and reason, even by nature given them,

---

[1] Bind.   [2] Admit.   [3] Frivolous.

Now to say one thing, and another now,
As best may serve their profitable ends.

    Ma. By'r-lady, sound instructions to a son.

    Va. Nay, sir; he makes his claim by debt of
        friendship.

    Go. Tush; friendship's but a term, boy; the fond
        world
Like to a doting mother glozes over
Her children's imperfections with fine terms ;
What she calls friendship and true humane kindness,
Is only want of true experience :
Honesty is but a defect of wit ;
Respect but mere rusticity and clownery.

    Ma. Better and better.   Soft, here comes my son.

    Enter FORTUNIO, RINALDO, *and* GRATIANA.

    Ri. Fortunio, keep your countenance ; see, sir, here
The poor young married couple, which you pleased
To send for to your house.

    Go. Fortunio, welcome.
And in that welcome I imply your wife's,
Who I am sure you count your second self.

                         [He kisses her.

    Fo. Sir, your right noble favours do exceed
All power of worthy gratitude by words,
That in your care supply my father's place.

    Go. Fortunio, I cannot choose but love you,
Being son to him who long time I have loved :
From whose just anger my house shall protect you,
Till I have made a calm way to your meetings.

    Fo. I little thought, sir, that my father's love
Would take so ill so slight a fault as this.

    Go. Call you it slight ?   Nay, though his spirit
        take it

In higher manner than for your loved sake,
I would have wish'd him ; yet I make a doubt,
Had my son done the like, if my affection
Would not have turn'd to more spleen than your
    father's :
And yet I qualify him all I can,
And doubt not but that time and my persuasion,
Will work out your excuse : since youth and love
Were th' unresisted [1] organs to seduce you :
But you must give him leave, for fathers must
Be won by penitence and submission,
And not by force or opposition.

  Fo. Alas, sir, what advise you me to do ?
I know my father to be highly moved,
And am not able to endure the breath
Of his express'd displeasure, whose hot flames
I think my absence soonest would have quench'd.

  Go. True, sir, as fire with oil, or else like them,
That quench the fire with pulling down the house ;
You shall remain here in my house conceal'd
Till I have won your father to conceive
Kinder opinion of your oversight.
Valerio, entertain Fortunio
And his fair wife, and give them conduct in.

  Va. Y'are welcome, sir.

  Go. What, sirrah, is that all ?
No entertainment to the gentlewoman ?

  Va. Forsooth y'are welcome, by my father's leave.

  Go. What, no more compliment ?   Kiss her, you
    sheepshead.
Why, when ?   Go, go, sir, call your sister hither.

                              [Exit Val.
Lady, you'll pardon our gross bringing up ?

            [1] Irresistible.

We dwell far off from court, you may perceive:
The sight of such a blazing star as you
Dazzles my rude son's wits.

 Gr. Not so, good sir.
The better husband, the more courtly ever.

 Ri. Indeed a courtier makes his lips go far,
As he doth all things else.

Enter VALERIO, BELLANORA.

 Go. Daughter, receive
This gentlewoman home, and use her kindly.

[*She kisses her.*

 Be. My father bids you kindly welcome, lady,
And therefore you must needs come well to me.

 Gr. Thank you, forsooth.

 Go. Go, dame, conduct 'em in.

[*Exeunt* RINALDO, FORTUNIO, BELL., GRAT.

Ah, errant sheepshead, hast thou lived thus long,
And darest not look a woman in the face?
Though I desire especially to see
My son a husband, shall I therefore have him
Turn absolute cullion?[1]　Let's see, kiss thy hand.
Thou kiss thy hand? thou wipest thy mouth, by
  th' mass.
Fie on thee, clown! They say the world's grown
  finer;
But I for my part never saw young men
Worse fashion'd and brought up than now-a-days.
'Sfoot, when myself was young, was not I kept
As far from Court as you? I think I was;
And yet my father on a time invited
The Duchess of his house; I being then
About some five-and-twenty years of age,

[1] Base fellow.

Was thought the only man to entertain her;
I had my congé; [1] plant myself of one leg,
Draw back t'other with a deep-fetch'd honour;
Then with a bel regard advant [2] mine eye
With boldness on her very visnomy. [3]
Your dancers all were counterfeits to me:
And for discourse in my fair mistress' presence
I did not, as you barren gallants do,
Fill my discourses up drinking [4] tobacco;
But on the present furnish'd evermore
With tales and practised speeches; as sometimes,
" What is't a clock?"   " What stuff's this petticoat?"
" What cost the making?   What the fringe and all?"
And " what she under her petticoat?"
And such-like witty compliments: and for need,
I could have written as good prose and verse
As the most beggarly poet of 'em all,
Either acrostic, *Exordion*,
Epithalamions, Satires, Epigrams,
Sonnets in Dozens, or your Quatorzains
In any rhyme, Masculine, Feminine,
Or Sdruciolla, [5] *or couplets,* Blank Verse.
Y'are but bench-whistlers now-a-days to them
That were in our times.   Well, about your husbandry,
Go, for i' faith th'art fit for nothing else.

        Exit VALERIO, *prodit* MARC ANTONIO.

  Ma. By'r-lady, you have play'd the courtier rarely.
  Go. But did you ever see so blank a fool,
When he should kiss a wench, as my son is?
  Ma. Alas, 'tis but a little bashfulness.
You let him keep no company, nor allow him
Money to spend at fence and dancing-schools;

---

  [1] Courteous bow.   [2] Raised.   [3] Face.
  [4] Smoking.   [5] Dactyls.

Y'are too severe, i'faith.

Go. And you, too supple.
Well, sir, for your sake I have stay'd your son
From flying to the wars; now see you rate [1] him,
To stay him yet from more expenseful courses,
Wherein your lenity will encourage him.

Ma. Let me alone; I thank you for this kindness.

[*Exeunt.*

Enter VALERIO *and* RINALDO.

Ri. So! are they gone? Now tell me, brave
    Valerio,
Have I not won the wreath from all your wits,
Brought thee t'enjoy the most desired presence
Of thy dear love at home? and with one labour,
My brother to enjoy thy sister, where
It had been her undoing t'have him seen,
And make thy father crave what he abhors;
T'entreat my brother home t'enjoy his daughter,
Command thee kiss thy wench, chide for not kissing,
And work all this out of a Machiavel,
A miserable politician?
I think the like was never play'd before!

Va. Indeed, I must commend thy wit, of force,
And yet I know not whose deserves most praise,
Of thine or my wit: thine for plotting well,
Mine, that durst undertake and carry it
With such true form.

Ri. Well, the evening crowns the day:
Perséver to the end, my wit hath put
Blind Fortune in a string into your hand;
Use it discreetly, keep it from your father,
Or you may bid all your good days good-night.

[1] Scold.

Va. Let me alone, boy.

Ri. Well, sir, now to vary
The pleasures of our wits ; thou know'st, Valerio,
Here is the new-turn'd gentleman's fair wife,
That keeps thy wife and sister company
With whom the amorous courtier Dariotto
Is far in love, and of whom her sour husband
Is passing jealous, puts on eagle's eyes,
To pry into her carriage.[1] Shall we see
If he be now from home and visit her ?

Enter GAZETTA *sewing*, CORNELIO *following*.

See, see, the prisoner comes.

Va. But soft, sir, see
Her jealous jailor follows at her heels.
Come, we will watch some fitter time to board[2] her,
And in the meantime seek out our mad crew :
My spirit longs to swagger.

Ri. Go to, youth,
Walk not too boldly ; if the sergeants meet you,
You may have swaggering work your bellyfull.

Va. No better copesmates ;[3]

[GAZETTA *sits and sings sewing.*

I'll go seek 'em out with this light in my hand,
The slaves grow proud with seeking out of us.

[*Exeunt.*

Co. A pretty work ; I pray what flowers are these ?

Ga. The pansy this.

Co. Oh, that's for lover's thoughts.
What's that, a columbine ?[4]

---

[1] Conduct.   [2] Accost.   [3] Associates.

[4] Compare Ophelia's speech in *Hamlet* (act iv., sc. 5) :—

" There is pansies, that's for thoughts ; there's fennel for you, and
columbines."

E

Ga. No, that thankless flower fits not my garden.

Co. Him ? yet it may mine ?
This were a pretty present for some friend,
Some gallant courtier, as for Dariotto,
One that adores you in his soul, I know.

Ga. Me ?   Why me more than yourself, I pray ?

Co. Oh yes, he adores you, and adhorns me :
I'faith, deal plainly, do not his kisses relish
Much better than such peasants as I am ?

Ga. Whose kisses ?

Co. Dariotto's ; does he not
The thing you wot on ?

Ga. What thing, good lord ?

Co. Why, lady, lie with you.

Ga. Lie with me ?

Co. Ay, with you.

Ga. You with me, indeed.

Co. Nay, I am told that he lies with you too,
And that he is the only whoremaster
About the city.

Ga. If he be so only,
'Tis a good hearing that there are no more.

Co. Well, mistress, well, I will not be abused ;[1]
Think not you dance in nets ; for though you do not
Make broad profession of your love to him,
Yet do I understand your darkest language,
Your treads a'th'toe, your secret jogs and wrings,
Your intercourse of glances ; every tittle
Of your close[2] amorous rites I understand.
They speak as loud to me, as if you said,
" My dearest Dariotto, I am thine."

Ga. Jesus ! what moods are these ? did ever husband
Follow his wife with jealousy so unjust ?

---

¹ Deceived.   ² Secret.

That once I loved you, you yourself will swear;
And if I did, where did you lose my love?
Indeed, this strange and undeserved usage
Hath power to shake a heart were ne'er so settled;
But I protest, all your unkindness never
Had strength to make me wrong you but in thought.

 Co. No, not with Dariotto?

 Ga. No, by heaven.

 Co. No letters pass'd, nor no designs for meeting?

 Ga. No, by my hope of heaven.

 Co. Well, no time past,
Go, go; go in and sew.

 Ga. Well, be it so.   [*Exit* GA.

 Co. Suspicion is (they say) the first degree
Of deepest wisdom; and however others
Inveigh against this mood of jealousy,
For my part I suppose it the best curb,
To check the ranging appetites that reign
In this weak sex; my neighbours point at me
For this my jealousy; but should I do,
As most of them do, let my wife fly out
To feasts and revels, and invite home gallants,
Play Menelaus, give them time and place,
While I sit like a well-taught waiting-woman
Turning her eyes upon some work or picture,
Read in a book, or take a feigned nap,
While her kind lady takes one to her lap.
No, let me still be pointed at, and thought
A jealous ass, and not a wittolly [1] knave.
I have a show of courtiers haunt my house,
In show my friends, and for my profit too;
But I perceive 'em, and will mock their aims,
With looking to their mark, I warrant 'em:

     [1] Witless.

I am content to ride abroad with them,
To revel, dice, and fit their other sports ;
But by their leaves I'll have a vigilant eye
To the main chance still.   See, my brave comrades.

Enter DARIOTTO, CLAUDIO, *and* VALERIO : VALERIO
putting up his sword.

Da. Well, wag, well ; wilt thou still deceive thy
father,
And being so simple a poor soul before him,
Turn swaggerer in all companies besides ?

Cl. Hadst thou been 'rested, all would have come
forth.

Va. Soft, sir, there lies the point, I do not doubt,
But t'have my pennyworths of these rascals one day,
I'll smoke the buzzing hornets from their nests,
Or else I'll make their leather jerkins stay.
The whoreson hungry horse-flies ; foot, a man
Cannot so soon, for want of almanacks,
Forget his day but three or four bare months,
But straight he sees a sort of corporals,
To lie in ambuscado to surprise him.

Da. Well, thou hadst happy fortune to escape 'em.

Va. But they thought theirs was happier to 'scape
me.
I walking in the place, where men's law-suits
Are heard and pleaded, not so much as dreaming
Of any such encounter, steps me forth
Their valiant foreman, with the word, " I 'rest you."
I made no more ado, but laid these paws
Close on his shoulders, tumbling him to earth ;
And there sate he on his posteriors,
Like a baboon ; and turning me about,
I straight espied the whole troop issuing on me.

I stept me back, and drawing my old friend [1] here,
Made to the midst of them, and all unable
T'endure the shock, all rudely fell in rout,
And down the stairs they ran with such a fury,
As meeting with a troop of lawyers there,
Mann'd by their clients : some with ten, some twenty,
Some five, some three ; he that had least, had one ;
Upon the stairs they bore them down afore them ;
But such a rattling then was there amongst them
Of ravish'd declarations, replications,
Rejoinders and petitions ; all their books
And writings torn and trod on, and some lost,
That the poor lawyers coming to the bar,
Could say nought to the matter, but instead,
Were fain to rail and talk beside their books
Without all order.

   Cl. Faith, that same vein of railing became
Now most applausive ; your best poet is
He that rails grossest.

    Da. True, and your best fool is your broad railing
      fool.

    Va. And why not, sir ?
For by the gods, to tell the naked truth,
What objects see men in this world, but such
As would yield matter to a railing humour ?
When he, that last year carried after one
An empty buckram bag, now fills a coach,
And crowds the senate with such troops of clients
And servile followers as would put a mad spleen
Into a pigeon.

    Da. Come, pray leave these cross capers ;
Let's make some better use of precious time,
See, here's Cornelio ; come, lad, shall we to dice ?

                  [1] His sword.

 Co. Anything I.

 Cl. Well said; how does thy wife?

 Co. In health, God save her.

 Va. But where is she, man?

 Co. Abroad about her business.

 Va. Why, not at home?

Foot, my masters, take her to the Court;
And this rare lad, her husband: and dost hear?
Play me no more the miserable farmer;
But be advised by friends, sell all i' th' country;
Be a flat courtier, follow some great man,
Or bring thy wife there, and she'll make thee great.

 Co. What, to the Court? then take me for a gull;

 Va. Nay, never shun it to be call'd a gull;
For I see all the world is but a gull;
One man gull to another in all kinds:
A merchant to a courtier is a gull;
A client to a lawyer is a gull;
A married man to a bachelor, a gull;
A bachelor to a cuckold is a gull;
All to a poet, or a poet to himself.

 Co. Hark, Dariotto; shall we gull this guller?

 Da. He gulls his father, man; we cannot gull him.

 Co. Let me alone. Of all men's wits alive,
I most admire Valerio's, that hath stolen
By his mere industry, and that by spurts,
Such qualities as no wit else can match,
With plodding at perfection every hour;
Which, if his father knew each gift he has,
Were like enough to make him give all from him:
I mean, besides his dicing and his wenching,
He has stolen languages; th' Italian, Spanish,
And some spice of the French; besides his dancing,
Singing, playing on choice instruments:

These has he got, almost against the hair.[1]

Cl. But hast thou stolen all these, Valerio?

Va. Toys, toys, a pox : and yet they be such toys
As every gentleman would not be without.

Co. Vain-glory makes ye judge on light i'faith.[2]

Da. Afore heaven, I was much deceived in him ;
But he's the man indeed that hides his gifts,
And sets them not to sale in every presence.
I would have sworn his soul were far from music,
And that all his choice music was to hear
His fat beasts bellow.

Co. Sir, your ignorance
Shall eftsoon be confuted. Prithee, Val,
Take thy theorbo,[3] for my sake a little.

Va. By heaven ! this month I touch'd not a theorbo.

Co. Touch'd a theorbo ? mark the very word.
Sirrah, go fetch. [*Exit Page.*

Va. If you will have it, I must need confess
I am no husband of my qualities.

[*He untrusses and capers.*

Co. See what a caper there was !

Cl. See again.

Co. The best that ever ; and how it becomes him !

Da. Oh that his father saw these qualities !

Enter a Page *with an instrument.*

Co. Nay, that's the very wonder of his wit
To carry all without his father's knowledge.

Da. Why, we might tell him now.

Co. No, but we could not,
Although we think we could ; his wit doth charm us.
Come, sweet Val, touch and sing.

---

[1] Against the grain.   [2] "You pretend it's nothing."
[3] A musical instrument, like a large lute. Pepys played it.

Da. 'Foot, will you hear
The worst voice in Italy ?

Enter RINALDO.

Co. O God, sir !   [*He sings.*]   Courtiers, how like
     you this ?

Da. Believe it excellent.

Co. Is it not natural ?

Va. If my father heard me,
'Foot, he'd renounce me for his natural [1] son.

     Da. By heaven, Valerio, and [2] I were thy father,
And loved good qualities as I do my life,
I'd disinherit thee ; for I never heard
Dog howl with worse grace.

     Co. Go to, Signor Courtier,
You deal not courtly now to be so plain,
Nor nobly, to discourage a young gentleman
In virtuous qualities, that has but stolen 'em.

     Cl. Call you this touching a theorbo ?

     Omnes. Ha, ha, ha.   [*Exeunt all but* VAL. *and* RIN.

     Va. How now, what's here ?

     Ri. Zoons, a plot laid to gull thee.
Could thy wit think thy voice was worth the hearing ?
This was the courtier's and the cuckold's project.

     Va. And is't e'en so ?   'Tis very well, master
     Courtier, and Dan Cornuto ; I'll cry quit with
     both ;
And first, I'll cast a jar betwixt them both,
With firing the poor cuckold's jealousy.
I have a tale will make him mad,
And turn his wife divorced loose amongst us.
But first let's home, and entertain my wife ;
Oh father, pardon, I was born to gull thee.   [*Exeunt.*

        [1] Own   [2] Same as *an*=if.

ACT THE THIRD

SCENE I

Enter FORTUNIO, BELLANORA, GRATIANA, GOSTANZO
following closely.

O. How happy am I, that by this sweet
means,
 I gain access to your most loved sight,
  And therewithal to utter my full love,
Which but for vent would burn my entrails up.

 Go. By th' mass they talk too softly.

 Be. Little thinks
The austere mind my thrifty father bears
That I am vow'd to you, and so am bound
From him, who for more riches he would force
On my disliking fancy.

 Fo. 'Tis no fault,
With just deeds to defraud an injury.

 Go. My daughter is persuading him to yield
In dutiful submission to his father.

Enter VALERIO.

Va. Do I not dream ? do I behold this sight
With waking eyes ? or from the ivory gate
Hath Morpheus sent a vision to delude me ?
Is't possible that I, a mortal man,
Should shrine within mine arms so bright a goddess,
The fair Gratiana, beauty's little world?

Go. What have we here ?

Va. My dearest mine of gold,
  All this that thy white arms enfold,
  Account it as thine own freehold.

Go. God's my dear soul, what sudden change is
  here ?
I smell how this gear [1] will fall out, i'faith.

Va. Fortunio, sister, come, let's to the garden.

            [*Exeunt.*

Go. Sits the wind there, i'faith ? see what example
Will work upon the dullest appetite.
My son, last day so bashful, that he durst not
Look on a wench, now courts her ; and by'r lady,
Will make his friend Fortunio wear his head
Of the right modern fashion.[2] What, Rinaldo !

Enter RINALDO.

Ri. I fear I interrupt your privacy.

Go. Welcome, Rinaldo, would 'thad been your hap
To come a little sooner, that you might
Have seen a handsome sight : but let that pass :
The short is that your sister Gratiana
Shall stay no longer here.

Ri. No longer, sir ?
Repent you then so soon your favour to her,

     [1] Business.   [2] Horned.

And to my brother?

  Go. Not so, good Rinaldo;
But to prevent a mischief that I see
Hangs over your abused brother's head;
In brief, my son has learn'd but too much courtship.
It was my chance even now to cast mine eye
Into a place whereto your sister enter'd:
My metamorphosed son: I must conceal
What I saw there: but to be plain, I saw
More than I would see.   I had thought to make
My house a kind receipt for your kind brother;
But I'd be loth his wife should find more kindness
Than she had cause to like of.

  Ri. What's the matter?
Perhaps a little compliment or so.

  Go. Well, sir, such compliment perhaps may cost
Married Fortunio the setting on.
Nor can I keep my knowledge; he that lately
Before my face I could not get to look
Upon your sister, by this light, now kiss'd her,
Embraced and courted with as good a grace
As any courtier could: and I can tell you
(Not to disgrace her) I perceived the dame
Was as far forward as himself, by the mass.

  Ri. You should have school'd him for't.

  Go. No, I'll not see't:
For shame once found, is lost; I'll have him think
That my opinion of him is the same
That it was ever; it will be a mean
To bridle this fresh humour bred in him.

  Ri. Let me then school him; foot, I'll rattle him up.

  Go. No, no, Rinaldo, th' only remedy
Is to remove the cause; carry the object
From his late tempted eyes.

Ri. Alas, sir, whither?
You know my father is incensed so much
He'll not receive her.

Go. Place her with some friend
But for a time, till I reclaim your father:
Meantime your brother shall remain with me.

Ri. [*to himself.*] The care's the less then; he has
    still his longing
To be with this gull's daughter.

Go. What resolve you?
I am resolved she lodges here no more:
My friend's son shall not be abused by mine.

Ri. Troth, sir, I'll tell you what a sudden toy
Comes in my head. What think you if I brought her
Home to my father's house?

Go. Ay, marry, sir;
Would he receive her?

Ri. Nay, you hear not all:
I mean, with use of some device or other.

Go. As how, Rinaldo?

Ri. Marry, sir, to say
She is your son's wife, married past your knowledge.

Go. I doubt, last day he saw her, and will know her
    to be Fortunio's wife.

Ri. Nay, as for that
I will pretend she was even then your son's wife,
But feign'd by me to be Fortunio's.
Only to try how he would take the matter.

Go. 'Fore heaven 'twere pretty.

Ri. Would it not do well?

Go. Exceeding well, in sadness.[1]

Ri. Nay, good sir.
Tell me unfeignedly, do ye like't indeed?

           [1] Earnest.

Go. The best that e'er I heard.

Ri. And do you think
He'll swallow down the gudgeon?[1]

Go. A my life,
It were a gross gob would not down with him;
An honest knight, but simple; not acquainted
With the fine sleights and policies of the world,
As I myself am.

Ri. I'll go fetch her straight;
And this jest thrive, 'twill make us princely sport;
But you must keep our counsel, second all;
Which to make likely, you must needs sometimes
Give your son leave (as if you knew it not)
To steal and see her at my father's house.

Go. Ay, but see you then that you keep good guard
Over his forward new-begun affections:
For, by the Lord, he'll teach your brother else,
To sing the cuckoo's note; spirit will break out,
Though never so suppress'd and pinioned.

Ri. Especially your son's; what would he be
If you should not restrain him by good counsel?

Go. I'll have an eye on him, I warrant thee.
I'll in and warn the gentlewoman to make ready.

Ri. Well, sir, and I'll not be long after you.

[*Exit* GOSTANZO.

Heaven, heaven, I see these politicians
(Out of blind Fortune's hands) are our most fools.
'Tis she that gives the lustre to their wits,
Still plodding at traditional devices:
But take 'em out of them to present actions,
A man may grope and tickle 'em like a trout,[2]
And take 'em from their close deer holes as fat
As a physician, and as giddy-headed,

---

[1] A fish used for bait.   [2] Fish were caught by tickling.

As if by miracle heaven had taken from them
Even that which commonly belongs to fools.
Well, now let's note what black ball of debate
Valerio's wit hath cast betwixt Cornelio
And the enamour'd courtier; I believe
His wife and he will part; his jealousy
Hath ever watch'd occasion of divorce;
And now Valerio's villany will present it.
See, here comes the twin-courtier, his companion.

Enter CLAUDIO.

Cl. Rinaldo, well encounter'd.

Ri. Why? what news?

Cl. Most sudden and infortunate, Rinaldo;
Cornelio is incensed so 'gainst his wife
That no man can procure her quiet with him.
I have assay'd him, and made Marc Antonio,
With all his gentle rhetoric, second me;
Yet all, I fear me, will be cast away.
See, see, they come; join thy wit, good Rinaldo,
And help to pacify his yellow fury.

Ri. With all my heart. I consecrate my wit
To the wish'd comfort of distressed ladies.

Enter CORNELIO, MARC ANTONIO, VALERIO, Page.

Co. Will any man assure me of her good behaviour?

Va. Who can assure a jealous spirit? you may be afraid of the shadow of your ears, and imagine them to be horns; if you will assure yourself, appoint keepers to watch her.

Co. And who shall watch the keepers?

Ma. To be sure of that, be you her keeper.

Va. Well said; and share the horns yourself; for that's the keeper's fee.

Co. But say I am gone out of town, and must trust others; how shall I know if those I trust be trusty to me?

Ri. Marry, sir, by a singular instinct given naturally to all you married men, that if your wives play leger-deheel, though you be a hundred miles off, yet you shall be sure instantly to find it in your foreheads.

Co. Sound doctrine, I warrant you; I am resolved, i'faith.

Page. Then give me leave to speak, sir, that hath all this while been silent; I have heard you with extreme patience; now, therefore, prick up your ears, and vouchsafe me audience.

Cl. Good boy, a mine honour.

Co. Pray, what are you, sir?

Pa. I am here, for default of better, of counsel with the fair Gazetta, and though herself had been best able to defend herself if she had been here, and would have pleased to put forth the buckler which Nature hath given all women, I mean her tongue——

Va. Excellent, good boy.

Pa. Yet, since she either vouchsafes it not, or thinks her innocence a sufficient shield against your jealous accusations, I will presume to undertake the defence of that absent and honourable lady, whose sworn knight I am; and in her of all that name (for lady is grown a common name to their whole sex), which sex I have ever loved from my youth, and shall never cease to love, till I want wit to admire.

Ma. An excellent spoken boy.

Va. Give ear, Cornelio; here is a young Mercurio sent to persuade thee.

Co. Well, sir, let him say on.

Pa. It is a heavy case, to see how this light sex is

tumbled and tossed from post to pillar, under the unsavoury breath of every humorous peasant. Gazetta,
you said, is unchaste, disloyal, and I wot not what;
alas! is it her fault? is she not a woman? did she
not suck it (as others of her sex do) from her mother's
breast? and will you condemn that as her fault which
is her nature? Alas! sir, you must consider a woman
is an unfinished creature, delivered hastily to the
world, before Nature had set to that seal which should
have made them perfect. Faults they have, no doubt,
but are we free? Turn your eye into yourself (good
Signor Cornelio), and weigh your own imperfections
with hers. If she be wanton abroad, are not you
wanting at home? if she be amorous, are not you
jealous? if she be high set, are not you taken down?
if she be a courtezan, are not you a cuckold?

Co. Out, you rogue.

Ri. On with thy speech, boy.

Ma. You do not well, Cornelio, to discourage the
bashful youth.

Cl. Forth, boy, I warrant thee.

Pa. But if our own imperfections will not teach us
to bear with theirs, yet let their virtues persuade us:
let us endure their bad qualities for their good; allow
the prickle for the rose, the brack [1] for the velvet, the
paring for the cheese, and so forth: if you say they
range abroad, consider it is nothing but to avoid idleness
at home; their nature is still to be doing; keep 'em
a-doing at home; let them practise one good quality
or other, either sewing, singing, playing, chiding,
dancing, or so; and these will put such idle toys out
of their heads into yours; but if you cannot find them
variety of business within doors, yet, at least, imitate

[1] Any flaw: here, a cracking; common defect of velvet.

the ancient wise citizens of this city, who used carefully to provide their wives gardens near the town to
plant, to graft in, as occasion served, only to keep 'em
from idleness.

Va. Everlasting good boy.

Co. I perceive your knavery, sir, and will yet have
patience.

Ri. Forth, my brave Curio.

Pa. As to her unquietness (which some have rudely
termed shrewishness), though the fault be in her, yet
the cause is in you. What so calm as the sea of its
own nature? Art was never able to equal it; your
dicing-tables nor your bowling-alleys are not com-
parable to it; yet, if a blast of wind do but cross it,
not so turbulent and violent an element in the world.
So (Nature in lieu of women's scarcity of wit, having
indued them with a large portion of will) if they
may (without impeach) enjoy their wills, no quieter
creatures under heaven; but if the breath of their
husbands' mouths once cross their wills, nothing more
tempestuous. Why then, sir, should you husbands
cross your wives' wills thus, considering the law allows
them no wills at all at their deaths, because it intended
they should have their wills while they lived?

Va. Answer him but that, Cornelio.

Co. All shall not serve her turn; I am thinking of
other matters.

Ma. Thou hast half won him, wag; ply him yet a
little further.

Pa. Now, sir, for these cuckooish songs of yours, of
cuckolds, horns, grafting, and such-like; what are
they but mere imaginary toys, bred out of your own
heads, as your own, and so by tradition delivered from
man to man, like scarecrows, to terrify fools from this

F

earthly paradise of wedlock, coined at first by some spent poets, superannuated bachelors, or some that were scarce men of their hands; who, like the fox having lost his tail, would persuade others to lose theirs for company? Again, for your cuckold, what is it but a mere fiction? show me any such creature in nature; if there be, I could never see it; neither could I ever find any sensible difference betwixt a cuckold and a Christian creature. To conclude, let poets coin, or fools credit, what they list: for mine own part, I am clear of this opinion, that your cuckold is a mere chimera, and that there are no cuckolds in the world but those that have wives: and so I will leave them.

Co. 'Tis excellent good, sir; I do take you, sir, d'ye see, to be, as it were, bastard to the saucy courtier, that would have me father more of your fraternity, d'ye see? and so are instructed (as we hear) to second that villain with your tongue, which he has acted with his tenure [1] piece, d'ye see?

Pa. No such matter, a my credit, sir.

Co. Well, sir, be as be may, I scorn to set my head against yours, d'ye see? when in the meantime I will firk [2] your father, whether you see or no.

[*Exit drawing his raiper.*

Ri. God's my life, Cornelio! [*Exit.*

Va. Have at your father, i'faith, boy, if he can find him.

Ma. See, he comes here: he has missed him.

Enter DARIOTTO.

Da. How now, my hearts, what, not a wench amongst you?

[1] For a consideration.   [2] Strike.

'Tis a sign y'are not in the grace of wenches
That they will let you be thus long alone.

Va. Well, Dariotto, glory not too much,
That for thy brisk attire and lips perfumed,
Thou play'st the stallion ever where thou comest ;
And like the husband of the flock, runn'st through
The whole town herd, and no man's bed secure :
No woman's honour unattempted by thee.
Think not to be thus fortunate for ever :
But in thy amorous conquests at the last
Some wound will slice your mazer : Mars himself
Fell into Vulcan's snare, and so may you.

Da. Alas, alas, faith, I have but the name ;
I love to court and win ; and the consent
Without the act obtain'd, is all I seek ;
I love the victory that draws no blood.

Cl. Oh, 'tis a high desert in any man
To be a secret lecher ; I know some
That (like myself) are true in nothing else.

Ma. And methinks it is nothing, if not told ;
At least the joy is never full before.

Va. Well, Dariotto, th'hadst as good confess,
The sun shines broad upon your practices.[1]
Vulcan will wake and intercept you one day.

Da. Why, the more jealous knave and coxcomb he.
What, shall the shaking of his bed a little
Put him in motion ?   It becomes him not ;
Let him be dull'd and stall'd, and then be quiet.
The way to draw my custom to his house,
Is to be mad and jealous ; 'tis the sauce
That whets my appetite.

Va. Or any man's :
Sine periculo friget lusus.

[1] Plots.

They that are jealous, use it still of purpose
To draw you to their houses.

    Da. Ay, by heaven,
I am of that opinion. Who would steal
Out of a common orchard? Let me gain
My love with labour, and enjoy't with fear,
Or I am gone.

Enter RINALDO.

    Ri. What, Dariotto here?
'Foot, darest thou come near Cornelio's house?

    Da. Why? is the bull run mad? what ails he,
        trow?

    Ri. I know not what he ails; but I would wish you
To keep out of the reach of his sharp horns,
For by this hand he'll gore you.

    Da. And why me,
More than thyself, or these two other whelps?
You all have basted him as well as I.
I wonder what's the cause?

    Ri. Nay, that he knows,
And swears withal, that whereso'er he meets you,
He'll mark you for a marker of men's wives.

    Va. Pray heaven he be not jealous by some tales
That have been told him lately; did you never
Attempt his wife? hath no love's harbinger,
No looks, no letters, pass'd 'twixt you and her?

    Da. For look I cannot answer; I bestow them
At large, and carelessly, much like the sun;
If any be so foolish to apply them
To any private fancy of their own
(As many do), it's not my fault, thou knowest.

    Va. Well, Dariotto, this set face of thine,
If thou be guilty of offence to him)

Comes out of very want of wit and feeling
What danger haunts thee; for Cornelio
Is a tall [1] man, I tell you; and 'twere best.
You shunn'd his sight awhile, till we might get
His patience, or his pardon; for past doubt
Thou diest, if he but see thee.

Enter CORNELIO.

Ri. 'Foot, he comes.

Da. Is this the cockatrice that kills with sight?
How dost thou, boy? ha?

Co. Well.

Da. What, lingering still
About this paltry town? hadst thou been ruled
By my advice, thou hadst by this time been
A gallant courtier, and at least a knight;
I would have got thee dubb'd by this time certain.

Co. And why then did you not yourself that
honour?

Da. Tush; 'tis more honour still to make a knight
Than 'tis to be a knight; to make a cuckold
Than 'tis to be a cuckold.

Co. Y'are a villain.

Da. God shield, man! villain?

Co. Ay, I'll prove thee one.

Da. What, wilt thou prove a villain? By this light
thou deceivest me, then.

Co. Well, sir, thus I prove it.   [*Draws.*

Omnes. Hold, hold! raise the streets.

Cl. Cornelio.

Ri. Hold, Dariotto, hold.

Va. What, art thou hurt?

Da. A scratch, a scratch.

----

[1] Powerful.

Va. Go, sirrah, fetch a surgeon.

Co. You'll set a badge on the jealous fool's head, sir ; now set a coxcomb on your own.

Va. What's the cause of these wars, Dariotto ?

Da. 'Foot, I know not.

Co. Well, sir, know and spare not. I will presently [1] be divorced, and then take her amongst ye.

Ri. Divorced ? nay, good Cornelio.

Co. By this sword I will ; the world shall not dissuade me. [*Exit.*

Va. Why, this has been your fault now, Dariotto,
You youths have fashions ; when you have obtain'd
A lady's favour, straight your hat must wear it ;
Like a jackdaw, that when he lights upon
A dainty morsel, kaas and makes his brags,
And then some kite doth scoop it from him straight ;
When, if he fed without his dawish noise,
He might fare better and have less disturbance.
Forbear it in this case ; and when you prove
Victorious over fair Gazetta's fort,
Do not for pity sound your trump for joy,
But keep your valour close, and 'tis your honour.

Enter Page *and* POCK.

Po. God save you, Signor Dariotto.

Da. I know you not, sir ; your name, I pray ?

Po. My name is Pock, sir ; a practitioner in surgery.

Da. Pock, the surgeon ; y'are welcome, sir ; I know a doctor of your name, master Pock.

Po. My name has made many doctors, sir.

Ri. Indeed, 'tis a worshipful name.

Va. Marry is it, and of an ancient descent.

[1] Instantly.

Po. 'Faith, sir, I could fetch my pedigree far, if I were so disposed.

Ri. Out of France, at least.

Po. And if I stood on my arms, as others do—

Da. No, do not, Pock; let others stand a their arms, and thou a thy legs, as long as thou canst.

Po. Though I live by my bare practice, yet I could show good cards for my gentility.

Va. Tush, thou canst not shake off thy gentry, Pock; 'tis bred i' th' bone. But to the main, Pock. What thinkest thou of this gentleman's wound, Pock; canst thou cure it, Pock?

Po. The incision is not deep, nor the orifice exorbitant; the pericranion is not dislocated. I warrant his life for forty crowns, without perishing of any joint.

Da. 'Faith, Pock; 'tis a joint I would be loth to lose for the best joint of mutton in Italy.

Ri. Would such a scratch as this hazard a man's head?

Po. Ay, by'r-lady, sir; I have known some have lost their heads for a less matter, I can tell you; therefore, sir, you must keep good diet; if you please to come home to my house till you be perfectly cured, I shall have the more care on you.

Va. That's your only course to have it well quickly.

Po. By what time would he have it well, sir?

Da. A very necessary question; canst thou limit the time?

Po. Oh, sir, cures are like causes in law, which may be lengthened or shortened at the discretion of the lawyer; he can either keep it green with replications or rejoinders, or sometimes skin it fair a' th' outside for fashion sake; but so he may be sure 'twill break

out again by a writ of error, and then has he his suit
new to begin ; but I will covenant with you, that by
such a time I'll make your head as sound as a bell ; I
will bring it to suppuration, and after I will make it
coagulate and grow to a perfect cicatrice,[1] and all within
these ten days, so you keep a good diet.

Da. Well, come, Pock, we'll talk farther on't within ; it draws near dinner-time.   What's o'clock, boy ?

Pa. By your clock, sir, it should be almost one,
for your head rung noon some half hour ago.

Da. Is't true, sir ?

Va. Away, let him alone ; though he came in at
the window he sets the gates of your honour open, I
can tell you.

Da. Come in, Pock, come, apply ; and for this
        deed
I'll give the knave a wound shall never bleed :
So, sir, I think this knock rings loud acquittance
For my ridiculous—

                    [*Exeunt all but* RINAL. *and* VALER.

Ri. Well, sir, to turn our heads to salve your
        licence,
Since you have used the matter so unwisely
That now your father has discern'd your humour
In your too careless usuage in his house,
Your wife must come from his house to Antonio's,
And he, to entertain her must be told
She is not wife to his son, but to you :
Which news will make his simple wit triumph
Over your father ; and your father thinking
He still is gull'd, will still account him simple.
Come, sir, prepare your villanous wit to feign
A kind submission to your father's fury,

                    [1] Scar.

And we shall see what hearty policy
He will discover, in his feigned anger,
To blind Antonio's eyes, and make him think
He thinks her heartily to be your wife.

   Va. Oh, will I gull him rarely with my wench,
Low kneeling at my heels before his fury,
And injury shall be salved with injury.

To find Antonio's eyes, and make him think
He thinks her heartily to be your wife:
To Oh, will I get him truly with my wench,
Now kneeling at my feet before his eyes,
And injury shall be salved with injury.

ACT THE FOURTH

SCENE I

MARC ANTONIO: GOSTANZO.

A. You see how too much wisdom ever-
more
    Out-shoots the truth: you were so for-
wards still
To tax my ignorance, my green experience
In these gray hairs, for giving such advantage
To my son's spirit, that he durst undertake
A secret match, so far short of his worth:
Your son so season'd with obedience,
Even from his youth, that all his actions relish
Nothing but duty, and your anger's fear.
What shall I say to you, if it fall out
That this most precious son of yours has play'd
A part as bad as this, and as rebellious:
Nay, more, has grossly gull'd your wit withal.
What if my son has undergone the blame
That appertain'd to yours? and that this wench
With which my son is charged, may call you father:
Shall I then say you want experience?

Y'are green, y'are credulous; easy to be blinded.

Go. Ha, ha, ha.
Good Marc Antonio, when't comes to that,
Laugh at me, call me fool, proclaim me so,
Let all the world take knowledge I am an ass.

Ma. Oh! the good God of Gods,
How blind is pride! what eagles we are still
In matters that belong to other men,
What beetles in our own! I tell you, knight,
It is confess'd to be as I have told you;
And Gratiana is by young Rinaldo
And your white son, brought to me as his wife.
How think you now, sir?

Go. Even just as before,
And have more cause to think honest Credulity
Is a true loadstone to draw on Decrepity!
You have a heart too open to embrace
All that your ear receives: alas! good man,
All this is but a plot for entertainment
Within your house; for your poor son's young wife
My house, without huge danger, cannot hold.

Ma. Is't possible; what danger, sir, I pray?

Go. I'll tell you, sir; 'twas time to take her thence;
My son, that last day you saw could not frame
His looks to entertain her, now, by'r-lady,
Is grown a courtier; for myself, unseen,
Saw when he courted her, embraced and kiss'd her,
And, I can tell you, left not much undone,
That was the proper office of your son.

Ma. What world is this?

Go. I told this to Rinaldo,
Advising him to fetch her from my house;
And his young wit, not knowing where to lodge her
Unless with you, and saw that could not be

Without some wile : I presently suggested
This quaint device—to say she was my son's ;
And all this plot, good Marc Antonio,
Flow'd from this fount, only to blind our eyes.

    Ma. Out of how sweet a dream have you awaked
      me !
By heaven, I durst have laid my part in heaven
All had been true ; it was so lively handled,
And drawn with such a seeming face of truth ;
Your son had cast a perfect veil of grief
Over his face, for his so rash offence,
To seal his love with act of marriage
Before his father had subscribed his choice.
My son (my circumstance lessening the fact)
Entreating me to break the matter to you,
And joining my effectual persuasions
With your son's penitent submission,
Appease your fury : I at first assented,
And now expect their coming to that purpose.

    Go. 'Twas well, 'twas well ; seem to believe it still,
Let art end what credulity began ;
When they come, suit your words and looks to theirs,
Second my sad son's feign'd submission,
And see in all points how my brain will answer
His disguised grief, with a set countenance
Of rage and choler ; now observe and learn
To school your son by me.

    Intrant RINALDO, VALERIO, GRATIANA.

    Ma. On with your mask ; here come the other
      maskers, sir.
    Ri. Come on, I say,
Your father with submission will be calm'd ;
Come on ; down a your knees.

Go. Villain, durst thou
Presume to gull thy father? Dost thou not
Tremble to see my bent and cloudy brows
Ready to thunder on thy graceless head,
And with the bolt of my displeasure cut
The thread of all my living from thy life,
For taking thus a beggar to thy wife?

Va. Father, if that part I have in your blood,
If tears, which so abundantly distil
Out of my inward eyes, and for a need
Can drown these outward (lend me thy handkercher)
And being, indeed, as many drops of blood
Issuing from the creator of my heart,
Be able to beget so much compassion,
Not on my life, but on this lovely dame,
Whom I hold dearer?

Go. Out upon thee, villain!

Ma. Nay, good Gostanzo; think, you are a father.

Go. I will not hear a word: out, out upon thee!
Wed without my advice, my love, my knowledge,
Ay, and a beggar, too, a trull, a blowse![1]

Ri. You thought not so last day, when you offer'd
  her
A twelvemonths' board for one night's lodging with
  her.

Go. Go to, no more of that; peace, good Rinaldo,
It is a fault that only she and you know.

Ri. Well, sir, go on, I pray,

Go. Have I, fond[2] wretch,
With utmost care and labour brought thee up,
Ever instructing thee, omitting never
The office of a kind and careful father,
To make thee wise and virtuous like thy father,

---

[1] Ruddy wench. [2] Foolish.

And hast thou in one act everted all?
Proclaim'd thyself to all the world a fool,
To wed a beggar?

 Va. Father, say not so.

 Go. Nay, she's thy own; here, rise, fool, take her
  to thee,

Live with her still, I know thou count'st thyself
Happy in soul, only in winning her:
Be happy still; here, take her hand, enjoy her.
Would not a son hazard his father's wrath,
His reputation in the world, his birthright,
To have but such a mess of broth as this?

 Ma. Be not so violent, I pray you, good Gostanzo,
Take truce with passion, license your sad son
To speak in his excuse.

 Go. What? what excuse?
Can any orator in this case excuse him?
What can he say? what can be said of any?

 Va. Alas, sir, hear me; all that I can say
In my excuse, is but to show love's warrant.

 Go. Notable wag!

 Va. I know I have committed
A great impiety, not to move you first
Before the dame I meant to make my wife.
Consider what I am, yet young, and green,
Behold what she is. Is there not in her,
Ay, in her very eye, a power to conquer
Even age itself and wisdom? Call to mind,
Sweet father, what yourself being young have been,
Think what you may be, for I do not think
The world so far spent with you, but you may
Look back on such a beauty, and I hope
To see you young again, and to live long
With young affections; wisdom makes a man

Live young for ever : and where is this wisdom
If not in you ?   Alas, I know not what
Rests in your wisdom to subdue affections,
But I protest it wrought with me so strongly
That I had quite been drown'd in seas of tears
Had I not taken hold in happy time
Of this sweet hand ; my heart had been consumed
T'a heap of ashes with the flames of love,
Had it not sweetly been assuaged and cool'd
With the moist kisses of these sugar'd lips.

  Go. O puissant wag ; what huge large thongs he
    cuts
Out of his friend Fortunio's stretching-leather.

  Ma. He knows he does it but to blind my eyes.

  Go. Oh, excellent ! these men will put up anything.

  Va. Had I not had her, I had lost my life,
Which life indeed I would have lost before
I had displeased you, had I not received it
From such a kind, a wise, and honoured father.

  Go. Notable boy !

  Va. Yet do I here renounce
Love, life, and all, rather than one hour longer
Endure to have your love eclipsed from me.

  Gr. Oh, I can hold no longer ; if thy words
Be used in earnest, my Valerio,
Thou wound'st my heart, but I know 'tis in jest.

  Go. No, I'll be sworn she has her lyripoop [1] too.

  Gr. Didst thou not swear to love, spite of father and
all the world ?
That nought should sever us but death itself ?

  Va. I did, but if my father
Will have his son forsworn, upon his soul
The blood of my black perjury shall lie ;

      [1] A silly person.

For I will seek his favour though I die.

    Go. No, no ; live still, my son ; thou well shalt
        know
I have a father's heart ; come join your hands,
Still keep thy vows, and live together still,
Till cruel death set foot betwixt you both.

    Va. Oh, speak you this in earnest?

    Go. Ay, by heaven.

    Va. And never to recall it?

    Go. Not till death.

    Ri. Excellent, sir ; you have done like yourself,
What would you more, Valerio?

    Va. Worshipful father.

    Ri. Come, sir, come you in, and celebrate your joys.
                      [Exeunt all save the old men.

    Go. O Marc Antonio,
Had I not arm'd you with an expectation,
Would not this make you pawn your very soul
The wench had been my son's wife?

    Ma. Yes, by heaven :
A knavery thus effected might deceive
A wiser man than I, for I, alas !
Am no good politician : plain believing,
Simple honesty, is my policy still.

    Go. The visible marks of folly, honesty,
And quick credulity his younger brother.
I tell you, Marc Antonio, there is much
In that young boy, my son.

    Ma. Not much honesty, if I may speak without
        offence to his father.

    Go. O God, you cannot please me better, sir.
H'as honesty enough to serve his turn,
The less honesty ever the more wit ;
But go you home, and use your daughter kindly ;

Meantime I'll school your son ; and do you still
Dissemble what you know, keep off your son ;
The wench at home must still be my son's wife ;
Remember that, and be you blinded still.

   Ma. You must remember too to let your son
Use his accustom'd visitations,
Only to blind my eyes.

   Go. He shall not fail ;
But still take you heed, have a vigilant eye
On that sly child of mine, for by this light,
He'll be too bold with your son's forehead else.

   Ma. Well, sir, let me alone, I'll bear a brain.

                                 [Exeunt.

      Enter VALERIO, RINALDO.

   Va. Come, they are gone.

   Ri. Gone ? they were far gone here.

   Va. Gull'd I my father, or gull'd he himself ?
Thou told'st him Gratiana was my wife,
I have confessed it, he has pardon'd it.

   Ri. Nothing more true, enow can witness it.
And therefore when he comes to learn the truth,
(As certainly for all these sly disguises,
Time will strip truth into her nakedness),
Thou hast good plea against him to confess
The honour'd action, and to claim his pardon.

   Va. 'Tis true, for all was done, he deeply swore,
Out of his heart.

   Ri. He has much faith the whiles,
That swore a thing so quite against his heart.

   Va. Why, this is policy.

   Ri. Well, see you repair
To Gratiana daily, and enjoy her
In her true kind ; and now we must expect
The resolute and ridiculous divorce

  G

Cornelio hath sued against his wedlock.

　Va. I think it be not so ; the ass dotes on her.

　Ri. It is too true, and thou shalt answer it
For setting such debate 'twixt man and wife :
See, we shall see the solemn manner of it.

Enter CORNELIO, DARIOTTO, CLAUDIO, NOTARY, Page,
GAZETTA, BELLANORA, GRATIANA.

　Be. Good Signor Cornelio, let us poor gentlewomen
entreat you to forbear.

　Co. Talk no more to me, I'll not be made cuckold
in my own house ; notary, read me the divorce.

　Ga. My dear Cornelio, examine the cause better
before you condemn me.

　Co. Sing to me no more, siren, for I will hear thee
no more ; I will take no compassion on thee.

　Pa. Good Signor Cornelio, be not too mankind
against your wife ; say y'are a cuckold (as the best that
is may be so at a time) will you make a trumpet of your
own horns ?

　Co. Go to, sir, y'are a rascal ; I'll give you a fee for
pleading for her one day.　Notary, do you your office.

　Va. Go to, signor, look better to your wife and be
better advised, before you grow to this extremity.

　Co. Extremity ! Go to, I deal but too mercifully
with her.　If I should use extremity with her I might
hang her, and her copesmate my drudge here.　How
say you, master Notary, might I not do it by law ?

　No. Not hang 'em, but you may bring them both to a
white sheet.

　Co. Nay, by the mass ! they have had too much of
the sheet already.

　No. And besides, you may set capital letters on their
foreheads.

Co. What's that to the capital letter that's written in mine? I say, for all your law, master Notary, that I may hang 'em. May I not hang him that robs me of mine honour, as well as he that robs me of my horse?

No. No, sir, your horse is a chattel.

Co. So is honour. A man may buy it with his penny, and if I may hang a man for stealing my horse, as I say, much more for robbing me of my honour; for why? if my horse be stolen it may be my own fault; for why? either the stable is not strong enough, or the pasture not well fenced, or watched, or so forth. But for your wife that keeps the stable of your honour; let her be locked in a brazen tower, let Argus himself keep her, yet can you never be secure of your honour; for why? she can run through all with her serpent noddle; besides, you may hang a lock upon your horse, and so can you not upon your wife.

Ri. But I pray you, sir, what are the presumptions on which you will build this divorce?

Co. Presumption enough, sir, for besides their intercourse, or commerce of glances that passed betwixt this cockrill-drone [1] and her at my table last Sunday night at supper, their winks, their becks, due guard, their treads a'the toe (as by heaven I swear she trod once upon my toe instead of his), this is chiefly to be noted, the same night she would needs lie alone; and the same night her dog barked. Did not you hear him, Valerio?

Va. And understand him too, I'll be sworn of a book.

Co. Why, very good; if these be not manifest presumptions now, let the world be judge. Therefore

[1] Young bantam.

without more ceremony, master Notary, pluck out
your instrument.

No. I will, sir, if there be no remedy.

Co. Have you made it strong in law, Master Notary?
have you put in words enough?

No. I hope so, sir; it has taken me a whole skin of
parchment, you see.

Co. Very good; and is egress and regress in?

No. I'll warrant you, sir, it is *forma juris*.

Co. Is there no hole to be found in the orthography?

No. None in the world, sir.

Co. You have written *Sunt* with an *S*, have you
not?

No. Yes, that I have.

Co. You have done the better for quietness' sake;
and are none of the authentical dashes over the head
left out? if there be, master Notary, an error will lie
out.

No. Not for a dash over head, sir, I warrant you, if
I should oversee. I have seen that tried in Butiro and
Caseo, in Butler and Cason's case, *Decimo sexto* of
Duke Anonimo.

Ri. Y'ave gotten a learned notary, Signor Cornelio.

Co. He's a shrewd fellow indeed. I had as lieve
have his head in a matter of felony, or treason, as
any notary in Florence. Read out, master Notary.
Hearken you, mistress; gentlemen, mark, I beseech
you.

Omnes. We will all mark you, sir, I warrant you.

No. I think it would be something tedious to read
all, and therefore, gentlemen, the sum is this: That
you, Signor Cornelio, Gentleman, for divers and
sundry weighty and mature considerations, you
especially moving, specifying all the particulars of

your wife's enormities in a schedule hereunto annexed,
the transcript whereof is in your own tenure, custody,
occupation, and keeping : That for these, the aforesaid
premises, I say, you renounce, disclaim, and discharge
Gazetta from being your leeful or your lawful wife :
And that you eftsoons divide, disjoin, separate, remove,
and finally eloigne, sequester, and divorce her, from your
bed and your board ; That you forbid her all access,
repair, egress or regress to your person or persons,
mansion or mansions, dwellings, habitations, remain-
ences or abodes, or to any shop, cellar, sollar,[1] ease-
ments' chamber, dormer, and so forth, now in the
tenure, custody, occupation, or keeping of the said
Cornelio ; notwithstanding all former contracts, cove-
nants, bargains, conditions, agreements, compacts,
promises, vows, affiances, assurances, bonds, bills,
indentures, poledeeds, deeds of gift, defesances, feoff-
ments, endowments, vouchers, double vouchers, privy
entries, actions, declarations, explications, rejoinders,
surrejoinders, rights, interests, demands, claims, or
titles whatsoever, heretofore betwixt the one and the
other party, or parties, being had, made, passed,
covenanted, and agreed, from the beginning of the
world till the day of the date hereof. Given the
seventeenth of November, fifteen hundred and so
forth. Here, sir, you must set to your hand.

Co. What else, master Notary ? I am resolute,
i'faith.

Ga. Sweet husband, forbear.

Co. Avoid, I charge thee in name of this divorce ;
thou mightst have looked to it in time, yet this I will
do for thee ; if thou canst spy out any other man that
thou wouldst cuckold, thou shalt have my letter to

[1] A garret.

him. I can do no more. More ink, master Notary;
I write my name at large.

No. Here is more, sir.

Co. Ah, ass, that thou couldst not know thy
happiness till thou hadst lost it! How now? my
nose bleed?[1] Shall I write in blood? What! only
three drops? 'Sfoot, 'tis ominous: I will not set my
hand to't now certain, master Notary, I like not this
abodement; I will defer the setting to of my hand
till the next court day. Keep the divorce, I pray you,
and the woman in your house together.

Omnes. Burn the divorce, burn the divorce!

Co. Not so, sir, it shall not serve her turn. Master
Notary, keep it at your peril, and, gentlemen, you may
begone a God's name; what have you to do to flock
about me thus? I am neither howlet nor cuckoo.
Gentlewomen, for God's sake meddle with your own
cases, it is not fit you should haunt these public
assemblies.

Omnes. Well, farewell, Cornelio.

Va. Use the gentlewoman kindly, master Notary.

No. As mine own wife, I assure you, sir.   [*Exeunt.*

Cl. Signor Cornelio, I cannot but in kindness
tell you that Valerio, by counsel of Rinaldo, hath
whispered all this jealousy into your ears; not that
he knew any just cause in your wife, but only to be
revenged on you for the gull you put upon him when
you drew him with his glory to touch the theorbe.

Co. May I believe this?

Cl. As I am a gentleman; and if this accident of
your nose had not fallen out, I would have told you
this before you set to your hand.

Co. It may well be, yet have I cause enough

---

[1] An ill omen.

To perfect my divorce; but it shall rest
Till I conclude it with a counterbuff
Given to these noble rascals.   Claudio, thanks:
What comes of this, watch but my brain a little,
And ye shall see, if like two parts in me,
I leave not both these gullers' wits imbrier'd;
Now I perceive well where the wild wind sits,
Here's gull for gull, and wits at war with wits.

                                        [*Exeunt.*

ACT THE FIFTH

SCENE I

RINALDO *solus*.

ORTUNE, the great commandress of the world,
    Hath divers ways to advance her followers :
To some she gives honour without deserving,
To other some, deserving without honour ;
Some wit, some wealth, and some wit without wealth ;
Some wealth without wit, some nor wit nor wealth,
But good smock-faces ; or some qualities,
By nature without judgment, with the which
They live in sensual acceptation
And make show only, without touch of substance.
My fortune is to win renown by gulling
Gostanzo, Dariotto, and Cornelio ;
All which suppose, in all their different kinds,
Their wits entire, and in themselves no piece ;
All at one blow, my helmet, yet unbruised,
I have unhorsed, laid flat on earth for gulls :
Now in what taking poor Cornelio is

Betwixt his large divorce and no divorce,
I long to see, and what he will resolve ;
I lay my life he cannot chew his meat,
And look much like an ape had swallow'd pills ;
And all this comes of bootless jealousy,
And see, where bootless jealousy appears.

Enter CORNELIO.

I'll board him straight : how now, Cornelio,
Are you resolved on the divorce, or no ?

Co. What's that to you ?   Look to your own affairs,
The time requires it : are not you engaged
In some bonds forfeit for Valerio ?

Ri. Yes, what of that ?

Co. Why, so am I myself,
And both our dangers great ; he is arrested
On a recognizance, by a usuring slave.

Ri. Arrested ?   I am sorry with my heart,
It is a matter may import me much.
May not our bail suffice to free him, think you ?

Co. I think it may, but I must not be seen in't,
Nor would I wish you, for we both are parties,
And liker far to bring ourselves in trouble,
Than bear him out ; I have already made
Means to the officers to sequester him
In private for a time, till some in secret
Might make his father understand his state,
Who would perhaps take present order for him,
Rather than suffer him t'endure the shame
Of his imprisonment.   Now, would you but go
And break the matter closely[1] to his father,
(As you can wisely do't) and bring him to him,
This were the only way to save his credit,

                    [1] Secretly.

And to keep off a shrewd blow from ourselves.

Ri. I know his father will be moved past measure.

Co. Nay, if you stand on such nice ceremonies,
Farewell our substance ; extreme diseases
Ask extreme remedies : better he should storm
Some little time than we be beat for ever
Under the horrid shelter of a prison.

Ri. Where is the place ?

Co. 'Tis at the Half Moon Tavern.
Haste, for the matter will abide no stay.

Ri. Heaven send my speed be equal with my haste.

            [*Exit.*

Co. Go, shallow scholar, you that make all gulls,
You that can out-see clear-eyed jealousy,
Yet make this slight a milestone, where your brain
Sticks in the midst amazed[1] ; this gull to him
And to his fellow guller, shall become
More bitter than their baiting of my humour ;
Here at this tavern shall Gostanzo find
Fortunio, Dariotto, Claudio,
And amongst them, the ringleader his son,
His husband, and his Saint Valerio,
That knows not of what fashion dice are made,
Nor ever yet look'd towards a red lattice[2]
(Thinks his blind sire), at drinking and at dice,
With all their wenches, and at full discover
His own gross folly and his son's distempers.
And both shall know (although I be no scholar)
Yet I have thus much Latin, as to say,
Jam sumus ergo pares.   [*Exit*

   [1] Bewildered.   [2] A tavern.

Enter VALERIO, FORTUNIO, CLAUDIO, Page, GRATIANA,
GAZETTA, BELLANORA. *A* Drawer *or two, setting
a table.*

Va. Set me the table here, we will shift rooms
To see if fortune will shift chances with us ;
Sit, ladies, sit ; Fortunio, place thy wench,
And Claudio place you Dariotto's mistress.
I wonder where that neat spruce slave becomes ;
I think he was some barber's son, by th' mass,
'Tis such a picked fellow, not a hair
About his whole bulk, but it stands in print.
Each pin hath his due place, not any point
But hath his perfect tie, fashion, and grace ;
A thing whose soul is specially employ'd
In knowing where best gloves, best stockings, waist
    coats
Curiously wrought, are sold ; sacks milliners' shops
For all new tires and fashions, and can tell ye
What new devices of all sorts there are,
And that there is not in the whole Rialto
But one new-fashion'd waistcoat, or one night-cap,
One pair of gloves, pretty or well perfumed,
And from a pair of gloves of half-a-crown
To twenty crowns, will to a very scute [1]
Smell out the price ; and for these womanly parts
He is esteem'd a witty gentleman.

Enter DARIOTTO.

Fo. See, where he comes.

Da. God save you, lovely ladies.

Va. Ay, well said, lovely Paris ; your wall eye
Must ever first be gloating on men's wives ;
You think to come upon us, being half drunk

---

[1] A French coin.

And so to part the freshest man among us,
But you shall overtake us, I'll be sworn.

Da. Tush, man; where are your dice?
Let's fall to them.

Cl. We have been at 'em.   Drawer, call for more.

Va. First, let's have wine; dice have no perfect
    edge
Without the liquid whetstone of the syrup.

Fo. True; and to welcome Dariotto's lateness,
He shall (unpledged) carouse one crowned cup
To all these ladies' health.

Da. I am well pleased.

Va. Come on, let us vary our sweet time
With sundry exercises.   Boy! tobacco.
And drawer, you must get us music too;
Call's in a cleanly noise,[1] the slaves grow lousy.

Dr. You shall have such as we can get for you, sir.
                                          [*Exit.*

Da. Let's have some dice; I pray thee they are
cleanly.

Va. Page, let me see that leaf.

Pa. It is not leaf, sir; 'tis pudding cane tobacco.

Va. But I mean your linstock,[2] sir; what leaf is
that, I pray?

Pa. I pray you see, sir, for I cannot read.

Va. 'Sfoot, a rank, stinking Satyr; this had been
Enough to have poison'd every man of us.

Da. And now you speak of that, my boy once
    lighted
A pipe of cane tobacco with a piece
Of a vile ballad, and I'll swear I had

---

[1] Musician.

[2] Stick to hold gunner's match: here used for the wisp of paper
he held for a light for his pipe.

A singing in my head a whole week after.

Va. Well, th' old verse is, *A potibus incipe io-c-um.*

Enter Drawer, *with wine and a cup.*

Va. Drawer, fill out this gentleman's carouse,
And harden him for our society.

Da. Well, ladies, here is to your honour'd healths.

Fo. What, Dariotto, without hat or knee?

Va. Well said, Fortunio; oh, y'are a rare courtier,
Your knee, good signor, I beseech, your knee.

Da. Nay, pray you, let's take it by degrees, Valerio;
on our feet first, for this will bring's too soon upon our
knees.

Va. Sir, there are no degrees of order in a tavern;
Here you must, I charge ye, run all ahead.
'Slight, courtier, down,
I hope you are no elephant, you have joints.

Da. Well, sir, here's to the ladies, on my knees.

Va. I'll be their pledge.

Enter GOSTANZO *and* RINALDO.

Fo. Not yet, Valerio;
This he must drink unpledged.

Va. He shall not; I will give him this advantage.

Go. How now, what's here? Are these the officers?

Ri. 'Slight, I would all were well.

Enter CORNELIO.

Va. Here is his pledge;
Here's to our common friend, Cornelio's health.

Cl. Health to Gazetta, poison to her husband.

                                        [*He kneels*

Co. Excellent guests; these are my daily guests.

Va. Drawer, make even th' impartial scales of
  justice,
Give it to Claudio, and from him fill round.
Come, Dariotto, set [1] me, let me rest,
Come in when they have done the ladies right.

 Go. Set me ; do you know what belongs to setting ?

 Ri. What a dull slave was I to be thus gull'd.

 Co. Why, Rinaldo, what meant you to entrap your
  friend,
And bring his father to this spectacle ?
You are a friend indeed.

 Ri. 'Tis very good, sir ;
Perhaps my friend, or I, before we part,
May make even with you,

 Fo. Come, let's set him round.

 Va. Do so ; at all. A plague upon these dice !
Another health, 'sfoot, I shall have no luck
Till I be drunk : come on, here's to the comfort
The cavalier, my father, should take in me
If he now saw me, and would do me right.

 Fo. I'll pledge it, and his health, Valerio.

 Go. Here's a good husband.

 Ri. I pray you have patience, sir.

 Va. Now have at all, and 'twere a thousand pounds.

 Go. Hold, sir ; I bar the dice.

 Va. What, sir, are you there ?
Fill's a fresh bottle ; by this light, sir knight,
You shall do right.

Enter MARC ANTONIO.

 Go. O thou ungracious villain !

 Va. Come, come, we shall have you now thunder
  forth

[1] Put up the stake.

Some of your thrifty sentences, as gravely :

"For as much, Valerius, as everything has time, and
a pudding has two ; yet ought not satisfaction to swerve
so much from defalcation of well-disposed people, as
that indemnity should prejudice what security doth
insinuate ;" a trial yet once again.

Ma. Here's a good sight ; y'are well encounter'd,
    sir ;
Did not I tell you you'd o'ershoot yourself
With too much wisdom ?

Va. Sir, your wisest do so ;
Fill the old man some wine.

Go. Here's a good infant.

Ma. Why, sir ; alas ! I'll wager with your wisdom,
His consorts drew him to it, for of himself
He is both virtuous, bashful, innocent ;
Comes not at city ; knows no city art,
But plies your husbandry ; dares not view a wench.

Va. Father, he comes upon you.[1]

Go. Here's a son.

Ma. Whose wife is Gratiana, now, I pray ?

Go. Sing your old song no more ; your brain's too
    short
To reach into these policies.

Ma. 'Tis true,
Mine eye's soon blinded ; and yourself would say so
If you knew all. Where lodged your son last night ?
Do you know that, with all your policy ?

Go. You'll say he lodged with you ; and did not I
Foretell you all this must for colour sake
Be brought about, only to blind your eyes ?

Ma. By heaven ! I chanced this morn, I know not
    why,

---

[1] He's got the best of you.

To pass by Gratiana's bedchamber ;
And whom saw I fast by her naked side
But your Valerio?

Go. Had you not warning given ?
Did not I bid you watch my courtier well,
Or he would set a crest a your son's head ?

Ma. That was not all, for by them on a stool,
My son sat laughing, to see you so gull'd.

Go. 'Tis too, too plain.

Ma. Why, sir, do you suspect it the more for that ?

Go. Suspect it ? is there any
So gross a wittoll, as if 'twere his wife,
Would sit by her so tamely ?

Ma. Why not, sir, to blind my eyes ?

Go. Well, sir, I was deceived,
But I shall make it prove a dear deceit
To the deceiver.

Ri. Nay, sir, let's not have
A new infliction set on an old fault :
He did confess his fault upon his knees,
You pardon'd it, and swore 'twas from your heart.

Go. Swore ; a great piece of work, the wretch shall
   know
I have a daughter here to give my land to,
I'll give my daughter all : the prodigal
Shall not have one poor house to hide his head in.

Fo. I humbly thank you, sir, and vow all duty
My life can yield you.

Go. Why are you so thankful ?

Fo. For giving to your daughter all your lands ;
Who is my wife, and so you gave them me.

Go. Better, and better.

Fo. Pray, sir, be not moved,
You drew me kindly to your house, and gave me

Access to woo your daughter, whom I loved:
And since (by honour'd marriage) made my wife.

Go. Now all my choler fly out in your wits:
Good tricks of youth, i' faith no indecorum,
Knight's son, knight's daughter; Marc Antonio,
Give me your hand; there is no remedy;
Marriage is ever made by destiny.

Ri. Silence, my masters; now here all are pleased,
Only Cornelio; who lacks but persuasion
To reconcile himself to his fair wife:
Good sir, will you (of all men our best speaker)
Persuade him to receive her into grace?

Go. That I will gladly; and he shall be ruled.
Good Cornelio, I have heard of your wayward jealousy,
and I must tell you plain as a friend, y'are an ass; you
must pardon me, I knew your father.

Ri. Then you must pardon him, indeed, sir.

Go. Understand me: put case Dariotto loved your
wife, whereby you would seem to refuse her; would
you desire to have such a wife as no man could love
but yourself?

Ma. Answer but that, Cornelio.

Go. Understand me; say Dariotto hath kissed your
wife, or performed other offices of that nature, whereby
they did converse together at bed and at board, as
friends may seem to do.

Ma. Mark but the "now understand me."

Go. Yet if there come no proofs but that her actions
were cleanly, or indiscreet private, why, 'twas a sign
of modesty; and will you blow the horn yourself,
when you may keep it to yourself? Go to, you are a
fool; understand me.

Va. Do understand him, Cornelio.

Go. Nay, Cornelio, I tell you again, I knew your

H

father; he was a wise gentleman and so was your mother; methinks I see her yet; a lusty stout woman, bore great children, you were the very scoundrel of 'em all; but let that pass; as for your mother, she was wise; a most flippant tongue she had, and could set out her tail with as good grace as any she in Florence, come cut and long tail; and she was honest [1] enough too. But yet by your leave she would tickle Dob now and then, as well as the best on 'em: by Jove! it's true, Cornelio, I speak it not to flatter you; your father knew it well enough, and would he do as you do, think you? Set rascals to undermine her, or look to her water (as they say)? No; when he saw 'twas but her humour, for his own quietness' sake he made a back-door to his house for convenience, got a bell to his fore door, and had an odd fashion in ringing, by which she and her maid knew him; and would stand talking to his next neighbour to prolong time, that all things might be rid cleanly out a the way before he came, for the credit of his wife. This was wisdom now, for a man's own quiet.

Ma. Here was a man, Cornelio.

Go. What, I say! Young men think old men are fools; but old men know young men are fools.

Co. Why, hark you, you two knights; do you think I will forsake Gazetta?

Go. And will you not?

Co. Why, there's your wisdom; why did I make show of divorce, think you?

Ma. Pray you why, sir?

Co. Only to bridle her stout stomach; and how did I draw on the colour for my divorce? I did train the woodcock [2] Dariotto into the net, drew him to my

---

[1] Virtuous.   [2] Fool.

house, gave him opportunity with my wife (as you say my father dealt with his wife's friends), only to train [1] him in; let him alone with my wife in her bed-chamber, and sometimes found him a bed with her, and went my way back again softly, only to draw him into the pit.

Go. This was well handled indeed, Cornelio.

Ma. Ay marry, sir, now I commend your wisdom.

Co. Why, if I had been so minded as you think, I could have flung his pantable [2] down the stairs, or done him some other disgrace; but I winked at it, and drew on the good fool more and more, only to bring him within my compass.

Go. Why, this was policy in grain.

Co. And now shall the world see I am as wise as my father.

Va. Is't come to this? then will I make a speech in praise of this reconcilement, including therein the praise and honour of the most fashionable and auten-tical *HORN:* stand close, gentles, and be silent.

[*He gets into a chair.*

Go. Come on, let's hear his wit in this potable humour.

Va. The course of the world (like the life of man) is said to be divided into several ages. As we into infancy, childhood, youth, and so forward, to old age; so the world into the golden age, the silver, the brass, the iron, the leaden, the wooden, and now into this present age, which we term the *horned age:* not that but former ages have enjoyed this benefit as well as our times, but that in ours it is more common, and nevertheless precious. It is said, that in the golden age of the world, the use of gold was not then known;

---

[1] Deceive him.   [2] Slipper.

an argument[1] of the simplicity of that age, lest therefore succeeding ages should hereafter impute the same
fault to us, which we lay upon the first age; that we,
living in the horned age of the world should not understand the use, the virtue, the honour, and the very
royalty of the horn, I will, in brief, sound the praises
thereof; that they, who are already in possession of
it, may bear their heads aloft, as being proud of such
lofty accoutrements; and they that are but in possi-
bility, may be ravished with a desire to be in possession. A trophy so honourable, and unmatchably
powerful, that it is able to raise any man from a
beggar to an emperor's fellow,[2] a duke's fellow, a
nobleman's fellow, alderman's fellow; so glorious, that
it deserves to be worn (by most opinions) in the most
conspicuous place about a man: for what worthier
crest can you bear than the horn? which if it might
be seen with our mortal eyes, what a wonderful spectacle would there be! and how highly they would
ravish the beholders. But their substance is incorporal,
not falling under sense, nor mixed of the gross con-
cretion of elements, but a quintessence beyond them;
a spiritual essence invisible and everlasting. And this
hath been the cause that many men have called their
being in question, whether there be such a thing in
rerum naturâ, or not; because they were not to be
seen, as though nothing were that were not to be seen.
Who ever saw the wind? yet what wonderful effects
are seen of it! it drives the clouds, yet no man sees
it; it rocks the house, bears down trees, castles,
steeples, yet who sees it? In like sort does your
horn: it swells the forehead, yet none sees it; it rocks
the cradle, yet none sees it; so that you plainly per-

[1] Proof. [2] Companion.

ceive sense is no judge of essence. The moon to any
man's sense seems to be horned; yet who knows not
the moon to be ever perfectly round? so, likewise your
heads seem ever to be round, when indeed they are
oftentimes horned. For their original it is unsearch-
able; natural they are not; for there[1] is beast born
with horns more than with teeth? created they were
not, for *Ex nihilo nihil fit;* then will you ask me,
how came they into the world? I know not; but I
am sure women brought them into this part of the
world; howsoever, some doctors are of opinion that
they came in with the devil, and not unlike;[2] for as
the devil brought sin into the world, but the woman
brought it to the man; so it may very well be that
the devil brought horns into the world, but the woman
brought them to the man. For their power, it is
general over the world: no nation so barbarous, no
country so proud, but doth equal homage to the horn.
Europa, when she was carried through the sea by the
Saturnian bull, was said (for fear of falling) to have
held by the horn; and what is this but a plain showing to us, that all Europe, which took name from that
Europa, should likewise hold by the horn. So that I
say, it is universal over the face of the world, general
over the face of Europe, and common over the face
of this country. What city, what town, what village,
what street, nay, what house, can quit itself of this
prerogative? I have read that the lion once made a
proclamation through all the forest, that all horned
beasts should depart forthwith upon pain of death;
if this proclamation should be made through our
forest, Lord! what pressing, what running, what flying
would there be even from all the parts of it! He that

---

[1] Where.   [2] Improbable.

had but a bunch of flesh in his head would away ; and
some foolishly fearful, would imagine the shadow of
his ears to be horns ; alas ! how desert would this
forest be left ! To conclude : for their force it is
irrevitable, for were they not irrevitable, then might
either properness [1] of person secure a man, or wisdom
prevent 'em ; or greatness exempt, or riches redeem
them ; but present experience hath taught us, that in
this case, all these stand in no stead ; for we see the
properest men take part of them, the best wits cannot
avoid them (for then should poets be no cuckolds), nor
can money redeem them, for then would rich men
fine [2] for their horns, as they do for offices ; but this
is held for a maxim, that there are more rich cuckolds
than poor. Lastly, for continuance of the horn, it is
undeterminable till death ; neither do they determine [3]
with the wife's death (howsoever, ignorant writers hold
opinion they do), for as when a knight dies his lady
still retains the title of lady ; when a company is cast [4]
yet the captain still retains the title of captain ; so
though the wife die by whom this title came to her
husband, yet by the courtesy of the city, he shall be a
cuckold during life, let all ignorant asses prate what
they list.

Go. Notable wag ; come, sir, shake hands with him
In whose high honour you have made this speech.

Ma. And you, sir, come, join hands ; y'are one
　　amongst them.

Go. Very well done ; now take your several wives,
And spread like wild-geese, though you now grow
　　tame ;
Live merrily together, and agree.
Horns cannot be kept off with jealousy.

　　　[1] Beauty.　　　[2] Pay fines.　　　[3] Cease.　　　[4] Disbanded.

EPILOGUE

INCE all our labours are as you can like,
    We all submit to you ; nor dare presume
    To think there's any real worth in them ;
    Sometimes feasts please the cooks, and not
       the guests ;
Sometimes the guests, and curious cooks contemn
   them.
Our dishes we entirely dedicate
To our kind guests ; but since ye differ so,
Some to like only mirth without taxations,[1]
Some to count such works trifles, and such-like,
We can but bring you meat, and set you stools,
And to our best cheer say, you all are—[2] welcome.

     [1] Personal remarks.
     [2] The dash indicates the suggested rime.

BUSSY D'AMBOIS

USSY D'AMBOIS, the most popular tragedy that Chapman ever wrote, was first published in 1607 ; other editions appeared in 1608, 1616, 1641, and 1657. The edition of 1641 is the one usually followed by modern editors, "being much corrected and amended by the author before his death." In 1691 Durfey produced an amended and altered version. The part of *Bussy* was one of Nathaniel Field's most popular impersonations.

Chapman drew his material for *Bussy* and the *Revenge* partly from De Thou's *Historiae sui temporis*, a contemporary work written in Latin. Chapman also used some other authorities, but he treated all his material with great freedom.

PROLOGUE

NOT out of confidence that none but we
 Are able to present this tragedy,
 Nor out of envy at the grace of late
 It did receive, nor yet to derogate
From their deserts, who give out boldly, that
They move with equal feet on the same flat;
Neither for all, nor any of such ends,
We offer it, gracious and noble friends,
To your review; we, far from emulation
(And charitably judge from imitation),
With this work entertain you, a piece known
And still believed in Court to be our own,
To quit our claim, doubting our right or merit,
Would argue in us poverty of spirit
Which we must not subscribe to: Field [1] is gone,
Whose action first did give it name, and one
Who came the nearest to him, is denied
By his gray beard to show the height and pride
Of D'Ambois' youth and bravery; yet to hold
Our title still a-foot, and not grow cold
By giving it o'er, a third man with his best
Of care and pains defends our interest;

---

[1] Nathaniel Field; this was his first recorded part.

As Richard he was liked, nor do we fear
In personating D'Ambois he'll appear
To faint, or go less, so[1] your free consent
As heretofore give him encouragement.[2]

[1] So long as.

[2] This Prologue, prefixed to the 1641 edition, is one of the most difficult things to explain in all English dramatic literature. If it was written by Chapman, who died in 1634, the "third man" would probably be Ilyard Swanston (see Fleay, *Biog. Chron. of Drama*, i., 60), for Swanston had acted Ricardo in Massinger's *Picture* in 1629, and this might explain the "Richard." Of the "gray beard" we have no record. Joseph Taylor was not old enough. The problem has never been satisfactorily solved.

DRAMATIS PERSONÆ [1]

HENRY III., King of France.
Monsieur, his brother.
THE DUKE OF GUISE.
MONTSURRY, an Earl.
BUSSY D'AMBOIS.
BARRISOR, ⎫
L'ANOU, ⎬ Warriors.
PYRRHOT, ⎭
BRISAC, ⎫
MELYNELL, ⎬ friends of Bussy D'Ambois.
FRIAR COMOLET
MAFFE, confidential servant to Monsieur.
NUNTIUS.
Murderers.
BEHEMOTH, a Spirit.
UMBRA FRIAR.
ELENOR, Duchess of Guise.
TAMYRA, Countess of Montsurry.
BEAUPRE.
PERO.
CHARLOTTE.
PYRA.
ANNABELLE.
Lords, Ladies, Pages, &c.

[1] Now first printed.

BUSSY D'AMBOIS

ACT THE FIRST

SCENE I

Enter BUSSY D'AMBOIS, *poor.*

U. Fortune, not Reason, rules the state of things,
    Reward goes backwards, Honour on his head ;
Who is not poor, is monstrous ; only need
Gives form and worth to every humane seed.
As cedars beaten with continual storms,
So great men flourish ; and do imitate
Unskilful statuaries, who suppose,
In forming a Colossus, if they make him
Straddle enough, strut, and look big, and gape,
Their work is goodly : so men merely great
In their affected gravity of voice,
Sourness of countenance, manners' cruelty,
Authority, wealth, and all the spawn of fortune,

127

Think they bear all the kingdom's worth before
    them ;
Yet differ not from those colossic statues,
Which, with heroic forms without o'erspread,
Within are nought but mortar, flint, and lead.
Man is a torch borne in the wind ; a dream
But of a shadow, summ'd with all his substance :
And as great seamen, using their wealth
And skills in Neptune's deep invisible paths,
In tall ships richly built and ribb'd with brass,
To put a girdle round about the world ; [1]
When they have done it (coming near their haven)
Are glad to give a warning-piece, and call
A poor, staid fisherman, that never past
His country's sight, to waft and guide them in :
So when we wander furthest through the waves
Of glassy Glory, and the gulfs of State,
Topt with all titles, spreading all our reaches,
As if each private arm would sphere the earth,
We must to Virtue for her guide resort,
Or we shall shipwrack in our safest port.   [*Procumbit.*

      Enter Monsieur, *with two* Pages.

Mo. There is no second place in numerous State
That holds more than a cipher ; in a king
All places are contain'd.   His word and looks
Are like the flashes and the bolts of Jove ;
His deeds inimitable, like the sea
That shuts still as it opes, and leaves no tracts
Nor prints of precedent for poor men's facts : [2]
There's but a thread betwixt me and a crown ·
I would not wish it cut, unless by nature ;
Yet to prepare me for that possible fortune,

    [1] Cf. *Midsummer Night's Dream*, I. i. 175.   [2] Deeds.

'Tis good to get resolved spirits about me.
I follow'd D'Ambois to this green retreat;
A man of spirit beyond the reach of fear,
Who (discontent with his neglected worth)
Neglects the light, and loves obscure abodes;
But he is young and haughty, apt to take
Fire at advancement, to bear state and flourish;
In his rise therefore shall my bounties shine:
None loathes the world so much, nor loves to scoff it,
But gold and grace will make him surfeit of it.
What, D'Ambois?

    Bu. He, sir.

    Mo. Turn'd to earth, alive?
Up, man: the sun shines on thee.

    Bu. Let it shine:
I am no more to play in't, as great men are.

    Mo. Think'st thou men great in state, motes in the
        sun?
They say so that would have thee freeze in shades,
That (like the gross Sicilian Gourmandist)
Empty their noses in the cates they love,
That none may eat but they.   Do thou but bring
Light to the banquet Fortune sets before thee,
And thou wilt loathe lean darkness like thy death.
Who would believe thy mettle could let sloth
Rust and consume it?   If Themistocles
Had lived obscured thus in th'Athenian State,
Xerxes had made both him and it his slaves.
If brave Camillus had lurk'd so in Rome,
He had not five times been Dictator there,
Nor four times triumph'd.   If Epaminondas
(Who lived twice twenty years obscured in Thebes)
Had lived so still, he had been still unnamed,
And paid his country nor himself their right:

  I

But putting forth his strength, he rescued both
From imminent ruin ; and like burnish'd steel,
After long use he shined ; for as the light
Not only serves to show, but render us
Mutually profitable ; so our lives
In acts exemplary, not only win
Ourselves good names, but doth to others give
Matter for virtuous deeds, by which we live.

   Bu. What would you wish me ?

   Mo. Leave the troubled streams,
And live, as thrivers do, at the well-head.

   Bu. At the well-head ?   Alas, what should I do
With that enchanted glass ? See devils there ?
Or, like a strumpet, learn to set my looks
In an eternal brake,[1] or practise juggling,
To keep my face still fast, my heart still loose ;
Or bear (like dames schoolmistresses their riddles)
Two tongues, and be good only for a shift ;
Flatter great lords, to put them still in mind
Why they were made lords ; or please humorous
    ladies
With a good carriage, tell them idle tales
To make their physic work ; spend a man's life
In sights and visitations, that will make
His eyes as hollow as his mistress' heart :
To do none good, but those that have no need ;
To gain being forward, though you break for haste
All the commandments ere you break your fast ;
But believe backwards, make your period
And creed's last article, " I believe in God : "
And (hearing villanies preach'd) t'unfold their art,
Learn to commit them ; 'tis a great man's part.
Shall I learn this there ?

             [1] Frame ; perfectly fixed.

Mo. No, thou need'st not learn,
Thou hast the theory ; now go there and practise.

Bu. Ay, in a threadbare suit; when men come
there,
They must have high naps,[1] and go from thence bare :
A man may drown the parts of ten rich men
In one poor suit ; brave barks[2] and outward gloss
Attract Court loves, be in parts ne'er so gross.

Mo. Thou shalt have gloss enough, and all things
fit
T'enchase in all show thy long-smother'd spirit :
Be ruled by me then. The rude Scythians
Painted blind Fortune's powerful hands with wings
To show her gifts come swift and suddenly,
Which, if her favourite be not swift to take,
He loses them for ever. Then be wise :

[*Exit* Monsieur.
Stay but awhile here, and I'll send to thee.

[*Manet* BUSSY.

Bu. What will he send ? Some crowns ? it is to
sow them
Upon my spirit, and make them spring a crown
Worth millions of the seed-crowns he will send :
Like to disparking[3] noble husbandmen,
He'll put his plow into me, plow me up.
But his unsweating thrift is policy,
And learning-hating policy is ignorant
To fit his seed-land soil ; a smooth plain ground
Will never nourish any politic seed ;
I am for honest actions, not for great :
If I may bring up a new fashion,
And rise in Court for virtue, speed his plow ;

---

[1] Clothes with fine gloss.   [2] Fine coverings.
[3] Those who change parks into fields for plowing.

The King hath known me long as well as he,
Yet could my fortune never fit the length
Of both their understandings till this hour.
There is a deep nick in time's restless wheel
For each man's good, when which nick comes, it
     strikes,
As rhetoric, yet works not persuasion,
But only is a mean to make it work :
So no man riseth by his real merit,
But when it cries clink in his raiser's spirit.
Many will say, that cannot rise at all,
Man's first hour's rise is first step to his fall.
I'll venture that ; men that fall low must die,
As well as men cast headlong from the sky.

Enter MAFFE.

Ma. Humour of princes !   Is this wretch endued
With any merit worth a thousand crowns ?
Will my lord have me be so ill a steward
Of his revenue, to dispose a sum
So great with so small cause as shows in him ?
I must examine this.   Is your name D'Ambois ?
     Bu. Sir ?
     Ma. Is your name D'Ambois ?
     Bu. Who have we here ?
Serve you the Monsieur ?
     Ma. How ?
     Bu. Serve you the Monsieur ?
     Ma. Sir, y'are very hot.   I do serve the Monsieur,
But in such place as gives me the command
Of all his other servants.   And because
His grace's pleasure is to give your good,
His pass through my command, methinks you might
Use me with more respect.

[*Table, Chess-board, and Tapers behind the arras.*

Bu. Cry you mercy;
Now you have open'd my dull eyes, I see you,
And would be glad to see the good you speak of;
What might I call your name?

Ma. Monsieur Maffe.

Bu. Monsieur Maffe? then, good Monsieur Maffe,
Pray let me know you better.

Ma. Pray do so,
That you may use me better; for yourself,
By your no better outside, I would judge you
To be some poet; have you given my lord
Some pamphlet?

Bu. Pamphlet?

Ma. Pamphlet, sir, I say.

Bu. Did your great master's goodness leave the
good
That is to pass your charge to my poor use,
To your discretion?

Ma. Though he did not, sir,
I hope 'tis no bad office to ask reason
How that his grace gives me in charge, goes from
me?

Bu. That's very perfect, sir.

Ma. Why, very good, sir;
I pray then give me leave; if for no pamphlet,
May I not know what other merit in you,
Makes his compunction willing to relieve you?

Bu. No merit in the world, sir.

Ma. That is strange.
Y'are a poor soldier, are you?

Bu. That I am, sir.

Ma. And have commanded?

Bu. Ay, and gone without, sir.

Ma. I see the man; a hundred crowns will make
    him
Swagger and drink healths to his grace's bounty,
And swear he could not be more bountiful;
So there's nine hundred crowns saved; here, tall
    soldier,
His grace hath sent you a whole hundred crowns.

Bu. A hundred, sir? Nay, do his highness right;
I know his hand is larger, and perhaps
I may deserve more than my outside shows;
I am a scholar, as I am a soldier,
And I can poetise; and (being well encouraged)
May sing his fame for giving; yours for delivering
(Like a most faithful steward) what he gives.

Ma. What shall your subject be?

Bu. I care not much
If to his bounteous grace I sing the praise
Of fair great noses, and to you of long ones.
What qualities have you, sir, beside your chain
And velvet jacket? Can your worship dance?

Ma. A merry fellow, 'faith; it seems my lord
Will have him for his jester; and by'r lady,
Such men are now no fools; 'tis a knight's place:
If I (to save my lord some crowns) should urge him
T'abate his bounty, I should not be heard;
I would to heaven I were an errant ass.
For then I should be sure to have the ears
Of these great men, where now their jesters have them.
'Tis good to please him, yet I'll take no notice
Of his preferment, but in policy
Will still be grave and serious, lest he think
I fear his wooden dagger.[1] Here, sir Ambo!

---

[1] The Vice, the comic character of the morality plays, carried a
wooden dagger.

Bu. How, Ambo, sir?

Ma. Ay, is not your name Ambo?

Bu. You call'd me lately D'Ambois; has your
    worship
So short a head?

Ma. I cry thee mercy, D'Ambois.
A thousand crowns I bring you from my lord:
If you be thrifty, and play the good husband, you may
    make
This a good standing living: 'tis a bounty
His highness might perhaps have bestow'd better.

Bu. Go, y'are a rascal; hence, away, you rogue!

Ma. What mean you, sir?

Bu. Hence! prate no more!
Or, by thy villain's blood, thou pratest thy last!
A barbarous groom grudge at his master's bounty!
But since I know he would as much abhor
His hind should argue what he gives his friend,
Take that, sir, for your aptness to dispute.   [*Exit.*

Ma. These crowns are sown in blood; blood be
    their fruit.   [*Exit.*

HENRY, GUISE, MONTSURRY, ELENOR, TAMYRA,
BEAUPRE, PERO, CHARLOTTE, PYRA, ANNABELLE.

He. Duchess of Guise, your grace is much enrich'd
In the attendance of that English virgin,
That will initiate her prime of youth
(Disposed to Court conditions) under hand
Of your preferr'd instructions and command,
Rather than any in the English Court,
Whose ladies are not match'd in Christendom
For graceful and confirm'd behaviours;
More than the Court, where they are bred, is equall'd.

Gu. I like not their Court form; it is too crestfall'n

In all observance, making demigods
Of their great nobles ; and of their old queen,
An ever-young and most immortal goddess.

Mo. No question she's the rarest queen in Europe.

Gu. But what's that to her immortality ?

He. Assure you, cousin Guise, so great a courtier,
So full of majesty and royal parts,
No queen in Christendom may vaunt herself.
Her Court approves it, that's a Court indeed,
Not mixt with clowneries used in common houses,
But, as Courts should be, th' abstracts of their king-
        doms,
In all the beauty, state, and worth they hold ;
So is hers, amply, and by her inform'd.
The world is not contracted in a man
With more proportion and expression,
Than in her Court, her kingdom.   Our French Court
Is a mere mirror of confusion to it :
The king and subject, lord and every slave,
Dance a continual hay ; our rooms of state
Kept like our stables ; no place more observed
Than a rude market-place : and though our custom
Keep this assured confusion from our eyes
'Tis ne'er the less essentially unsightly,
Which they would soon see, would they change their
        form
To this of ours, and then compare them both ;
Which we must not affect, because in kingdoms
Where the king's change doth breed the subject's
        terror,
Pure innovation is more gross than error.

Mo. No question we shall see them imitate
(Though afar off) the fashions of our Courts,
As they have ever aped us in attire.

; he's so at first greets
n, which becomes t
e attires of men.

He. No quest h wrong their real worth
In affectation of outli m ;
But they have faults, ve more ; they foolish
proud
To jet[1] in others plumes so hau ily ;
We proud, that they are proud of foolery,
Holding our worths more complete for their vaunts.

Enter Monsieur, D'AMBOIS.

Mo. Come, mine own sweetheart, I will enter thee.
Sir, I have brought a gentleman to Court,
And pray you would vouchsafe to do him grace.

He. D'Ambois, I think ?

Bu. That's still my name, my lord,
Though I be something alter'd in attire.

He. I like your alteration, and must tell you
I have expected th' offer of your service ;
For we (in fear to make mild virtue proud)
Use not to seek her out in any man.

Bu. Nor doth she use to seek out any man :
He that will win must woo her.

Mo. I urged her modesty in him, my lord,
And gave her those rites that he says she merits.

[1] Strut.

en, brother, wear

See, here's the

Tharreau, Beaupres.

thee; ladies, y'are too many
ncil; I have here a friend
uld gladly enter in your graces.
Save you, ladies.

Du. If you enter him in our graces, my lord, methinks by his blunt behaviour he should come out of himself.

Ta. Has he never been courtier, my lord?

Mo. Never, my lady.

Be. And why did the toy take him in th' head now?

Bu. 'Tis leap-year, lady, and therefore very good to enter a courtier.

He. Mark, Duchess of Guise, there is one is not bashful.

Du. No, my lord, he is much guilty of the bold extremity.

Ta. The man's a courtier at first sight.

Bu. I can sing pricksong,[1] lady, at first sight; and why not be a courtier as suddenly?

Be. Here's a courtier rotten before he be ripe.

Bu. Think me not impudent, lady; I am yet no courtier; I desire to be one, and would gladly take entrance, madam, under your princely colours.

Enter BARRISOR, L'ANOU, PYRRHOT.

Du. Soft, sir, you must rise by degrees, first being the servant[2] of some common lady, or knight's wife,

---

[1] Music written with points, or dots.   [2] Lover.

then a little higher to a lord's wife; next a little
higher to a countess; yet a little higher to a duchess,
and then turn the ladder.

Bu. Do you allow a man, then, four mistresses, when
the greatest mistress is allowed but three servants?

Du. Where find you that statute, sir?

Bu. Why, be judged by the groom-porters.

Du. The groom-porters?

Bu. Ay, madam; must not they judge of all
gamings i' th' Court?

Du. You talk like a gamester.

Gu. Sir, know you me?

Bu. My lord?

Gu. I know not you. Whom do you serve?

Bu. Serve, my lord?

Gu. Go to, companion, your courtship's too saucy.

Bu. Saucy! Companion! 'Tis the Guise, but yet
those terms might have been spared of the Guiserd.
Companion! He's jealous, by this light. Are you
blind of that side, duke? I'll to her again for that.
Forth, princely mistress, for the honour of courtship.
Another riddle!

Gu. Cease your courtship, or by heaven I'll cut
your throat.

Bu. Cut my throat? cut a whetstone. Good
Accius Nævius, do as much with your tongue, as he
did with a razor: cut my throat!

Ba. What new-come gallant have we here, that
dares mate the Guise thus?

L'A. 'Sfoot, 'tis D'Ambois. The duke mistakes
him, on my life, for some knight of the new edition.

Bu. Cut my throat! I would the king feared thy
cutting of his throat no more than I fear thy cutting
of mine.

Gu. I'll do't, by this hand.

Bu. That hand dares not do't—y'ave cut too many throats already, Guise ; and robbed the realm of many thousand souls, more precious than thine own. Come, madam, talk on. 'Sfoot, can you not talk? Talk on, I say ; another riddle.

Py. Here's some strange distemper.

Ba. Here's a sudden transmigration with D'Ambois —out of the knight's ward into the duchess' bed.

L'A. See what a metamorphosis a brave suit can work.

Py. 'Slight, step to the Guise and discover him.

Ba. By no means; let the new suit work, we'll see the issue.

Gu. Leave your courting.

Bu. I will not. I say, mistress, and I will stand unto it, that if a woman may have three servants, a man may have three-score mistresses.

Gu. Sirrah, I'll have you whipped out of the Court for this insolence.

Bu. Whipped? Such another syllable out a th' presence, if thou darest for thy dukedom.

Gu. Remember, poltroon.

Mo. Pray thee, forbear.

Bu. Passion of death ! Were not the king here, he should strow the chamber like a rush.

Mo. But leave courting his wife, then.

Bu. I will not. I'll court her in despite of him. Not court her ! Come, madam, talk on, fear me nothing ; well may'st thou drive thy master from the Court, but never D'Ambois.

Mo. His great heart will not down, 'tis like the sea,
That partly by his own internal heat,
Partly the stars' daily and nightly motion,

Their heat and light, and partly of the place,
The divers frames; but chiefly by the moon,
Bristled with surges, never will be won,
(No, not when th' hearts of all those powers are burst)
To make retreat into his settled home,
Till he be crown'd with his own quiet foam.

He. You have the mate.[1]   Another.

Gu. No more.   [*Flourish short.*

[*Exit* GUISE, *after him the* King, Monsieur
whispering.

Ba. Why, here's the lion, scared with the throat of a dunghill cock; a fellow that has newly shaken off his shackles; now does he crow for that victory.

L'A 'Tis one of the best jigs that ever was acted.

Py. Whom does the Guise suppose him to be, trow?

L'A. Out of doubt, some new denizen'd lord, and thinks that suit newly drawn out a th' mercer's books.

Ba. I have heard of a fellow, that by a fixed imagination looking upon a bull-baiting, had a visible pair of horns grew out of his forehead; and I believe this gallant, overjoyed with the conceit of Monsieur's cast [2] suit, imagines himself to be the Monsieur.

L'A. And why not? as well as the ass, stalking in the lion's case,[3] bear himself like a lion, braying all the huger beasts out of the forest?

Py. Peace, he looks this way.

Ba. Marry, let him look, sir; what will you say now if the Guise be gone to fetch a blanket [4] for him?

L'A. Faith, I believe it for his honour sake.

Py. But, if D'Ambois carry it clean?

Ba. True, when he curvets in the blanket.

Py. Ay, marry, sir.

---

[1] Checkmate : they are playing chess.   [2] Cast off.
[3] Skin.   [4] To toss him.

L'A. 'Sfoot, see how he stares on's.

Ba. Lord bless us, let's away.

Bu. Now, sir, take your full view; how does the object please ye?

Ba. If you ask my opinion, sir, I think your suit fits as well as if't had been made for you.

Bu. So, sir, and was that the subject of your ridiculous jollity?

L'A. What's that to you, sir?

Bu. Sir, I have observed all your fleerings;[1] and resolve yourselves ye shall give a strict account for't.

Enter BRISAC, MELYNELL.

Ba. Oh, miraculous jealousy! do you think yourself such a singular subject for laughter that none can fall into the matter of our merriment but you?

L'A. This jealousy of yours, sir, confesses some close defect in yourself, that we never dreamed of.

Py. We held discourse of a perfumed ass, that being disguised with a lion's case, imagined himself a lion : I hope that touched not you.

Bu. So, sir; your descants do marvellous well fit this ground; we shall meet where your buffoonly laughters will cost ye the best blood in your bodies.

Ba. For life's sake let's be gone; he'll kill's outright.

Bu. Go, at your pleasures, I'll be your ghost to haunt you; and ye sleep an't, hang me.

L'A. Go, go, sir; court your mistress.

Py. And be advised; we shall have odds against you.

Bu. Tush! valour stands not in number; I'll maintain it, that one man may beat three boys.

[1] Sneers.

Br. Nay, you shall have no odds of him in number, sir; he's a gentleman as good as the proudest of you, and ye shall not wrong him.

Ba. Not, sir?

Me. Not, sir: though he be not so rich, he's a better man than the best of you; and I will not endure it.

L'A. Not you, sir?

Br. No, sir, nor I.

Bu. I should thank you for this kindness, if I thought these perfumed musk-cats (being out of this privilege) durst but once mew at us.

Ba. Does your confident spirit doubt that, sir? Follow us and try.

L'A. Come, sir, we'll lead you a dance.   [*Exeunt.*

ACT THE SECOND

SCENE I

Enter HENRY, GUISE, MONTSURRY, *and* Attendants.

E. This desperate quarrel sprung out of
their envies
To D'Ambois' sudden bravery,[1] and
great spirit.
Gu. Neither is worth their envy.
He. Less than either
Will make the gall of envy overflow ;
She feeds on outcast entrails like a kite ;
In which foul heap, if any ill lies hid,
She sticks her beak into it, shakes it up,
And hurls it all abroad, that all may view it.
Corruption is her nutriment ; but touch her
With any precious ointment, and you kill her :
When she finds any filth in men, she feasts,
And with her black throat bruits it through the world
(Being sound and healthful).   But if she but taste
The slenderest pittance of commended virtue,
She surfeits on it, and is like a fly
That passes all the body's soundest parts,

And dwells upon the sores; or if her squint eye
Have power to find none there, she forges some:
She makes that crooked ever which is straight;
Calls valour giddiness, justice tyranny;
A wise man may shun her, she not herself:
Whithersoever she flies from her harms,
She bears her foes still clasp'd in her own arms;
And therefore, cousin Guise, let us avoid her.

Enter NUNTIUS.

Nu. What Atlas or Olympus lifts his head
So far past covert, that with air enough
My words may be inform'd, and from his height
I may be seen, and heard through all the world?
A tale so worthy, and so fraught with wonder
Sticks in my jaws, and labours with event.

   He. Comest thou from D'Ambois?

   Nu. From him, and the rest,
His friends and enemies; whose stern fight I saw,
And heard their words before and in the fray.

   He. Relate at large what thou hast seen and heard.

   Nu. I saw fierce D'Ambois and his two brave
      friends
Enter the field, and at their heels their foes;
Which were the famous soldiers, Barrisor,
L'Anou, and Pyrrhot, great in deeds of arms:
All which arrived at the evenest piece of earth
The field afforded, the three challengers
Turn'd head, drew all their rapiers, and stood rank'd:
When face to face the three defendants met them,
Alike prepared, and resolute alike.
Like bonfires of contributory wood
Every man's look show'd, fed with either's spirit;
As one had been a mirror to another,

   K

Like forms of life and death, each took from other ;
And so were life and death mix'd at their heights,
That you could see no fear of death, for life,
Nor love of life, for death ; but in their brows
Pyrrho's opinion in great letters shone :
That life and death in all respects are one.

    He. Pass'd there no sort of words at their en-
counter ?

    Nu. As Hector, 'twixt the hosts of Greece and
Troy,
(When Paris and the Spartan king should end
The nine years' war) held up his brazen lance
For signal that both hosts should cease from arms,
And hear him speak : so Barrisor (advised)
Advanced his naked rapier 'twixt both sides,
Ripp'd up the quarrel, and compared six lives
Then laid in balance with six idle words ;
Offer'd remission and contrition too ;
Or else that he and D'Ambois might conclude
The others' dangers.   D'Ambois liked the last ;
But Barrisor's friends (being equally engaged
In the main quarrel) never would expose
His life alone to that they all deserved.
And (for the other offer of remission)
D'Ambois (that like a laurel put in fire
Sparkled and spit) did much more than scorn
That his wrong should incense him so like chaff
To go so soon out ; and like lighted paper
Approve his spirit at once both fire and ashes ;
So drew they lots and in them fates appointed
That Barrisor should fight with fiery D'Ambois ;
Pyrrhot with Melynell ; with Brisac L'Anou :
And then like flame and powder they commixt,
So spritely, that I wish'd they had been spirits,

That the ne'er-shutting wounds, they needs must
    open,
Might as they open'd, shut and never kill :
But D'Ambois' sword (that lighten'd as it flew)
Shot like a pointed comet at the face
Of manly Barrisor ; and there it stuck :
Thrice pluck'd he at it, and thrice drew on thrusts,
From him that of himself was free as fire ;
Who thrust still as he pluck'd, yet (past belief)
He with his subtle eye, hand, body, 'scaped :
At last the deadly bitten point tugged off,
On fell his yet undaunted foe so fiercely
That (only made more horrid with his wound)
Great D'Ambois shrunk, and gave a little ground ;
But soon return'd, redoubled in his danger,
And at the heart of Barrisor seal'd his anger :
Then, as in Arden I have seen an oak
Long shook with tempests, and his lofty top
Bent to his root, which being at length made loose
(Even groaning with his weight) he 'gan to nod
This way and that : as loth his curled brows
(Which he had oft wrapt in the sky with storms)
Should stoop : and yet, his radical fibres burst,
Storm-like he fell, and hid the fear-cold earth ;
So fell stout Barrisor, that had stood the shocks
Of ten set battles in your highness' war,
'Gainst the sole soldier of the world, Navarre.

    Gu. Oh, piteous and horrid murder !
    Be. Such a life
Methinks had metal in it to survive
An age of men.
    He. Such often soonest end :
Thy felt report calls on, we long to know
On what events the other have arrived.

Nu. Sorrow and fury, like two opposite fumes,
Met in the upper region of a cloud,
At the report made by this worthy's fall,
Brake from the earth, and with them rose Revenge,
Entering with fresh powers his two noble friends;
And under that odds fell surcharged Brisac,
The friend of D'Ambois, before fierce L'Anou;
Which D'Ambois seeing, as I once did see
In my young travels through Armenia,
An angry unicorn in his full career
Charge with too swift a foot a jeweller
That watch'd him for the treasure of his brow,[1]
And ere he could get shelter of a tree,
Nail him with his rich antler to the earth:
So D'Ambois ran upon revenged L'Anou,
Who eyeing th' eager point borne in his face,
And giving back, fell back, and in his fall
His foe's uncurbed sword stopt in his heart;
By which time all the life-strings of the tw'other
Were cut, and both fell as their spirits flew
Upwards; and still hunt honour at the view:
And now, of all the six, sole D'Ambois stood
Untouch'd, save only with the others' blood.

He. All slain outright but he?

Nu. All slain outright but he.
Who kneeling in the warm life of his friends,
(All freckled with the blood his rapier rain'd)
He kiss'd their pale cheeks, and bade both farewell;
And see the bravest man the French earth bears.

Enter Monsieur, D'Ambois *bare.*

Bu. Now is the time, y'are princely vow'd, my
   friend,

[1] The horn.

Perform it princely, and obtain my pardon.

Mo. Else heaven forgive not me; come on, brave
    friend.

If ever nature held herself her own,

When the great trial of a king and subject

Met in one blood, both from one belly springing;

Now prove her virtue and her greatness one,

Or make the one the greater with the t'other,

(As true kings should) and for your brother's love,

(Which is a special species of true virtue)

Do that you could not do, not being a king.

He. Brother, I know your suit; these wilful
    murders

Are ever past our pardon.

Mo. Manly slaughter

Should never bear th'account of wilful murder;

It being a spice of justice, where with life

Offending past law, equal life is laid

In equal balance, to scourge that offence

By law of reputation, which to men

Exceeds all positive law, and what that leaves

To true men's valours (not prefixing rights

Of satisfaction, suited to their wrongs)

A free man's eminence may supply and take.

He. This would make every man that thinks him
    wrong'd

Or is offended, or in wrong or right,

Lay on this violence, and all vaunt themselves

Law-menders and suppliers,[1] though mere butchers;

Should this fact (though of justice) be forgiven?

Mo. Oh, no, my lord; it would make cowards
    fear

To touch the reputations of true men

          [1] Substitutes, deputies.

When only they are left to imp the law.
Justice will soon distinguish murderous minds
From just revengers : had my friend been slain,
(His enemy surviving) he should die,
Since he had added to a murder'd fame
(Which was in his intent) a murder'd man ;
And this had worthily been wilful murder ;
But my friend only saved his fame's dear life,
Which is above life, taking th'under value,
Which in the wrong it did, was forfeit to him ;
And in this fact only preserves a man
In his uprightness ; worthy to survive
Millions of such as murder men alive.

   He. Well, brother, rise, and raise your friend
       withal
From death to life ; and D'Ambois, let your life
(Refined by passing through this merited death)
Be purged from more such foul pollution ;
Nor on your 'scape, nor valour more presuming
To be again so daring.

   Bu. My lord,
I loathe as much a deed of unjust death
As law itself doth ; and to tyrannize,
Because I have a little spirit to dare
And power to do, as to be tyrannized ;
This is a grace that (on my knees redoubled),
I crave to double this, my short life's gift :
And shall your royal bounty centuple,
That I may so make good what God and nature
Have given me for my good ; since I am free,
(Offending no just law), let no law make
By any wrong it does, my life her slave :
When I am wrong'd, and that law fails to right me,
Let me be king myself (as man was made),

And do a justice that exceeds the law ;
If my wrong pass the power of single valour
To right and expiate ; then be you my king,
And do a right, exceeding law and nature :
Who to himself is law, no law doth need,
Offends no law, and is a king indeed.

    He. Enjoy what thou entreat'st ; we give but ours.

    Bu. What you have given, my lord, is ever yours.

                         [Exit Rex *cum* NUNTIUS.

    Gu. Who would have pardon'd such a murder ?
                                   [Exit.

    Mo. Now vanish horrors into Court attractions,
For which let this balm make thee fresh and fair.
And now forth with thy service to the duchess,
As my long love will to Montsurry's countess.   *[Exit.*

    Bu. To whom my love hath long been vow'd in
        heart,
Although in hand for show I held the duchess,
And now through blood and vengeance, deeds of
        height
And hard to be achieved, 'tis fit I make
Attempt of her perfection ; I need fear
No check in his rivality, since her virtues
Are so renown'd, and he of all dames hated.   *[Exit.*

MONTSURRY, TAMYRA, BEAUPRE, PERO, CHARLOTTE,
                  PYRA.

    Mont. He will have pardon, sure.

    Ta. 'Twere pity, else :
For though his great spirit something overflow,
All faults are still borne, that from greatness grow ;
But such a sudden courtier saw I never.

    Be. He was too sudden, which indeed was rudeness.

Ta. True, for it argued his no due conceit[1]
Both of the place and greatness of the persons,
Nor of our sex: all which (we all being strangers
To his encounter) should have made more manners
Deserve more welcome.

Mont. All this fault is found
Because he loved the duchess and left you.

Ta. Alas, love give her joy: I am so far
From envy of her honour, that I swear,
Had he encounter'd me with such proud slight,
I would have put that project face of his
To a more test than did her duchesship.

Be. Why (by your leave, my lord) I'll speak it here,
Although she be my aunt, she scarce was modest,
When she perceived the duke her husband take
Those late exceptions to her servant's courtship,
To entertain him.

Ta. Ay, and stand him still,
Letting her husband give her servant place;
Though he did manly, she should be a woman.

Enter GUISE.

Gu. D'Ambois is pardon'd; where's a king? where
law?
See how it runs, much like a turbulent sea;
Here high, and glorious as it did contend
To wash the heavens and make the stars more pure;
And here so low, it leaves the mud of hell
To every common view; come, Count Montsurry,
We must consult of this.

Ta. Stay not, sweet lord.

Mont. Be pleased. I'll straight return.
[*Exit cum* GUISE.

___
[1] Conception.

Ta. Would that would please me!

Be. I'll leave you, madam, to your passions;
I see there's change of weather in your looks.

[*Exit cum suis.*

Ta. I cannot cloak it; but, as when a fume,
Hot, dry, and gross, within the womb of earth
Or in her superficies begot,
When extreme cold hath struck it to her heart,
The more it is compress'd, the more it rageth;
Exceeds his prison's strength that should contain it,
And then it tosseth temples in the air,
All bars made engines to his insolent fury;
So, of a sudden, my licentious fancy
Riots within me; not my name and house
Nor my religion, to this hour observed,
Can stand above it; I must utter that
That will in parting break more strings in me
Than death when life parts; and that holy man
That, from my cradle, counsell'd for my soul,
I now must make an agent for my blood.

Enter Monsieur.

Mo. Yet, is my mistress gracious?

Ta. Yet unanswer'd?

Mo. Pray thee regard thine own good, if not
mine,
And cheer my love for that; you do not know
What you may be by me, nor what without me;
I may have power t'advance and pull down any.

Ta. That's not my study; one way I am sure
You shall not pull down me; my husband's height
Is crown to all my hopes; and his retiring
To any mean state, shall be my aspiring;
Mine honour's in mine own hands, spite of kings

Mo. Honour, what's that : your second maiden-
    head :
And what is that ? a word : the word is gone,
The thing remains : the rose is pluck'd, the stalk
Abides ; an easy loss where no lack's found :
Believe it, there's as small lack in the loss
As there is pain i'th' losing ; archers ever
Have two strings to a bow ; and shall great Cupid
(Archer of archers both in men and women,)
Be worse provided than a common archer ?
A husband and a friend all wise wives have.

    Ta. Wise wives they are that on such strings
    depend,
With a firm husband joining a loose friend.

    Mo. Still you stand on your husband, so do all
The common sex of you, when y'are encounter'd
With one ye cannot fancy : all men know
You live in Court, here, by your own election,
Frequenting all our solemn sports and triumphs,
All the most youthful company of men :
And wherefore do you this ? To please your
    husband ?
'Tis gross and fulsome : if your husband's pleasure
Be all your object, and you aim at honour
In living close to him, get you from Court ;
You may have him at home ; these common put-offs
For common women serve : my honour ? husband ?
Dames maritorious ne'er were meritorious :
Speak plain, and say " I do not like you, sir,
Y'are an ill-favour'd fellow in my eye ; "
And I am answer'd.

    Ta. Then, I pray, be answer'd :
For in good faith, my lord, I do not like you
In that sort you like.

Mo. Then have at you, here :
Take (with a politic hand) this rope of pearl,
And though you be not amorous, yet be wise :
Take me for wisdom ; he that you can love
Is ne'er the further from you.

Ta. Now it comes
So ill prepared, that I may take a poison,
Under a medicine as good cheap as it ;
I will not have it were it worth the world.

Mo. Horror of death ; could I but please your eye,
You would give me the like, ere you would lose me :
Honour and husband !

Ta. By this light, my lord,
Y'are a vile fellow, and I'll tell the king
Your occupation of dishonouring ladies
And of his Court : a lady cannot live
As she was born, and with that sort of pleasure
That fits her state, but she must be defamed
With an infamous lord's detraction.
Who would endure the Court if these attempts
Of open and profess'd lust must be borne ?
Who's there ?   Come on, dame, you are at your book
When men are at your mistress ; have I taught you
Any such waiting-woman's quality ?

Mo. Farewell, good husband.   [*Exit* Monsieur.

Mont. Farewell, wicked lord.

Enter MONTSURRY.

Mont. Was not the Monsieur here ?

Ta. Yes, to good purpose :
And your cause is as good to seek him too,
And haunt his company.

Mont. Why, what's the matter ?

Ta. Matter of death, were I some husband's wife :

I cannot live at quiet in my chamber,
For opportunities almost to rapes
Offer'd me by him.

   Mont. Pray thee bear with him ;
Thou know'st he is a bachelor and a courtier,
Ay, and a prince ; and their prerogatives
Are to their laws, as to their pardons are
Their reservations, after Parliaments
One quits another ; form gives all their essence :
That prince doth high in virtue's reckoning stand
That will entreat a vice, and not command.
So far bear with him ; should another man
Trust to his privilege, he should trust to death :
Take comfort, then, my comfort, nay, triumph
And crown thyself, thou part'st with victory ;
My presence is so only dear to thee
That other men's appear worse than they be.
For this night yet, bear with my forced absence ;
Thou know'st my business ; and with how much
     weight
My vow hath charged it.

   Ta. True, my lord, and never
My fruitless love shall let [1] your serious honour ;
Yet, sweet lord, do not stay ; you know my soul
Is so long time without me, and I dead
As you are absent.

   Mont. By this kiss, receive
My soul for hostage, till I see my love.

   Ta. The morn shall let me see you.

   Mont. With the sun
I'll visit thy more comfortable [2] beauties.

   Ta. This is my comfort, that the sun hath left
The whole world's beauty ere my sun leaves me.

       [1] Hinder.   [2] Comforting.

Mont. 'Tis late night now indeed; farewell, my light.
[*Exit.*

Ta. Farewell, my light and life; but not in him,
In mine own dark love and light bent to another.
Alas that in the wave of our affections
We should supply it with a full dissembling,
In which each youngest maid is grown a mother;
Frailty is fruitful, one sin gets another:
Our loves like sparkles are that brightest shine
When they go out; most vice shows most divine.
Go, maid, to bed; lend me your book, I pray;
Not like yourself for form; I'll this night trouble
None of your services: make sure the doors,
And call your other fellows to their rest.

Pe. I will, yet I will watch to know why you watch.
[*Exit.*

Ta. Now all ye peaceful regents of the night,
Silently-gliding exhalations,
Languishing winds, and murmuring falls of waters,
Sadness of heart and ominous secureness,
Enchantments, dead sleeps, all the friends of rest,
That ever wrought upon the life of man,
Extend your utmost strengths; and this charm'd hour
Fix like the Centre [1]; make the violent wheels
Of Time and Fortune stand; and great Existence
(The Maker's treasury) now not seem to be,
To all but my approaching friends and me.
They come, alas! they come; fear, fear and hope
Of one thing, at one instant fight in me;
I love what most I loathe, and cannot live
Unless I compass that which holds my death:
For Life's mere death, loving one that loathes me,
And he I love, will loathe me, when he sees

[1] Centre of the earth.

I fly my sex, my virtue, my renown,
To run so madly on a man unknown.

[The vault opens.

See, see a vault is opening that was never
Known to my lord and husband, nor to any
But him that brings the man I love, and me ;
How shall I look on him ? how shall I live,
And not consume in blushes?   I will in,
And cast myself off, as I ne'er had been.   *[Exit.*

Ascendit Friar *and* D'Ambois.

Fr. Come, worthiest son, I am past measure glad,
That you (whose worth I have approved so long)
Should be the object of her fearful love ;
Since both your wit and spirit can adapt
Their full force to supply her utmost weakness :
You know her worths and virtues, for report
Of all that know, is to a man a knowledge :
You know besides, that our affections' storm,
Raised in our blood, no reason can reform.
Though she seek then their satisfaction
(Which she must needs, or rest unsatisfied)
Your judgment will esteem her peace thus wrought,
Nothing less dear than if yourself had sought :
And (with another colour, which my art
Shall teach you to lay on) yourself must seem
The only agent, and the first orb move
In this our set and cunning world of love.

Bu. Give me the colour, my most honour'd father,
And trust my cunning then to lay it on.

Fr. 'Tis this, good son ; Lord Barrisor (whom you
      slew)
Did love her dearly, and with all fit means
Hath urged his acceptation, of all which

She keeps one letter written in his blood :
You must say thus then, that you heard from me
How much herself was touch'd in conscience
With a report (which is in truth dispersed)
That your main quarrel grew about her love,
Lord Barrisor imagining your courtship
Of the great Guise's Duchess in the presence,
Was by you made to his elected mistress :
And so made me you mean now to resolve her,
Choosing (by my direction) this night's depth
For the more clear avoiding of all note,
Of your presumed presence, and with this
(To clear her hands of such a lover's blood)
She will so kindly thank and entertain you,
(Methinks I see how), ay, and ten to one,
Show you the confirmation in his blood,
Lest you should think report and she did feign,
That you shall so have circumstantial means
To come to the direct, which must be used ;
For the direct is crooked ; love comes flying ;
The height of love is still won with denying.

    Bu. Thanks, honour'd father.

    Fr. She must never know
That you know anything of any love
Sustain'd on her part : For learn this of me ;
In anything a woman does alone,
If she dissemble, she thinks 'tis not done ;
If not dissemble, nor a little chide,
Give her her wish, she is not satisfied ;
To have a man think that she never seeks,
Does her more good than to have all she likes :
This frailty sticks in them beyond their sex,
Which to reform, reason is too perplex :
Urge reason to them, it will do no good ;

Humour (that is the chariot of our food
In everybody) must in them be fed,
To carry their affections by it bred.
Stand close.

Enter TAMYRA *with a book.*

Ta. Alas, I fear my strangeness will retire him.
If he go back, I die ; I must prevent it,
And cheer his onset ; with my sight at least,
And that's the most ; though every step he takes
Goes to my heart, I'll rather die than seem
Not to be strange to that I most esteem.

Fr. Madam.

Ta. Ah !

Fr. You will pardon me, I hope,
That so beyond your expectation,
And at a time for visitants so unfit,
I (with my noble friend here) visit you :
You know that my access at any time
Hath ever been admitted ; and that friend
That my care will presume to bring with me
Shall have all circumstance of worth in him
To merit as free welcome as myself.

Ta. Oh, father ! but at this suspicious hour
You know how apt best men are to suspect us,
In any cause, that makes suspicion's shadow
No greater than the shadow of a hair :
And y'are to blame ; what though my lord and
      husband
Lie forth to-night ? and since I cannot sleep
When he is absent, I sit up to-night,
Though all the doors are sure, and all our servants
As sure bound with their sleeps ; yet there is One
That wakes above, whose eye no sleep can bind ;

He sees through doors, and darkness, and our thoughts;
And therefore as we should avoid with fear,
To think amiss ourselves before his search;
So should we be as curious to shun
All cause that other think not ill of us.

Bu. Madam, 'tis far from that; I only heard
By this my honour'd father, that your conscience
Made some deep scruple with a false report
That Barrisor's blood should something touch your
    honour;
Since he imagined I was courting you,
When I was bold to change words with the duchess,
And therefore made his quarrel; his long love
And service, as I hear, being deeply vow'd
To your perfections, which my ready presence,
Presumed on with my father at this season
For the more care of your so curious honour,
Can well resolve your conscience, is most false.

Ta. And is it therefore that you come, good sir?
Then crave I now your pardon and my father's,
And swear your presence does me so much good,
That all I have it binds to your requital;
Indeed, sir, 'tis most true that a report
Is spread, alleging that his love to me
Was reason of your quarrel, and because
You shall not think I feign it for my glory
That he importuned me for his court service,
I'll show you his own hand, set down in blood
To that vain purpose: good sir, then come in.
Father, I thank you now a thousand-fold.

                    [*Exit* TAMYRA *and* D'AMBOIS.

Fr. May it be worth it to you, honour'd daughter.

                    [*Descendit* Friar.

L

ACT THE THIRD

SCENE I

Enter D'AMBOIS, TAMYRA, *with a Chain of Pearl.*

U. Sweet mistress, cease, your conscience
is too nice,
And bites too hotly of the Puritan
spice.

Ta. Oh, my dear servant,[1] in thy close embraces,
I have set open all the doors of danger
To my encompass'd honour, and my life:
Before I was secure 'gainst death and hell;
But now am subject to the heartless fear
Of every shadow, and of every breath,
And would change firmness with an aspen leaf;
So confident a spotless conscience is,
So weak a guilty: oh, the dangerous siege
Sin lays about us! and the tyranny
He exercises when he hath expugn'd:
Like to the horror of a winter's thunder,
Mix'd with a gushing storm, that suffer nothing
To stir abroad on earth but their own rages,

[1] Lover.

Is sin, when it hath gather'd head above us :
No roof, no shelter can secure us so,
But he will drown our cheeks in fear or woe.

　Bu. Sin is a coward, madam, and insults
But on our weakness, in his truest valour :
And so our ignorance tames us, that we let
His shadows fright us : and like empty clouds,
In which our faulty apprehensions forge
The forms of dragons, lions, elephants,
When they hold no proportion, the sly charms
Of the witch policy makes him, like a monster
Kept only to show men for servile money :
That false hag often paints him in her cloth
Ten times more monstrous than he is in troth :
In three of us, the secret of our meeting
Is only guarded, and three friends as one
Have ever been esteem'd : as our three powers
That in our one soul are as one united :
Why should we fear then ? For myself I swear
Sooner shall torture be the sire to pleasure,
And health be grievous to one long time sick,
Than the dear jewel of your fame in me
Be made an outcast to your infamy ;
Nor shall my valour (sacred to your virtues)
Only give free course to it, from myself :
But make it fly out of the mouths of kings
In golden vapours and with awful wings.

　Ta. It rests as all kings' seals were set in thee.
Now let us call my father, whom I swear
I could extremely chide, but that I fear
To make him so suspicious of my love
Of which, sweet servant, do not let him know
For all the world.

　Bu. Alas ! he will not think it.

Ta. Come, then—ho!   Father, ope, and take your
　　friend. ··　　　　　　　　[*Ascendit* Friar.

Fr. Now, honour'd daughter, is your doubt resolved?

Ta. Ay, father, but you went away too soon.

Fr. Too soon?

Ta. Indeed you did, you should have stay'd ;
Had not your worthy friend been of your bringing,
And that contains all laws to temper me,
Not all the fearful danger that besieged us,
Had awed my throat from exclamation.

Fr. I know your serious disposition well.
Come, son, the morn comes on.

Bu. Now, honour'd mistress,
Till farther service call, all bliss supply you.

Ta. And you this chain of pearl, and my love only.
　　　　　　　　　　[*Descendit* Friar *and* D'Ambois.

Ta. It is not I, but urgent destiny,
That (as great statesmen for their general end
In politic justice, make poor men offend)
Enforceth my offence to make it just.
What shall weak dames do, when the whole work of
　　nature
Hath a strong finger in each one of us ?
Needs must that sweep away the silly cobweb
Of our still-undone labours ; that lays still
Our powers to it : as to the line, the stone,
Not to the stone, the line should be opposed ;
We cannot keep our constant course in virtue :
What is alike at all parts ?   Every day
Differs from other : every hour and minute ;
Ay, every thought in our false clock of life,
Ofttimes inverts the whole circumference :
We must be sometimes one, sometimes another :
Our bodies are but thick clouds to our souls,

Through which they cannot shine when they desire :
When all the stars, and even the sun himself,
Must stay the vapours' fumes that he exhales
Before he can make good his beams to us ;
Oh, how can we, that are but motes to him,
Wandering at random in his order'd rays,
Disperse our passions' fumes, with our weak labours,
That are more thick and black than all earth's
    vapours ?

Enter MONTSURRY.

Mont. Good day, my love ; what, up and ready [1] too !

Ta. Both, my dear lord ; not all this night made I
Myself unready, or could sleep a wink.

Mont. Alas ! what troubled my true love ? my peace,
From being at peace within her better self?
Or how could sleep forbear to seize thine eyes
When he might challenge them as his just prize?

Ta. I am in no power earthly, but in yours ;
To what end should I go to bed, my lord,
That wholly miss'd the comfort of my bed ?
Or how should sleep possess my faculties,
Wanting the proper closer of mine eyes ?

Mont. Then will I never more sleep night from
    thee ;
All mine own business, all the king's affairs,
Shall take the day to serve them ; every night
I'll ever dedicate to thy delight.

Ta. Nay, good my lord, esteem not my desires
Such doters on their humours that my judgment
Cannot subdue them to your worthier pleasure ;
A wife's pleased husband must her object be
In all her acts, not her soothed fantasy.

            [1] Dressed.

Mont. Then come, my love, now pay those rites to
    sleep
Thy fair eyes owe him ; shall we now to bed ?

Ta. Oh, no, my lord ; your holy friar says
All couplings in the day that touch the bed
Adulterous are, even in the married ;
Whose grave and worthy doctrine, well I know,
Your faith in him will liberally allow.[1]

Mont. He's a most learned and religious man ;
Come to the presence then, and see great D'Ambois
(Fortune's proud mushroom shot up in a night)
Stand like an Atlas under our King's arm ;
Which greatness with him Monsieur now envies
As bitterly and deadly as the Guise.

Ta. What, he that was but yesterday his maker,
His raiser and preserver ?

Mont. Even the same :
Each natural agent works but to this end,
To render that it works on like itself ;
Which since the Monsieur in his act on D'Ambois
Cannot to his ambitious end effect,
But that, quite opposite, the King hath power
In his love borne to D'Ambois, to convert
The point of Monsieur's aim on his own breast,
He turns his outward love to inward hate.
A prince's love is like the lightning's fume,
Which no man can embrace, but must consume.
                              [Exeunt.

Enter HENRY, D'AMBOIS, Monsieur, GUISE, Duchess,
    ANNABELLE, CHARLOTTE, Attendants.

He. Speak home, my Bussy ; thy impartial words
Are like brave falcons that dare truss a fowl

              [1] Approve.

Much greater than themselves ; flatterers are kites
That check [1] at sparrows ; thou shalt be my eagle,
And bear my thunder underneath thy wings ;
Truth's words, like jewels, hang in the ears of kings.

Bu. Would I might live to see no Jews hang there
Instead of jewels ; sycophants, I mean,
Who use truth like the devil, his true foe,
Cast by the angel to the pit of fears,
And bound in chains ; truth seldom decks kings' ears.
Slave flattery (like a rippier's [2] legs roll'd up
In boots of hay ropes) with kings' soothed guts
Swaddled and strappled, [3] now lives only free.
Oh, 'tis a subtle knave ; how like the plague
Unfelt he strikes into the brain of man,
And rageth in his entrails, when he can,
Worse than the poison of a red-hair'd man. [4]

He. Fly at him and his brood ; I cast thee off,
And once more give thee surname of mine eagle.

Bu. I'll make you sport enough, then ; let me have
My lucerns [5] too, or dogs inured to hunt
Beasts of most rapine, but to put them up,
And if I trust not, let me not be trusted.
Show me a great man (by the people's voice,
Which is the voice of God) that by his greatness
Bombasts [6] his private roofs with public riches ;
That affects royalty, rising from a clapdish ; [7]
That rules so much more by his suffering king,
That he makes kings of his subordinate slaves :
Himself and them graduate like woodmongers,
Piling a stack of billets from the earth,

---

[1] Pursue.   [2] Fisherman.   [3] Bound.
[4] A traitor : Judas's hair was supposed to be red.
[5] Hunting dogs.   [6] Stuffs out.
[7] Dish carried by beggars, who clapped the lid to attract notice.

Raising each other into steeples' heights;
Let him convey this on the turning props
Of Protean law, and, his own counsel keeping,
Keep all upright; let me but hawk at him,
I'll play the vulture, and so thump his liver,
That, like a huge unlading Argosy,
He shall confess all, and you then may hang him.
Show me a clergyman, that is in voice
A lark of heaven, in heart a mole of earth;
That hath good living, and a wicked life;
A temperate look, and a luxurious gut;
Turning the rents of his superfluous cures
Into your pheasants and your partridges;
Venting their quintessence as men read Hebrew;
Let me but hawk at him, and, like the other,
He shall confess all, and you then may hang him.
Show me a lawyer that turns sacred law
(The equal renderer of each man his own,
The scourge of rapine and extortion,
The sanctuary and impregnable defence
Of retired learning and besieged virtue)
Into a harpy, that eats all but's own,
Into the damned sins it punisheth;
Into the synagogue of thieves and atheists,
Blood into gold, and justice into lust;
Let me but hawk at him, as at the rest,
He shall confess all, and you then may hang him.

Enter MONTSURRY, TAMYRA, *and* PERO.

Gu. Where will you find such game as you would
hawk at?
Bu. I'll hawk about your house for one of them.
Gu. Come, y'are a glorious [1] ruffian, and run proud

---

[1] Boastful.

Of the King's headlong graces ; hold your breath,
Or, by that poison'd vapour, not the King
Shall back your murderous valour against me.

   Bu. I would the King would make his presence free
But for one bout betwixt us : by the reverence
Due to the sacred space 'twixt kings and subjects,
Here would I make thee cast that popular purple,
In which thy proud soul sits and braves thy sovereign.

   Mo. Peace, peace, I pray thee peace.

   Bu. Let him peace first that made the first war.

   Mo. He's the better man.

   Bu. And therefore may do worst ?

   Mo. He has more titles.

   Bu. So Hydra had more heads.

   Mo. He's greater known.

   Bu. His greatness is the people's ; mine's mine own.

   Mo. He's nobly born.

   Bu. He is not, I am noble.
And noblesse in his blood hath no gradation,
But in his merit.

   Gu. Th'art not nobly born,
But bastard to the Cardinal of Ambois.

   Bu. Thou liest, proud Guiserd ; let me fly, my lord.

   He. Not in my face, my eagle ; violence flies
The sanctuaries of a prince's eyes.

   Bu. Still shall we chide and foam upon this bit ?
Is the Guise only great in faction ?
Stands he not by himself ?   Proves he th' opinion
That men's souls are without them ?   Be a duke
And lead me to the field.

   Gu. Come, follow me.

   He. Stay them, stay, D'Ambois ; cousin Guise, I
      wonder
Your honour'd disposition brooks so ill

A man so good, that only would uphold
Man in his native noblesse, from whose fall
All our dimensions rise ; that in himself
(Without the outward patches of our frailty,
Riches and honour) knows he comprehends
Worth with the greatest ; kings had never borne
Such boundless empire over other men,
Had all maintain'd the spirit and state of D'Ambois ;
Nor had the full impartial hand of nature
That all things gave in her original,
Without these definite terms of mine and thine,
Been turn'd unjustly to the hand of Fortune,
Had all preserved her in her prime, like D'Ambois ;
No envy, no disjunction had dissolved,
Or pluck'd one stick out of the golden faggot
In which the world of Saturn bound our lives,
Had all been held together with the nerves,
The genius, and th'ingenuous soul of D'Ambois.
Let my hand therefore be the Hermean rod
To part and reconcile, and so conserve you,
As my combined embracers and supporters.

 Bu. 'Tis our king's motion, and we shall not seem
To worst eyes womanish, though we change thus soon
Never so great grudge for his greater pleasure.

 Gu. I seal to that, and so the manly freedom
That you so much profess, hereafter prove not
A bold and glorious license to deprave,
To me his hand shall hold the Hermean virtue
His grace affects, in which submissive sign
On this his sacred right hand, I lay mine.

 Bu. 'Tis well, my lord, and so your worthy greatness
Decline not to the greater insolence,
Nor make you think it a prerogative,
To rack men's freedoms with the ruder wrongs ;

My hand (stuck full of laurel, in true sign
'Tis wholly dedicate to righteous peace)
In all submission kisseth th'other side.

He. Thanks to ye both ; and kindly I invite ye
Both to banquet, where we'll sacrifice
Full cups to confirmation of your loves ;
At which, fair ladies, I entreat your presence ;
And hope you, madam, will take one carouse
For reconcilement of your lord and servant.

Du. If I should fail, my lord, some other lady
Would be found there to do that for my servant.

Mo. Any of these here ?

Du. Nay, I know not that.

Bu. Think your thoughts like my mistress', honour'd
    lady ?

Ta. I think not on you, sir ; y'are one I know not.

Bu. Cry you mercy, madam.

Mont. Oh, sir, has she met you ?

                            [*Exeunt* HENRY, D'AMBOIS, Ladies.

Mo. What had my bounty drunk when it raised
    him ?

Gu. Y'ave stuck us up a very worthy flag,
That takes more wind than we with all our sails.

Mo. Oh, so he spreads and flourishes.

Gu. He must down ;
Upstarts should never perch too near a crown.

Mo. 'Tis true, my lord ; and as this doting hand,
Even out of earth, like Juno, struck this giant,
So Jove's great ordinance shall be here implied
To strike him under th'Etna of his pride ;
To which work lend your hands, and let us cast
Where we may set snares for his ranging greatness ;
I think it best, amongst our greatest women :
For there is no such trap to catch an upstart

As a loose downfall ; for you know their falls
Are th'ends of all men's rising : if great men
And wise make scapes to please advantage
'Tis with a woman : women that worst may
Still hold men's candles ; they direct and know
All things amiss in all men ; and their women
All thing amiss in them ; through whose charm'd
    mouths,
We may see all the close scapes of the Court.
When the most royal beast of chase, the hart,
(Being old and cunning in his lairs and haunts)
Can never be discover'd to the bow,
The piece, or hound ; yet where, behind some quitch, [1]
He breaks his gall, and rutteth with his hind,
The place is mark'd, and by his venery
He still is taken.   Shall we then attempt
The chiefest mean to that discovery here,
And court our greatest ladies' chiefest women
With shows of love and liberal promises?
'Tis but our breath.   If something given in hand
Sharpens their hopes of more, 'twill be well ventured.

    Gu. No doubt of that ; and 'tis the cunning'st point
Of your devised investigation.

    Mo. I have broken
The ice to it already with the woman
Of our chaste lady, and conceive good hope
I shall wade thorough to some wished shore
At our next meeting.

    Mont. Nay, there's small hope there.

    Gu. Take say of her, my lord, she comes most fitly.

    Mo. Starting back ?

---

[1] Grass

Enter CHARLOTTE, ANNABELLE, PERO.

Gu. Y'are engaged, indeed.

An. Nay, pray, my lord, forbear.

Mont. What, skittish, servant?

An. No, my lord, I am not so fit for your service.

Ch. Pray pardon me now, my lord; my lady expects me.

Gu. I'll satisfy her expectation, as far as an uncle may.

Mo. Well said; a spirit of courtship of all hands. Now mine own Pero, hast thou remembered me for the discovery I entreated thee to make of thy mistress? speak boldly, and be sure of all things I have sworn to thee.

Pe. Building on that assurance, my lord, I may speak; and much the rather, because my lady hath not trusted me with that I can tell you; for now I cannot be said to betray her.

Mo. That's all one, so we reach our objects; forth, I beseech thee.

Pe. To tell you truth, my lord, I have made a strange discovery.

Mo. Excellent, Pero, thou revivest me; may I sink quick to perdition if my tongue discover [1] it.

Pe. 'Tis thus, then: this last night, my lord lay forth, and I watching my lady's sitting up, stole up at midnight from my pallet; and (having before made a hole both through the wall and arras to her inmost chamber) I saw D'Ambois and herself reading a letter.

Mo. D'Ambois?

Pe. Even he, my lord.

Mo. Dost thou not dream, wench?

_____
[1] Reveal.

Pe. I swear he is the man.

Mo. The devil he is, and thy lady his dam ; why, this was the happiest shot that ever flew ! The just plague of hypocrisy levelled it. Oh, the infinite regions betwixt a woman's tongue and her heart ! is this our goddess of chastity ? I thought I could not be so sleighted if she had not her fraught besides, and, therefore, plotted this with her woman, never dreaming of D'Ambois. Dear Pero, I will advance thee for ever ; but tell me now ; God's precious, it transforms me with admiration ;[1] sweet Pero, whom should she trust with his conveyance ? Or, all the doors being made sure, how should his conveyance be made ?

Pe. Nay, my lord, that amazes[2] me ; I cannot by any study so much as guess at it.

Mo. Well, let's favour our apprehensions with forbearing that a little ; for if my heart were not hooped with adamant, the conceit[3] of this would have burst it. But hark thee.   [*Whispers.*

Ch. I swear to your grace, all that I can conjecture touching my lady your niece, is a strong affection she bears to the English Mylor.

Gu. All, quod you ? 'Tis enough, I assure you, but tell me.

Mont. I pray thee, resolve me : the duke will never imagine that I am busy about's wife : hath D'Ambois any privy access to her ?

An. No, my lord ; D'Ambois neglects her, as she takes it, and is therefore suspicious that either your lady, or the Lady Beaupre hath closely[4] entertained him.

Mont. By'r lady, a likely suspicion, and very near the life, if she marks it, especially of my wife.

[1] Wonder.   [2] Bewilders.   [3] Thoughts.   [4] Secretly.

Mo. Come, we'll disguise all seeming only to have courted; away, dry palm: sh'as a liver as hard as a biscuit; a man may go a whole voyage with her, and get nothing but tempests from her windpipe.

Gu. Here's one, I think, has swallowed a porcupine, she casts pricks from her tongue so.

Mont. And here's a peacock seems to have devoured one of the Alps, she has so swelling a spirit, and is so cold of her kindness.

Ch. We are no windfalls, my lord ; ye must gather us with the ladder of matrimony, or we'll hang till we be rotten.

Mo. Indeed, that's the way to make ye right open-arses. But, alas! ye have no portions fit for such husbands as we wish you.

Pe. Portions, my lord? yes, and such portions as your principality cannot purchase.

Mo. What, woman? what are those portions?

Pe. Riddle my riddle, my lord.

Mo. Ay, marry wench, I think thy portion is a right riddle, a man shall never find it out. But let's hear it.

Pe. You shall, my lord.

> *What's that, that being most rare's most cheap?*
> *That when you sow, you never reap?*
> *That when it grow most, most you in it?*
> *And still you lose it when you win it;*
> *That when 'tis commonest, 'tis dearest,*
> *And when 'tis farthest off, 'tis nearest?*

Mo. Is this your great portion?

Pe. Even this, my lord.

Mo. Believe me, I cannot riddle it.

Pe. No, my lord : 'tis my chastity, which you shall neither riddle nor fiddle.

Mo. Your chastity? Let me begin with the end of it ; how is a woman's chastity nearest a man when 'tis furthest off ?

Pe. Why, my lord, when you cannot get it, it goes to th' heart on you : and that, I think, comes most near you : and I am sure it shall be far enough off ; and so we leave you to our mercies. [*Exeunt* Women.

Mo. Farewell, riddle.

Gu. Farewell, medlar.[1]

Mont. Farewell, winter plum.

Mo. Now, my lords, what fruit of our inquisition ? Feel you nothing budding yet? Speak, good my Lord Montsurry.

Mont. Nothing but this : D'Ambois is negligent in observing the duchess, and therefore she is suspicious that your niece or my wife closely entertains him.

Mo. Your wife, my lord? Think you that possible ?

Mont. Alas, I know she flies him like her last hour.

Mo. Her last hour? Why, that comes upon her the more she flies it. Does D'Ambois so, think you ?

Mont. That's not worth the answering. 'Tis miraculous to think with what monsters women's imaginations engross them when they are once enamoured, and what wonders they will work for their satisfaction. They will make a sheep valiant, a lion fearful.

Mo. And an ass confident. Well, my lord, more will come forth shortly ; get you to the banquet.

Gu. Come, my lord ; I have the blind side of one of them.   [*Exit* GUISE *cum* MONTSURRY.

Mo. Oh, the unsounded sea of women's bloods, That when 'tis calmest, is most dangerous ;

---

[1] A medlar was a fruit that became rotten before it was ripe.

Not any wrinkle creaming in their faces
When in their hearts are Scylla and Charybdis,
Which still are hid in dark and standing fogs,
Where never day shines, nothing never grows,
But weeds and poisons, that no statesman knows,
Nor Cerberus ever saw the damned nooks
Hid with the veils of women's virtuous looks ;
But what a cloud of sulphur have I drawn
Up to my bosom in this dangerous secret !
Which if my haste with any spark should light,
Ere D'Ambois were engaged in some sure plot,
I were blown up ; he would be sure my death.
Would I had never known it, for before
I shall persuade th'importance to Montsurry,
And make him with some studied stratagem
Train D'Ambois to his wreak, his maid may tell it,
Or I (out of my fiery thirst to play
With the fell tiger, up in darkness tied,
And give it some light) make it quite break loose.
I fear it afore heaven, and will not see
D'Ambois again, till I have told Montsurry
And set a snare with him to free my fears :
Who's there ?

Enter MAFFE.

Ma. My lord ?

Mo. Go call the Count Montsurry,
And make the doors fast ; I will speak with none
Till he come to me.

Ma. Well, my lord.   [*Exiturus.*

Mo. Or else
Send you some other, and see all the doors
Made safe yourself, I pray ; haste, fly about it.

Ma. You'll speak with none but with the Count
Montsurry ?

M

Mo. With none but he, except it be the Guise.

Ma. See even by this, there's one exception more!
Your grace must be more firm in the command,
Or else shall I as weakly execute.
The Guise shall speak with you?

Mo. He shall, I say.

Ma. And Count Montsurry?

Mo. Ay, and Count Montsurry.

Ma. Your grace must pardon me, that I am bold
To urge the clear and full sense of your pleasure;
Which whensoever I have known, I hope
Your grace will say, I hit it to a hair.

Mo. You have.

Ma. I hope so, or I would be glad—

Mo. I pray thee get thee gone, thou art so tedious
In the strict form of all thy services
That I had better have one negligent.
You hit my pleasure well, when D'Ambois hit you;
Did you not, think you?

Ma. D'Ambois? why, my lord?

Mo. I pray thee talk no more, but shut the doors:
Do what I charge thee.

Ma. I will, my lord, and yet
I would be glad the wrong I had of D'Ambois—

Mo. Precious! then it is a fate that plagues me
In this man's foolery; I may be murder'd
While he stands on protection of his folly.
Avaunt about thy charge.

Ma. I go, my lord.
I had my head broke in his faithful service;
I had no suit the more, nor any thanks,
And yet my teeth must still be hit with D'Ambois:
D'Ambois, my lord, shall know.

Mo. The devil and D'Ambois!   [*Exit* MAFFE.

How am I tortured with this trusty fool !
Never was any curious in his place
To do things justly, but he was an ass ;
We cannot find one trusty that is witty,
And therefore bear their disproportion.
Grant thou, great star and angel of my life,
A sure lease of it but for some few days,
That I may clear my bosom of the snake
I cherish'd there, and I will then defy
All check to it but Nature's, and her altars
Shall crack with vessels crown'd with every liquor
Drawn from her highest and most bloody humours.
I fear him strangely, his advanced valour
Is like a spirit raised without a circle,
Endangering him that ignorantly raised him,
And for whose fury he hath learned no limit.

Enter MAFFE *hastily.*

Ma. I cannot help it : what should I do more ?
As I was gathering a fit guard to make
My passage to the doors, and the doors sure,
The man of blood is enter'd.

Mo. Rage of death !
If I had told the secret, and he knew it,
Thus had I been endanger'd :—My sweet heart !
How now, what leap'st thou at ?

Enter D'AMBOIS.

Bu. O royal object !
Mo. Thou dream'st, awake ; object in th'empty air ?
Bu. Worthy the brows of Titan, worth his chair.
Mo. Pray thee, what mean'st thou ?
Bu. See you not a crown
Impale the forehead of the great King Monsieur ?

Mo. Oh, fie upon thee !

Bu. Sir, that is the subject
Of all these your retired and sole discourses.

Mo. Wilt thou not leave that wrongful supposition ?

Bu. Why wrongful, to suppose the doubtless right
To the succession worth the thinking on ?

Mo. Well, leave these jests ; how I am overjoy'd
With thy wish'd presence, and how fit thou comest,
For of mine honour I was sending for thee.

Bu. To what end ?

Mo. Only for thy company,
Which I have still in thought, but that's no payment
On thy part made with personal appearance.
Thy absence so long suffer'd, oftentimes
Put me in some little doubt thou dost not love me.
Wilt thou do one thing therefore now sincerely ?

Bu. Ay, anything, but killing of the King.

Mo. Still in that discord, an ill-taken note ?
How most unseasonable thou play'st the cuckoo,
In this thy fall of friendship !

Bu. Then do not doubt,
That there is any act within my nerves
But killing of the King, that is not yours.

Mo. I will not, then ; to prove which by my love
Shown to thy virtues, and by all fruits else
Already sprung from that still-flourishing tree,
With whatsoever may hereafter spring,
I charge thee utter (even with all the freedom
Both of thy noble nature and thy friendship)
The full and plain state of me in thy thoughts.

Bu. What, utter plainly what I think of you ?

Mo. Plain as truth.

Bu. Why, this swims quite against the stream of
greatness ;

Great men would rather hear their flatteries,
And if they be not made fools, are not wise.

Mo. I am no such great fool, and therefore charge
    thee
Even from the root of thy free heart, display me.

Bu. Since you affect [1] in it such serious terms,
If yourself first will tell me what you think
As freely and as heartily of me,
I'll be as open in my thoughts of you.

Mo. A bargain, of mine honour; and make this,
That prove we in our full dissection
Never so foul, live still the sounder friends.

Bu. What else, sir? Come, pay me home; I'll
    bide it bravely.

Mo. I will swear. I think thee then a man
That dares as much as a wild horse or tiger;
As headstrong and as bloody; and to feed
The ravenous wolf of thy most cannibal valour,
(Rather than not employ it) thou wouldst turn
Hackster to any whore, slave to a Jew
Or English usurer, to force possessions,
And cut men's throats of mortgaged estates;
Or thou wouldst 'tire thee like a tinker's strumpet,
And murder market-folks, quarrel with sheep,
And run as mad as Ajax; serve a butcher,
Do anything but killing of the King:
That in thy valour th'art like other naturals [2]
That have strange gifts in nature, but no soul
Diffused quite through, to make them of a piece,
But stop at humours that are more absurd,
Childish and villanous than that hackster, whore,
Slave, cut-throat, tinker's bitch, compared before;
And in those humours wouldst envy, betray,

         [1] Desire.   [2] Idiots.

Slander, blaspheme, change each hour a religion ;
Do anything but killing of the King :
That in thy valour (which is still the dung-hill,
To which hath reference all filth in thy house)
Thou art more ridiculous and vain-glorious
Than any mountebank ; and impudent
Than any painted bawd ; which, not to soothe
And glorify thee like a Jupiter Hammon,
Thou eat'st thy heart in vinegar ; and thy gall
Turns all thy blood to poison, which is cause
Of that toad-pool that stands in thy complexion,
And makes thee (with a cold and earthy moisture,
Which is the dam of putrefaction,
As plague to thy damn'd pride) rot as thou livest ;
To study calumnies and treacheries ;
To thy friends' slaughters like a screech-owl sing,
And do all mischiefs but to kill the King.

   Bu. So ! have you said ?

   Mo. How think'st thou ? Do I flatter ?
Speak I not like a trusty friend to thee ?

   Bu. That ever any man was blest withal ;
So here's for me. I think you are (at worst)
No devil, since y'are like to be no king ;
Of which, with any friend of yours, I'll lay
This poor stillado[1] here, 'gainst all the stars,
Ay, and 'gainst all your treacheries, which are more ;
That you did never good, but to do ill ;
But ill of all sorts, free and for itself :
That (like a murdering piece, making lanes in armies,
The first man of a rank, the whole rank falling)
If you have wrong'd one man, you are so far
From making him amends, that all his race,
Friends, and associates, fall into your chase :

             [1] Stiletto (?).

That y'are for perjuries the very prince
Of all intelligencers [1]; and your voice
Is like an eastern wind, that where it flies
Knits nets of caterpillars, with which you catch
The prime of all the fruits the kingdom yields.
That your political head is the cursed fount
Of all the violence, rapine, cruelty,
Tyranny, and atheism flowing through the realm.
That y'ave a tongue so scandalous, 'twill cut
A perfect crystal; and a breath that will
Kill to that wall a spider; you will jest
With God, and your soul to the devil tender
For lust; kiss horror, and with death engender.
That your foul body is a Lernean fen
Of all the maladies breeding in all men;
That you are utterly without a soul;
And, for your life, the thread of that was spun
When Clotho slept, and let her breathing rock
Fall in the dirt; and Lachesis still draws it,
Dipping her twisting fingers in a bowl
Defiled, and crown'd with virtue's forced soul.
And lastly (which I must for gratitude
Ever remember) that of all my height
And dearest life, you are the only spring,
Only in royal hope to kill the King.

 Mo. Why, now I see thou lovest me; come to the
banquet.   [*Exeunt.*

     [1] Spies.

ACT THE FOURTH

SCENE I

Enter HENRY, Monsieur, *with a letter ;* GUISE, MONT-
SURRY, BUSSY, ELENOR, TAMYRA, BEAUPRE, PERO,
CHARLOTTE, ANNABELLE, PYRA, *with four* Pages.

E. Ladies, ye have not done our banquet
right,
Nor look'd upon it with those cheerful
rays
That lately turn'd your breaths to floods of gold ;
Your looks, methinks, are not drawn out with
thoughts
So clear and free as heretofore, but foul,
As if the thick complexions of men
Govern'd within them.
    Bu. 'Tis not like, my lord,
That men in women rule, but contrary ;
For as the moon (of all things God created)
Not only is the most appropriate image
Or glass to show them how they wax and wane,
But in her height and motion likewise bears
Imperial influences that command
In all their powers, and make them wax and wane ;
So women, that (of all things made of nothing)

Are the most perfect idols of the moon
(Or still - unwean'd sweet moon - calves with white
  faces)
Not only are patterns of change to men,
But as the tender moonshine of their beauties
Clears, or is cloudy, make men glad or sad,
So then they rule in men, not men in them.

   Mo. But here the moons are changed, (as the King
  notes)
And either men rule in them, or some power
Beyond their voluntary faculty:
For nothing can recover their lost faces.

   Mont. None can be always one: our griefs and joys
Hold several sceptres in us, and have times
For their divided empires: which grief now, in them
Doth prove as proper to his diadem.

   Bu. And grief's a natural sickness of the blood,
That time to part asks, as his coming had,
Only slight fools grieved suddenly are glad;
A man may say to a dead man, " Be revived."
As well as to one sorrowful, " Be not grieved."
And therefore, princely mistress, in all wars
Against these base foes that insult on weakness,
And still fight housed behind the shield of Nature,
Of privilege, law, treachery, or beastly need,
Your servant cannot help; authority here
Goes with corruption: something like some States,
That back worst men: valour to them must creep
That, to themselves left, would fear him asleep.

   Du. Ye all take that for granted that doth rest
Yet to be proved; we all are as we were,
As merry and as free in thought as ever.

   Gu. And why then can ye not disclose your
  thoughts?

Ta. Methinks the man hath answer'd for us well.

Mo. The man? why, madam, d'ye not know his
  name?

Ta. Man is a name of honour for a king:
Additions [1] take away from each chief thing:
The school of modesty, not to learn, learns dames:
They sit in high forms there, that know men's names.

Mo. Hark! sweetheart, here's a bar set to your
  valour:
It cannot enter here: no, not to notice
Of what your name is; your great eagle's beak
(Should you fly at her) had as good encounter
An Albion cliff, as her more craggy liver.

Bu. I'll not attempt her, sir; her sight and name
(By which I only know her) doth deter me.

He. So they do all men else.

Mo. You would say so
If you knew all.

Ta. Knew all, my lord? What mean you?

Mo. All that I know, madam.

Ta. That you know? speak it.

Mo. No, 'tis enough. I feel it.

He. But, methinks
Her courtship is more pure than heretofore;
True courtiers should be modest, but not nice,
Bold, but not impudent, pleasure love, not vice.

Mo. Sweetheart! come hither, what if one should
  make
Horns at Montsurry? Would it not strike him
  jealous
Through all the proofs of his chaste lady's virtues?

Bu. If he be wise, not.

Mo. What? Not if I should name the gardener

     [1] Titles.

That I would have him think hath grafted him?

Bu. So the large licence that your greatness uses
To jest at all men, may be taught indeed
To make a difference of the grounds you play on,
Both in the men you scandal, and the matter.

Mo. As how? as how?

Bu. Perhaps led with a train, where you may have
Your nose made less and slit, your eyes thrust out.

Mo. Peace, peace, I pray thee peace.
Who dares do that? the brother of his king?

Bu. Were your king brother in you; all your
        powers
(Stretch'd in the arms of great men and their bawds),
Set close down by you; all your stormy laws
Spouted with lawyers' mouths; and gushing blood,
Like to so many torrents; all your glories
(Making you terrible, like enchanted flames
Fed with bare cockscombs; and with crooked hams),
All your prerogatives, your shames and tortures;
All daring heaven, and opening hell about you;
Were I the man ye wrong'd so and provoked,
Though ne'er so much beneath you, like a box-tree
I would (out of the roughness of my root)
Ram hardness, in my lowness, and like death
Mounted on earthquakes, I would trot through all
Honours and horrors: thorough foul and fair
And from your whole strength toss you into the air.

Mo. Go, th'art a devil; such another spirit
Could not be 'still'd from all th'Armenian dragons.
O my love's glory; heir to all I have;
That's all I can say, and that all I swear.
If thou outlive me, as I know thou must,
Or else hath nature no proportion'd end
To her great labours; she hath breathed a mind

Into thy entrails, of desert to swell
Into another great Augustus Cæsar;
Organs and faculties fitted to her greatness;
And should that perish like a common spirit,
Nature's a courtier and regards no merit.

   He. Here's nought but whispering with us; like a
      calm
Before a tempest, when the silent air
Lays her soft ear close to the earth to hearken
For that she fears steals on to ravish her;
Some fate doth join our ears to hear it coming.
Come, my brave eagle, let's to covert fly;
I see almighty Æther in the smoke
Of all his clouds descending; and the sky
Hid in the dim ostents [1] of tragedy.

        [*Exit* HENRY *with* D'AMBOIS *and* Ladies.

   Gu. Now stir the humour, and begin the brawl.
   Mont. The King and D'Ambois now are grown all
      one.
   Mo. Nay, they are two, my lord.
   Mont. How's that?
   Mo. No more.
   Mont. I must have more, my lord.
   Mo. What, more than two?
   Mont. How monstrous is this!
   Mo. Why?
   Mont. You make me horns.
   Mo. Not I; it is a work without my power,
Married men's ensigns are not made with fingers;
Of divine fabric they are, not men's hands;
Your wife, you know, is a mere [2] Cynthia,
And she must fashion horns out of her nature.

      [1] Manifestations.   [2] Absolute.

Mont. But doth she, dare you charge her? speak,
  false prince.

Mo. I must not speak, my lord; but if you'll use
The learning of a nobleman, and read,
Here's something to those points; soft, you must
  pawn [1]
Your honour having read it to return it.

Mont. Not I, I pawn my honour for a paper?

Mo. You must not buy it under.

　　　　　　　　　　　[*Exeunt* GUISE *and* Monsieur.

Mont. Keep it then,
And keep fire in your bosom.

Ta. What says he?

Mont. You must make good the rest.

Ta. How fares my lord?
Takes my love anything to heart he says?

Mont. Come y'are a——

Ta. What, my lord?

Mont. The plague of Herod
Feast in his rotten entrails.

Ta. Will you wreak
Your anger's just cause given by him, on me?

Mont. By him?

Ta. By him, my lord, I have admired [2]
You could all this time be at concord with him,
That still hath placed such discords on your honour.

Mont. Perhaps 'tis with some proud string of my
  wife's.

Ta. How's that, my lord?

Mont. Your tongue will still admire,
Till my head be the miracle of the world.

Ta. Oh, woe is me!

　　　　　　　　　　　　　　[*She seems to swound.*

　　¹ Pledge.　　　² Wondered.

Pe. What does your lordship mean?
Madam, be comforted; my lord but tries you;
Madam! help, good my lord, are you not moved?
Do your set looks print in your words your thoughts?
Sweet lord, clear up those eyes, unbend that masking
  forehead; whence is it
You rush upon her with these Irish wars,
More full of sound than hurt? But it is enough,
You have shot home, your words are in her heart;
She has not lived to bear a trial now.

 Mont. Look up, my love, and by this kiss receive
My soul amongst the spirits for supply
To thine, chased with my fury.

 Ta. Oh, my lord,
I have too long lived to hear this from you.

 Mont. 'Twas from my troubled blood, and not from
  me;
I know not how I fare; a sudden night
Flows through my entrails, and a headlong chaos
Murmurs within me, which I must digest;
And not drown her in my confusions,
That was my life's joy, being best inform'd;
Sweet, you must needs forgive me, that my love
(Like to a fire disdaining his suppression)
Raged being discouraged; my whole heart is wounded
When any least thought in you is but touch'd,
And shall be till I know your former merits;
Your name and memory altogether crave
In just oblivion their eternal grave;
And then you must hear from me, there's no mean
In any passion I shall feel for you;
Love is a razor cleansing being well used,
But fetcheth blood still being the least abused;
To tell you briefly all: the man that left me

When you appear'd, did turn me worse than woman,
And stabbed me to the heart thus, with his fingers.[1]

   Ta. Oh, happy woman! Comes my stain from
     him,
It is my beauty, and that innocence proves;
That slew Chimæra, rescued Peleus
From all the savage beasts in Pelion;
And raised the chaste Athenian prince from hell;
All suffering with me, they for women's lusts,
I for a man's, that the Augean stable
Of his foul sin would empty in my lap;
How his guilt shunn'd me! sacred innocence
That where thou fear'st, art dreadful; and his face
Turn'd in flight from thee, that had thee in chase;
Come, bring me to him; I will tell the serpent
Even to his venom'd teeth (from whose cursed seed
A pitch'd field starts up 'twixt my lord and me)
That his throat lies, and he shall curse his fingers,
For being so govern'd by his filthy soul.

   Mont. I know not if himself will vaunt t'have been
The princely author of the slavish sin,
Or any other; he would have resolved[2] me
Had you not come; not by his word, but writing,
Would I have sworn to give it him again,
And pawn'd mine honour to him for a paper.

   Ta. See how he flies me still; 'tis a foul heart
That fears his own hand; good, my lord, make haste
To see the dangerous paper; papers hold
Oft-times the forms and copies of our souls,
And, though the world despise them, are the prizes
Of all our honours; make your honour then
A hostage for it, and with it confer
My nearest woman here, in all she knows;

       [1] Making horns.   [2] Informed.

Who (if the sun or Cerberus could have seen
Any stain in me) might as much as they;
And, Pero, here I charge thee by my love,
And all proofs of it (which I might call bounties),
By all that thou hast seen seem good in me,
And all the ill which thou shouldst spit from thee,
By pity of the wound this touch hath given me,
Not as thy mistress now, but a poor woman,
To death given over; rid me of my pains,
Pour on thy powder; clear thy breast of me;
My lord is only here; here speak thy worst,
Thy best will do me mischief; if thou sparest me,
Never shine good thought on thy memory.
Resolve, my lord, and leave me desperate.

   Pe. My lord? my lord hath played a prodigal's
      part,
To break his stock for nothing; and an insolent,
To cut a gordian when he could not loose it;
What violence is this, to put true fire
To a false train? To blow up long-crown'd peace
With sudden outrage, and believe a man
Sworn to the shame of women, 'gainst a woman,
Born to their honours? But I will to him.

   Ta. No, I will write (for I shall never more
Meet with the fugitive) where I will defy him,
Were he ten times the brother of my king.
To him, my lord, and I'll to cursing him.

                         [Exeunt.

     Enter D'AMBOIS *and* Friar.

   Bu. I am suspicious, my most honour'd father,
By some of Monsieur's cunning passages,
That his still ranging and contentious nostrils,
To scent the haunts of mischief have so used
The vicious virtue of his busy sense,

That he trails hotly of him, and will rouse him,
Driving him all enraged and foaming, on us.
And therefore have entreated your deep skill
In the command of good ærial spirits,
To assume these magic rites, and call up one
To know if any have reveal'd unto him
Anything touching my dear love and me.

   Fr. Good son, you have amazed me but to make
The least doubt of it, it concerns so nearly
The faith and reverence of my name and order.
Yet will I justify, upon my soul,
All I have done; if any spirit i' th' earth or air
Can give you the resolve, do not despair.

   Music.   TAMYRA *enters with* PERO *and her maid,*
                  bearing a letter.

   Ta. Away, deliver it : O may my lines [*Exit* PERO.
(Fill'd with the poison of a woman's hate
When he shall open them), shrink up his eyes
With torturous darkness, such as stands in hell,
Stuck full of inward horrors, never lighted;
With which are all things to be fear'd, affrighted;
Father !

       Ascendit BUSSY *with* Friar.

   Bu. How is it with my honour'd mistress ?

   Ta. O servant, help, and save me from the gripes
Of shame and infamy.   Our love is known :
Your Monsieur hath a paper where is writ
Some secret tokens that decipher it.

   Bu. What cold dull northern brain, what fool but he
Durst take into his Epimethean breast
A box of such plagues as the danger yields
Incurr'd in this discovery ?   He had better

N

Ventured his breast in the consuming reach
Of the hot surfeits cast out of the clouds,
Or stood the bullets that (to wreak the sky)
The Cyclopes ram in Jove's artillery.

Fr. We soon will take the darkness from his face
That did that deed of darkness ; we will know
What now the Monsieur and your husband do ;
What is contain'd within the secret paper
Offer'd by Monsieur, and your love's events :
To which ends, honour'd daughter, at your motion,
I have put on these exorcising rites,
And, by my power of learned holiness
Vouchsafed me from above, I will command
Our resolution of a raised spirit.

Ta. Good father, raise him in some beauteous form
That with least terror I may brook his sight.

Fr. Stand sure together, then, whate'er ye see,
And stir not, as ye tender all our lives.

[*He puts on his robes.*

*Occidentalium legionum spiritualium imperator (magnus
ille Behemoth) veni, veni, comitatus cum Astaroth
locotenente invicto. Adjuro te per Stygis inscrutabilia
arcana, per ipsos irremeabiles anfractus Averni : adesto
ô Behemoth, tu cui pervia sunt Magnatum scrinia ; veni,
per Noctis & tenebrarum abdita profundissima ; per
labentia sidera; per ipsos motus horarum furtivos, Hecatesq;
altum silentium : Appare in forma spiritali, lucente,
splendida & amibili.*

[*Thunder.   Ascendit.*

Behemoth. What would the holy Friar ?

Fr. I would see
What now the Monsieur and Montsurry do ;
And see the secret paper that the Monsieur
Offer'd to Count Montsurry, longing much

To know on what events the secret loves
Of these two honour'd persons shall arrive.

    Beh. Why call'dst thou me to this accursed light
To these light purposes? I am Emperor
Of that inscrutable darkness where are hid
All deepest truths, and secrets never seen,
All which I know, and command legions
Of knowing spirits that can do more than these.
Any of this my guard that circle me
In these blue fires, and out of whose dim fumes
Vast murmurs use to break, and from their sounds
Articulate voices, can do ten parts more
Than open such slight truths as you require.

    Fr. From the last night's black depth I call'd up
        one
Of the inferior ablest ministers,
And he could not resolve me; send one then
Out of thine own command, to fetch the paper
That Monsieur hath to show to Count Montsurry.

    Beh. I will. Cartophylax, thou that properly
Hast in thy power all papers so inscribed,
Glide through all bars to it and fetch that paper.

    Cartoph. I will.   [*A torch removes.*

    Fr. Till he returns, great prince of darkness,
Tell me if Monsieur and the Count Montsurry
Are yet encounter'd?

    Beh. Both them and the Guise
Are now together.

    Fr. Show us all their persons,
And represent the place, with all their actions.

    Beh. The spirit will straight return; and then I'll
        show thee.
See, he is come; why brought'st thou not the paper?

    Cartoph. He hath prevented me, and got a spirit

Raised by another great in our command,
To take the guard of it before I came.

Beh. This is your slackness, not t'invoke our powers
When first your acts set forth to their effects ;
Yet shall you see it and themselves : behold
They come here, and the Earl now holds the paper.

Enter Monsieur, Guise, Montsurry, *with a paper.*

Bu. May we not hear them ?

Fr. No, be still and see.

Bu. I will go fetch the paper.

Fr. Do not stir ;
There's too much distance and too many locks
'Twixt you and them, how near so'er they seem,
For any man to interrupt their secrets.

Ta. O honour'd spirit, fly into the fancy
Of my offended lord, and do not let him
Believe what there the wicked man hath written.

Beh. Persuasion hath already enter'd him
Beyond reflection ; peace till their departure.

Mo. There is a glass of ink where you may see
How to make ready black-faced tragedy :
You now discern, I hope, through all her paintings,
Her gasping wrinkles, and fame's sepulchres.

Gu. Think you he feigns, my lord ?   What hold you
     now ?
Do we malign your wife, or honour you ?

Mo. What, stricken dumb ! Nay fie, lord, be not
     daunted ;
Your case is common ; were it ne'er so rare,
Bear it as rarely ; now to laugh were manly ;
A worthy man should imitate the weather
That sings in tempests, and being clear is silent.

Gu. Go home, my lord, and force your wife to write
Such loving lines to D'Ambois as she used
When she desired his presence.

Mo. Do, my lord,
And make her name her conceal'd messenger,
That close and most inennerable [1] pander,
That passeth all our studies to exquire; [2]
By whom convey the letter to her love :
And so you shall be sure to have him come
Within the thirsty reach of your revenge ;
Before which, lodge an ambush in her chamber
Behind the arras, of your stoutest men
All close and soundly arm'd ; and let them share
A spirit amongst them that would serve a thousand.

Enter PERO *with a letter.*

Gu. Yet a little ; see, she sends for you.
Mo. Poor, loving lady ; she'll make all good yet,
Think you not so, my lord ?

[Exit MONTSURRY *and stabs* PERO.

Gu. Alas, poor soul !
Mo. That was cruelly done, i'faith.
Pe. 'Twas nobly done.
And I forgive his lordship from my soul.

Mo. Then much good do't thee, Pero ! hast a letter ?
Pe. I hope it rather be a bitter volume
Of worthy curses for your perjury.

Gu. To you, my lord.
Mo. To me ? now, out upon her.
Gu. Let me see, my lord.
Mo. You shall presently : how fares my Pero ?

---

[1] Indescribable. [2] Search into.

Enter Servant.

Who's there? Take in this maid, sh'as caught a clap,
And fetch my surgeon to her ; come, my lord,
We'll now peruse our letter.

[*Exeunt* Monsieur, GUISE.

Pe. Furies rise   [*Lead her out.*
Out of the black lines, and torment his soul.

Ta. Hath my lord slain my woman ?

Beh. No, she lives.

Fr. What shall become of us ?

Beh. All I can say,
Being call'd thus late, is brief, and darkly this :
If D'Ambois' mistress stay not her white hand
In his forced blood, he shall remain untouch'd :
So, father, shall yourself, but by yourself :
To make this augury plainer : when the voice
Of D'Ambois shall invoke me, I will rise,
Shining in greater light : and show him all
That will betide ye all ; meantime be wise,
And curb his valour with your policies.

[*Descendit cum suis.*

Bu. Will he appear to me when I invoke him ?

Fr. He will, be sure.

Bu. It must be shortly then :
For his dark words have tied my thoughts on knots,
Till he dissolve, and free them.

Ta. In meantime,
Dear servant, till your powerful voice revoke [1] him,
Be sure to use the policy he advised :
Lest fury in your too quick knowledge taken
Of our abuse, and your defence of me
Accuse me more than any enemy ;
And, father, you must on my lord impose

[1] Call back.

Your holiest charges, and the Church's power
To temper his hot spirit and disperse
The cruelty and the blood I know his hand
Will shower upon our heads, if you put not
Your finger to the storm, and hold it up,
As my dear servant here must do with Monsieur.

 Bu. I'll soothe his plots ; and strow my hate with
   smiles.

Till all at once the close mines of my heart
Rise at full date, and rush into his blood :
I'll bind his arm in silk, and rub his flesh,
To make the vein swell, that his soul may gush
Into some kennel, where it longs to lie,
And policy shall be flank'd with policy.
Yet shall the feeling centre where we meet
Groan with the weight of my approaching feet ;
I'll make th'inspired thresholds of his court
Sweat with the weather of my horrid steps,
Before I enter ; yet will I appear
Like calm security, before a ruin ;
A politician must like lightning melt
The very marrow, and not taint the skin :
His ways must not be seen ; the superficies
Of the green centre must not taste his feet,
When hell is plow'd up with his wounding tracts ;
And all his harvest reap'd by hellish facts. [*Exeunt.*

ACT THE FIFTH

SCENE I

MONTSURRY *bare, unbraced, pulling* TAMYRA *in by the hair,* Friar. *One bearing a light, a standish* [1] *and a paper, which sets a table.*

A. Oh, help me, father.

    Fr. Impious earl, forbear.

    Take violent hand from her, or by mine order

The King shall force thee.

    Mont. 'Tis not violent; come ye not willingly?

    Ta Yes, good my lord.

    Fr. My lord, remember that your soul must seek

Her peace, as well as your revengeful blood;

You ever to this hour have proved yourself

A noble, zealous, and obedient son,

T'our holy mother; be not an apostate;

Your wife's offence serves not, were it the worst

You can imagine, without greater proofs,

To sever your eternal bonds and hearts;

Much less to touch her with a bloody hand;

Nor is it manly, much less husbandly,

               [1] Case for pen and ink.

To expiate any frailty in your wife
With churlish strokes or beastly odds of strength :
The stony birth of clouds will touch no laurel ;
Nor any sleeper ; your wife is your laurel,
And sweetest sleeper ; do not touch her then ;
Be not more rude than the wild seed of vapour,
To her that is more gentle than that rude ;
In whom kind nature suffer'd one offence
But to set off her other excellence.

   Mont. Good father, leave us ; interrupt no more
The course I must run for mine honour sake.
Rely on my love to her, which her fault
Cannot extinguish ; will she but disclose
Who was the secret minister of her love,
And through what maze he served it, we are friends.

   Fr. It is a damn'd work to pursue those secrets
That would ope more sin, and prove springs of
     slaughter ;
Nor is't a path for Christian feet to tread,
But out of all way to the health of souls,
A sin impossible to be forgiven ;
Which he that dares commit——

   Mont. Good father, cease ; your terrors
Tempt not a man distracted ; I am apt
To outrages that I shall ever rue ;
I will not pass the verge that bounds a Christian,
Nor break the limits of a man nor husband.

   Fr. Then God inspire you both with thoughts and
     deeds
Worthy his high respect, and your own souls.

   Ta. Father !

   Fr. I warrant thee, my dearest daughter,
He will not touch thee ; think'st thou him a pagan ?
His honour and his soul lies for thy safety.　　　[*Exit.*

Mont. Who shall remove the mountain from my
    breast?
Stand the opening furnace of my thoughts,
And set fit outcries for a soul in hell?

                         [MONTSURRY *turns a key.*

For now it nothing fits my woes to speak
But thunder, or to take into my throat
The trump of heaven, with whose determinate blast
The winds shall burst, and the devouring seas
Be drunk up in his sounds; that my hot woes
(Vented enough) I might convert to vapour,
Ascending from my infamy unseen;
Shorten the world, preventing the last breath
That kills the living, and regenerates death.

   Ta. My lord, my fault (as you may censure it
With too strong arguments) is past your pardon:
But how the circumstances may excuse me
Heaven knows, and your more temperate mind here-
    after
May let my penitent miseries make you know.

   Mont. Hereafter? 'Tis a supposed infinite,
That from this point will rise eternally:
Fame grows in going; in the 'scapes of virtue
Excuses damn her: they be fires in cities
Enraged with those winds that less lights extinguish
Come, syren, sing, and dash against my rocks
Thy ruffian galley, rigg'd with quench for lust;
Sing, and put all the nets into thy voice
With which thou drew'st into thy strumpet's lap
The spawn of Venus; and in which ye danced;
That, in thy lap's stead, I may dig his tomb,
And quit his manhood with a woman's sleight,
Who never is deceived in her deceit.
Sing (that is, write), and then take from mine eyes

The mists that hide the most inscrutable pander
That ever lapp'd up an adulterous vomit;
That I may see the devil, and survive
To be a devil, and then learn to wive:
That I may hang him, and then cut him down,
Then cut him up, and with my soul's beams search
The cranks and caverns of his brain, and study
The errant wilderness of a woman's face;
Where men cannot get out, for all the comets
That have been lighted at it; though they know
That adders lie a-sunning in their smiles,
That basilisks drink their poison from their eyes,
And no way there to coast out to their hearts;
Yet still they wander there, and are not stay'd
Till they be fetter'd, nor secure before
All cares devour them; nor in humane consort
Till they embrace within their wife's two breasts
All Pelion and Cythæron with their beasts.
Why write you not?

　　Ta. O good my lord, forbear
In wreak of great faults, to engender greater,
And make my love's corruption generate murder.

　　Mont. It follows needfully as child and parent
The chain-shot of thy lust is yet aloft,
And it must murder; 'tis thine own dear twin:
No man can add height to a woman's sin.
Vice never doth her just hate so provoke,
As when she rageth under virtue's cloak.
Write: for it must be; by this ruthless steel,
By this impartial torture, and the death
Thy tyrannies have invented in my entrails,
To quicken life in dying, and hold up
The spirits in fainting, teaching to preserve
Torments in ashes, that will ever last.

Speak!   Will you write?

   Ta. Sweet lord, enjoin my sin
Some other penance than what makes it worse ;
Hide in some gloomy dungeon my loathed face,
And let condemned murderers let me down
(Stopping their noses) my abhorred food.
Hang me in chains, and let me eat these arms
That have offended ; bind me face to face
To some dead woman, taken from the cart
Of execution, till death and time
In grains of dust dissolve me ; I'll endure ;
Or any torture that your wrath's invention
Can fright all pity from the world withal ;
But to betray a friend with show of friendship,
That is too common, for the rare revenge
Your rage affecteth ; here then are my breasts,
Last night your pillows ; here my wretched arms,
As late the wished confines of your life ;
Now break them as you please, and all the bounds
Of manhood, noblesse, and religion.

   Mont. Where all these have been broken, they are
     kept,
In doing their justice there with any show
Of the like cruel cruelty ; thine arms have lost
Their privilege in lust, and in their torture
Thus they must pay it.   [*Stabs her.*

   Ta. O Lord !

   Mont. Till thou writest,
I'll write in wounds (my wrong's fit characters)
Thy right of sufferance.   Write.

   Ta. Oh, kill me, kill me ;
Dear husband, be not crueller than death ;
You have beheld some Gorgon ; feel, oh, feel
How you are turn'd to stone ; with my heart-blood

Dissolve yourself again, or you will grow
Into the image of all tyranny.

Mont. As thou art of adultery, I will still
Prove thee my parallel, being most a monster ;
Thus I express thee yet.   [*Stabs her again.*

Ta. And yet I live.

Mont. Ay, for thy monstrous idol is not done yet ;
This tool hath wrought enough ; now, torture use.

Enter Servants.

This other engine on th'habituate powers
Of her thrice-damn'd and whorish fortitude.
Use the most madding pains in her that ever
Thy venoms soak'd through, making most of death ;
That she may weigh her wrongs with them, and then
Stand vengeance on thy steepest rock, a victor.

Ta. Oh, who is turn'd into my lord and husband ?
Husband !   My lord !   None but my lord and hus-
     band !
Heaven, I ask thee remission of my sins,
Not of my pains ; husband, oh, help me, husband !

Ascendit Friar *with a sword drawn.*

Fr. What rape of honour and religion—
Oh, wrack of nature !   [*Falls and dies.*

Ta. Poor man ; oh, my father,
Father, look up ; oh, let me down, my lord,
And I will write.

Mont. Author of prodigies !
What new flame breaks out of the firmament,
That turns up counsels never known before ?
Now is it true, earth moves, and heaven stands still ;
Even heaven itself must see and suffer ill ;
The too huge bias of the world hath sway'd
Her back part upwards, and with that she braves

This hemisphere, that long her mouth hath mock'd ;
The gravity of her religious face,
(Now grown too weighty with her sacrilege
And here discern'd sophisticate enough)
Turns to th'antipodes ; and all the forms
That her illusions have imprest in her,
Have eaten through her back ; and now all see,
How she is riveted with hypocrisy :
Was this the way ? was he the mean betwixt you ?

 Ta. He was, he was, kind worthy man, he was.

 Mont. Write, write a word or two.

 Ta. I will, I will.

I'll write, but with my blood, that he may see
These lines come from my wounds, and not from me.

           [*Writes.*

 Mont. Well might he die for thought ; methinks the
  frame
And shaken joints of the whole world should crack
To see her parts so disproportionate ;
And that his general beauty cannot stand
Without these stains in the particular man.
Why wander I so far ? here, here was she
That was a whole world without spot to me,
Though now a world of spots ; oh, what a lightning
Is man's delight in women ! what a bubble,
He builds his state, fame, life on, when he marries !
Since all earth's pleasures are so short and small,
The way t'enjoy it, is t'abjure it all ;
Enough : I must be messenger myself,
Disguised like this strange creature : in, I'll after,
To see what guilty light gives this cave eyes,
And to the world sing new impieties.

  [*Exeunt. He puts the* Friar *in the vault and follows.*
   She wraps herself in the Arras.

Enter Monsieur *and* Guise.

Mo. Now shall we see, that nature hath no end
In her great works, responsive to their worths,
That she that makes so many eyes, and souls,
To see and foresee, is stark blind herself ;
And as illiterate men say Latin prayers
By rote, of heart and daily iteration ;
Not knowing what they say ; so Nature lays
A deal of stuff together, and by use,
Or by the mere necessity of matter,
Ends such a work, fills it, or leaves it empty
Of strength or virtue, error or clear truth ;
Not knowing what she does ; but usually
Gives that which she calls merit to a man,
And belief must arrive him on huge riches,
Honour, and happiness, that effects his ruin ;
Even as in ships of war, whose lasts of powder
Are laid, men think, to make them last, and guards,
When a disorder'd spark that powder taking,
Blows up with sudden violence and horror
Ships that kept empty, had sail'd long with terror.
Gu. He that observes, but like a worldly man,
That which doth oft succeed, and by th'events
Values the worth of things ; will think it true
That nature works at random, just with you ;
But with as much proportion she may make
A thing that from the feet up to the throat
Hath all the wondrous fabric man should have,
And leave it headless for a perfect man,
As give a full man valour, virtue, learning,
Without an end more excellent than those,
On whom she no such worthy part bestows.
Mo. Yet shall you see it here, here will be one
Young, learned, valiant, virtuous, and full mann'd ;

One on whom Nature spent so rich a hand,
That, with an ominous eye, she wept to see
So much consumed her virtuous treasury.
Yet, as the winds sing through a hollow tree,
And (since it lets them pass through) lets it stand ;
But a tree solid (since it gives no way
To their wild rage) they rend up by the root ;
So this whole man,
(That will not wind with every crooked way,
Trod by the servile world) shall reel and fall
Before the frantic puffs of blind-born chance,
That pipes through empty men, and makes them
        dance ;
Not so the sea raves on the Lybian sands,
Tumbling her billows in each others' necks ;
Not so the surges of the Euxine sea
(Near to the frosty pole, where free Boötes
From those dark deep waves turns his radiant team)
Swell being enraged, even from their inmost drop,
As Fortune swings about the restless state
Of virtue, now thrown into all men's hate.

Enter MONTSURRY *disguised, with the* Murderers.

Away, my lord, you are perfectly disguised,
Leave us to lodge your ambush.

    Mont. Speed me, vengeance.   [*Exit.*

    Mo. Resolve, my masters, you shall meet with one
Will try what proofs your privy coats are made on
When he is enter'd, and you hear us stamp,
Approach, and make all sure.

    Murd. We will, my lord.   [*Exeunt.*

Enter D'AMBOIS *with two* Pages *with tapers.*

    Bu. Sit up to-night, and watch ; I'll speak with none

But the old Friar, who bring to me.

Pa. We will, sir. [*Exeunt.*

Bu. What violent heat is this? Methinks the fire
Of twenty lives doth on a sudden flash
Through all my faculties; the air goes high
In this close chamber, and the frighted earth

[*Thunder.*

Trembles, and shrinks beneath me; the whole house
Nods with his shaken burthen; bless me, heaven!

Enter Umbra Friar.

Um. Note what I want, my son, and be forewarn'd;
O there are bloody deeds past and to come:
I cannot stay; a fate doth ravish me;
I'll meet thee in the chamber of thy love. [*Exit.*

Bu. What dismal change is here; the good old
      Friar
Is murder'd; being made known to serve my love;
And now his restless spirit would forewarn me
Of some plot dangerous and imminent.
Note what he wants? He wants his upper weed,
He wants his life and body; which of these
Should be the want he means, and may supply me
With any fit forewarning? This strange vision
(Together with the dark prediction
Used by the Prince of Darkness that was raised
By this embodied shadow) stir my thoughts
With reminiscion of the spirit's promise,
Who told me, that by any invocation
I should have power to raise him, though it wanted
The powerful words and decent rites of art;
Never had my set brain such need of spirit
T'instruct and cheer it; now, then, I will claim
Performance of his free and gentle vow

o

T'appear in greater light, and make more plain
His rugged oracle.   I long to know
How my dear mistress fares, and be inform'd
What hand she now holds on the troubled blood
Of her incensed lord.   Methought the spirit
(When he had utter'd his perplex'd presage)
Threw his changed countenance headlong into clouds,
His forehead bent, as it would hide his face,
He knock'd his chin against his darken'd breast,
And struck a churlish silence through his powers.
Terror of darkness!   O, thou king of flames!
That with thy music-footed horse dost strike
The clear light out of crystal on dark earth,
And hurl'st instructive fire about the world,
Wake, wake the drowsy and enchanted night,
That sleeps with dead eyes in this heavy riddle;
Or thou great prince of shades where never sun
Sticks his far-darted beams, whose eyes are made
To shine in darkness, and see ever best
Where men are blindest: open now the heart
Of thy abashed oracle, that for fear,
Of some ill it includes, would fain lie hid,
And rise thou with it in thy greater light.

      [*Thunders.   Surgit Spiritus cum suis.*

 Sp. Thus to observe my vow of apparition,
In greater light, and explicate thy fate,
I come; and tell thee that if thou obey
The summons that thy mistress next will send thee,
Her hand shall be thy death.

 Bu. When will she send?

 Sp. Soon as I set again, where late I rose.

 Bu. Is the old Friar slain?

 Sp. No, and yet lives not.

 Bu. Died he a natural death?

Sp. He did.

Bu. Who then
Will my dear mistress send?

Sp. I must not tell thee.

Bu. Who lets [1] thee?

Sp. Fate.

Bu. Who are fate's ministers?

Sp. The Guise and Monsieur.

Bu. A fit pair of shears
To cut the threads of kings, and kingly spirits,
And consorts fit to sound forth harmony,
Set to the falls of kingdoms: shall the hand
Of my kind mistress kill me?   [*Thunders.*

Sp. If thou yield
To her next summons, y'are fair-warn'd: farewell!
     [*Exit.*

Bu. I must farewell, however: though I die,
My death consenting with his augury;
Should not my powers obey when she commands,
My motion must be rebel to my will:
My will to life: if, when I have obey'd,
Her hand should so reward me, they must arm it,
Bind me or force it: or, I lay my life,
She rather would convert it many times
On her own bosom, even to many deaths;
But were there danger of such violence,
I know 'tis far from her intent to send:
And who she should send is as far from thought,
Since he is dead, whose only mean she used.
     [*Knocks.*
Who's there! Look to the door, and let him in,
Though politic Monsieur or the violent Guise.

----

[1] Prevents.

Enter MONTSURRY, *like the* Friar, *with a letter written
in blood.*

Mont. Hail to my worthy son.

Bu. Oh, lying spirit !
To say the Friar was dead ; I'll now believe
Nothing of all his forged predictions.
My kind and honour'd father, well revived,
I have been frighted with your death, and mine,
And told my mistress' hand should be my death
If I obey'd this summons.

Mont. I believed
Your love had been much clearer than to give
Any such doubt a thought, for she is clear,
And having freed her husband's jealousy
(Of which her much abused hand here is witness)
She prays, for urgent cause, your instant presence.

Bu. Why, then your prince of spirits may be call'd
The prince of liars.

Mont. Holy Writ so calls him.

Bu. What, writ in blood ?

Mont. Ay, 'tis the ink of lovers.

Bu. O, 'tis a sacred witness of her love.
So much elixir of her blood as this
Dropt in the lightest dame, would make her firm
As heat to fire : and like to all the signs,
Commands the life confined in all my veins ;
O, how it multiplies my blood with spirit,
And makes me apt t'encounter death and hell.
But come, kind father, you fetch me to heaven,
And to that end your holy weed was given.

[*Exeunt.*

Thunder. **Intrat** Umbra Friar, *and discovers*
TAMYRA.

Um. Up with these stupid thoughts, still loved
    daughter,
And strike away this heartless trance of anguish.
Be like the sun, and labour in eclipses ;
Look to the end of woes : oh, can you sit
Mustering the horrors of your servant's slaughter
Before your contemplation, and not study
How to prevent it ? watch when he shall rise,
And with a sudden outcry of his murder,
Blow his retreat before he be revenged.

    Ta. O father ! have my dumb woes waked your
    death ?
When will our humane griefs be at their height ?
Man is a tree that hath no top in cares,
No root in comforts ; all his power to live
Is given to no end, but t'have power to grieve.

    Um. It is the misery of our creation.
Your true friend,
Led by your husband, shadow'd in my weed,
Now enters the dark vault.

    Ta. But, my dearest father,
Why will not you appear to him yourself,
And see that none of these deceits annoy [1] him ?

    Um. My power is limited ; alas ! I cannot.
All that I can do—See, the cave opens.

                [*Exit.* D'AMBOIS *at the gulf.*

    Ta. Away (my love), away ; thou wilt be murder'd !

Enter Monsieur *and* GUISE *above.*

    Bu. Murder'd ; I know not what that Hebrew
    means :

                [1] Destroy.

That word had ne'er been named had all been
  D'Ambois.
Murder'd? By heaven he is my murderer
That shows me not a murderer; what such bug
Abhorreth not the very sleep of D'Ambois?
Murder'd who dares give all the room I see
To D'Ambois' reach? or look with any odds
His fight i'th' face, upon whose hand sits death;
Whose sword hath wings, and every feather pierceth?
If i'scape Monsieur's 'pothecary shops,
Foutre [1] for Guise's shambles! 'twas ill plotted
They should have maul'd me here,
When I was rising. I am up and ready.
Let in my politic visitants, let them in,
Though entering like so many moving armours,
Fate is more strong than arms, and sly than treason,
And I at all parts buckled in my fate,

   Mo. ⎫
   Gu. ⎬ Why enter not the coward villains?

   Bu. Dare they not come?

   Enter Murderers *with* Friar *at the other door.*

   Ta. They come.
   1st Mu. Come all at once.
   Um. Back, coward murderers, back.
   Omn. Defend us, heaven. [*Exeunt all but the first.*
   1st. Come ye not on?
   Bu. No, slave, nor goest thou off.
Stand you so firm? Will it not enter here?
You have a face yet; so in thy life's flame
I burn the first rites to my mistress' fame.
   Um. Breathe thee, brave son, against the other
     charge.

            [1] An expression of contempt.

Bu. Oh, is it true then that my sense first told me?
Is my kind father dead?

Ta. He is, my love.
'Twas the Earl, my husband, in his weed that brought
    thee.

Bu. That was a speeding sleight, and well resembled.
Where is that angry Earl, my lord? Come forth
And show your own face in your own affair;
Take not into your noble veins the blood
Of these base villains, nor the light reports
Of blister'd tongues, for clear and weighty truth:
But me against the world, in pure defence
Of your rare lady, to whose spotless name
I stand here as a bulwark, and project
A life to her renown, that ever yet
Hath been untainted, even in envy's eye,
And where it would protect a sanctuary.
Brave Earl, come forth, and keep your scandal in:
'Tis not our fault if you enforce the spot
Nor the wreak yours if you perform it not.

     Enter MONTSURRY, *with all the* Murderers.

Mont. Cowards, a fiend or spirit beat ye off!
They are your own faint spirits that have forged
The fearful shadows that your eyes deluded:
The fiend was in you; cast him out then, thus.

                [D'AMBOIS *hath* MONT. *down.*

Ta. Favour my lord, my love, O, favour him!
                [*Pistols shot within.*

Bu. I will not touch him: take your life, my lord,
And be appeased: O, then the coward Fates
Have maim'd themselves, and ever lost their honour.

Um. What have ye done, slaves? irreligious lord!

Bu. Forbear them, father; 'tis enough for me

That Guise and Monsieur, death and destiny,
Come behind D'Ambois.   Is my body, then,
But penetrable flesh?   And must my mind
Follow my blood?   Can my divine part add
No aid to th'earthly in extremity?
Then these divines are but for form, not fact:
Man is of two sweet courtly friends compact,
A mistress and a servant; let my death
Define life nothing but a courtier's breath.
Nothing is made of nought, of all things made,
Their abstract being a dream but of a shade.
I'll not complain to earth yet, but to heaven,
And, like a man, look upwards even in death.
And if Vespasian thought in majesty
An emperor might die standing, why not I?
Nay, without help, in which I will exceed him;
For he died splinted with his chamber grooms.

                                   [*She offers to help him.*

Prop me, true sword, as thou hast ever done:
The equal thought I bear of life and death
Shall make me faint on no side; I am up;
Here like a Roman statue I will stand
Till death hath made me marble: oh, my fame,
Live in despite of murder; take thy wings
And haste thee where the grey-eyed morn perfumes
Her rosy chariot with Sabæan spices,
Fly, where the evening from th'Iberian vales,
Takes on her swarthy shoulders Hecate,
Crown'd with a grove of oaks: fly where men feel
The cunning axletree: and those that suffer
Beneath the chariot of the snowy Bear:
And tell them all that D'Ambois now is hasting
To the eternal dwellers; that a thunder
Of all their sighs together (for their frailties

Beheld in me) may quit my worthless fall
With a fit volley for my funeral.

Um. Forgive thy murderers.

Bu. I forgive them all;
And you, my lord, their fautor;[1] for true sign
Of which unfeign'd remission, take my sword;
Take it, and only give it motion,
And it shall find the way to victory
By his own brightness, and th'inherent valour
My fight hath still'd into't, with charms of spirit.
Now let me pray you that my weighty blood
Laid in one scale of your impartial spleen,
May sway the forfeit of my worthy love
Weigh'd in the other; and be reconciled
With all forgiveness to your matchless wife.

Ta. Forgive thou me, dear servant, and this hand
That led thy life to this unworthy end;
Forgive it, for the blood with which 'tis stain'd,
In which I writ the summons of thy death;
The forced summons, by this bleeding wound,
By this here in my bosom; and by this
That makes me hold up both my hands imbrued
For thy dear pardon.

Bu. O, my heart is broken;
Fate, nor these murderers, Monsieur, nor the Guise,
Have any glory in my death, but this,
This killing spectacle, this prodigy;
My sun is turn'd to blood, in whose red beams
Pindus and Ossa hid in drifts of snow,
Laid on my heart and liver; from their veins
Melt like two hungry torrents; eating rocks
Into the ocean of all humane life,
And make it bitter, only with my blood.

[1] Patron.

O frail condition of strength, valour, virtue,
In me, like warning fire upon the top
Of some steep beacon, on a steeper hill,
Made to express it : like a falling star
Silently glanced, that like a thunderbolt
Look'd to have stuck and shook the firmament.

[Moritur.

Um. My terrors are struck inward, and no more
My penance will allow they shall enforce
Earthly afflictions but upon myself.
Farewell, brave relics of a complete man ;
Look up and see thy spirit made a star,
Join flames with Hercules ; and when thou sett'st
Thy radiant forehead in the firmament,
Make the vast crystal crack with thy receipt ;
Spread to a world of fire ; and th'aged sky
Cheer with new sparks of old humanity.

Son of the earth, whom my unrested soul,
Rues t'have begotten in the faith of heaven ;
(Since thy revengeful spirit hath rejected
The charity it commands, and the remission
To serve and worship the blind rage of blood)
Assay to gratulate and pacify
The soul fled from this worthy by performing
The Christian reconcilement he besought
Betwixt thee and thy lady, let her wounds
Manlessly digg'd in her, be eased and cured
With blame of thine own tears ; or be assured
Never to rest free from my haunt and horror.

Mont. See how she merits this ; still sitting by,
And mourning his fall more than her own fault.

Um. Remove, dear daughter, and content thy
    husband ;

So piety wills thee, and thy servant's peace.

Ta. O wretched piety, that art so distract
In thine own constancy; and in thy right
Must be unrighteous; if I right my friend
I wrong my husband; if his wrong I shun,
The duty of my friend I leave undone;
Ill plays on both sides; here and there, it riseth;
No place, no good, so good, but ill compriseth;
My soul more scruple breeds, than my blood, sin.
Virtue imposeth more than any stepdame;
O had I never married but for form,
Never vow'd faith but purposed to deceive,
Never made conscience of any sin,
But cloak'd it privately and made it common;
Nor never honour'd been, in blood, or mind,
Happy had I been then, as others are
Of the like licence; I had then been honour'd;
Lived without envy; custom had benumb'd
All sense of scruple, and all note of frailty:
My fame had been untouch'd, my heart unbroken:
But (shunning all) I strike on all offence,
O husband! dear friend! O my conscience!

Mo. Come, let's away; my senses are not proof
Against those plaints.

[*Exeunt* GUISE, Monsieur: D'AMBOIS *is borne off.*

Mont. I must not yield to pity, nor to love
So servile and so traitorous: cease, my blood,
To wrastle with my honour, fame, and judgment:
Away, forsake my house, forbear complaints
Where thou hast bred them: here all things are full
Of their own shame and sorrow; leave my house.

Ta. Sweet lord, forgive me, and I will be gone,
And till these wounds, that never balm shall close
Till death hath enter'd at them, so I love them,

Being open'd by your hands, by death be cured,
I never more will grieve you with my sight,
Never endure that any roof shall part
Mine eyes and heaven ; but to the open deserts
(Like to hunted tigers) I will fly :
Eating my heart, shunning the steps of men,
And look on no side till I be arrived.

Mont. I do forgive thee, and upon my knees,
With hands held up to heaven, wish that mine honour
Would suffer reconcilement to my love ;
But since it will not, honour, never serve
My love with flourishing object till it sterve :[1]
And as this taper, though it upwards look,
Downwards must needs consume, so let our love ;
As having lost his honey, the sweet taste
Runs into savour, and will needs retain
A spice of his first parents, till, like life,
It sees and dies ; so let our love ; and lastly,
As when the flame is suffer'd to look up,
It keeps his lustre : but, being thus turn'd down,
His natural course of useful light inverted),
His own stuff puts it out ; so let our love :
Now turn from me, as here I turn from thee,
And may both points of heaven's straight axle-tree
Conjoin in one, before thyself and me.

[*Exeunt severally.*

[1] Perish.

EPILOGUE[1]

WITH many hands you have seen D'Ambois
    slain,
    Yet by your grace he may revive again,
    And every day grow stronger in his skill
To please, as we presume he is in will.
The best deserving actors of the time
Had their ascents ; and by degrees did climb
To their full height, a place to study due
To make him tread in their path lies in you ;
He'll not forget his makers ; but still prove
His thankfulness as you increase your love.

[1] First printed in the edition of 1641.

THE REVENGE OF BUSSY D'AMBOIS

THE *Revenge*, although nominally a sequel to *Bussy*, is really an entirely separate play; it was published in 1613. The dedication is particularly interesting as containing a definite statement of Chapman's theory of tragedy.

SIR THOMAS HOWARD, &c.

SIR,—

INCE works of this kind have been lately esteemed worthy the patronage of some of our worthiest nobles, I have made no doubt to prefer this of mine to your undoubted virtue, and exceeding true noblesse; as containing matter no less deserving your reading, and excitation to heroical life, than any such late dedication. Nor have the greatest Princes of Italy and other countries, conceived it any least diminution to their greatness to have their names winged with these tragic plumes, and dispersed by way of patronage through the most noble notices of Europe.

Howsoever therefore in the scenical presentation it might meet with some maligners, yet considering, even therein, it passed with approbation of more worthy judgments; the balance of their side (especially being held by your impartial hand) I hope will to no grain abide the out-weighing. And for the authentical truth of either person or action, who (worth the respecting) will expect it in a poem, whose subject is not truth, but things like truth? Poor envious souls they are that cavil at truth's want in these natural fictions; material instruction, elegant and sententious excitation to virtue, and deflec-

tion from her contrary, being the soul, limbs, and limits
of an authentical tragedy. But whatsoever merit of your
full countenance and favour suffers defect in this, I shall
soon supply with some other of more general account:
wherein your right-virtuous name made famous and preserved to posterity, your future comfort and honour in
your present acceptation, and love of all virtuous and
divine expression; may be so much past others of your
rank increased, as they are short of your judicial ingenuity
in their due estimation.

For, howsoever those ignoble and sour-browed world-
lings are careless of whatsoever future or present opinion
spreads of them; yet (with the most divine philosopher,
if Scripture did not confirm it) I make it matter of my
faith, that we truly retain an intellectual feeling of good
or bad after this life, proportionably answerable to the
love or neglect we bear here to all virtue, and truly
humane instruction. In whose favour and honour I
wish you most eminent; and rest ever,

> Your true Virtue's
> Most true observer,
> GEO. CHAPMAN.

DRAMATIS PERSONÆ

HENRY, the king.

Monsieur, his brother.

GUISE, Duke.

RENEL, a marquess,

MONTSURRY, an earl.

BALIGNY, Lord-lieutenant.

CLERMONT D'AMBOIS.

MAILLARD,
CHALON, } captains.
AUMALE,

ESPERNON.

SOISSON.

PERRICOT.

The Guard.

Soldiers.

Servants.

The Ghost of {
BUSSY.
Monsieur.
GUISE.
Cardinal GUISE.
CHATILLON.
}

Countess of CAMBRAY.

TAMYRA, wife to Montsurry.

CHARLOTTE, wife to Baligny.

RIOVA, a servant.

THE REVENGE OF BUSSY D'AMBOIS

ACT THE FIRST

SCENE I

Enter BALIGNY, RENEL.

A. To what will this declining kingdom turn,
Swingding in every licence, as in this
Stupid permission of brave D'Ambois'
murder?
Murder made parallel with law! Murder used
To serve the kingdom, given by suit to men
For their advancement! suffer'd scarecrowlike
To fright adultery! What will policy
At length bring under his capacity?

   Re. All things: for as when the high births of
kings,
Deliverances, and coronations,
We celebrate with all the cities' bells
(Jangling together in untuned confusion);

229

All order'd clocks are tied up : so when glory,
Flattery, and smooth applauses of things ill,
Uphold th'inordinate swindge of downright power,
Justice, and truth, that tell the bounded use,
Virtuous, and well-distinguish'd forms of Time
Are gagg'd and tongue-tied, but we have observed
Rule in more regular motion : things most lawful
Were once most royal, kings sought common good,
Men's manly liberties, though ne'er so mean,
And had their own swindge so : more free, and more.
But when pride enter'd them, and rule by power,
All brows that smiled beneath them, frown'd : hearts
		grieved
By imitation ; virtue quite was vanish'd,
And all men studied self-love, fraud, and vice ;
Then no man could be good but he was punish'd :
Tyrants being still more fearful of the good
Than of the bad ; their subjects' virtues ever
Managed with curbs and dangers, and esteem'd
As shadows and detractions to their own.

   Ba. Now all is peace, no danger : now what
		follows ?
Idleness rusts us ; since no virtuous labour
Ends ought rewarded : ease, security,
Now all the palm wears, we made war before
So to prevent war, men with giving gifts
More than receiving, made our country strong ;
Our matchless race of soldiers then would spend
In public wars, not private brawls, their spirits,
In daring enemies, arm'd with meanest arms ;
Not courting strumpets, and consuming birthrights
In apishness and envy of attire.
No labour then was harsh, no way so deep,
No rock so steep, but if a bird could scale it,

Up would our youth fly too.   A foe in arms
Stirr'd up a much more lust of his encounter,
Than of a mistress never so be-painted ;
Ambition then, was only scaling walls ;
And over-topping turrets ; fame was wealth ;
Best parts, best deeds, were best nobility ;
Honour with worth ; and wealth well got or none :
Countries we won with as few men as countries :
Virtue subdued all.

 Re. Just : and then our nobles
Loved virtue so, they praised and used it too :
Had rather do, than say ; their own deeds hearing
By others glorified, than be so barren,
That their parts only stood in praising others.

 Ba. Who could not do, yet praised, and envied
  not ;
Civil behaviour flourish'd ; bounty flow'd,
Avarice to upland boors, slaves, hangman, banish'd.

 Re. 'Tis now quite otherwise ; but to note the
  cause
Of all these foul digressions and revolts
From our first natures, this 'tis in a word ;
Since good arts fail, crafts and deceits are used ;
Men ignorant are idle ; idle men
Most practise what they most may do with ease,
Fashion, and favour ; all their studies aiming
At getting money, which no wise man ever
Fed his desires with.

 Ba. Yet now none are wise
That think not heaven's true foolish, weigh'd with
  that.
Well, thou most worthy to be greatest Guise,
Make with thy greatness a new world arise.
Such depress'd nobles, followers of his,

As you, myself, my lord, will find a time
When to revenge your wrongs.

Re. I make no doubt;
In mean time, I could wish the wrong were righted
Of your slain brother-in-law, brave Bussy D'Ambois.

Ba. That one accident was made my charge.
My brother Bussy's sister, now my wife,
By no suit would consent to satisfy
My love of her with marriage, till I vow'd
To use my utmost to revenge my brother;
But Clermont D'Ambois, Bussy's second brother,
Had since his apparition, and excitement
To suffer none but his hand in his wreak,
Which he hath vow'd, and so will needs acquit
Me of my vow, made to my wife, his sister,
And undertake himself Bussy's revenge;
Yet loathing any way to give it act,
But in the noblest and most manly course;
If th'earl dares take it, he resolves to send
A challenge to him, and myself must bear it,
To which delivery I can use no means;
He is so barricado'd in his house,
And arm'd with guard still.

Re. That means lay on me,
Which I can strangly make. My last lands' sale,
By his great suit, stands now on price with him,
And he, as you know, passing covetous,
With that blind greediness that follows gain,
Will cast no danger, where her sweet feet tread.
Besides, you know, his lady by his suit,
(Wooing as freshly, as when first love shot
His faultless arrows from her rosy eyes)
Now lives with him again, and she, I know,
Will join with all helps in her friend's revenge.

Ba. No doubt, my lord, and therefore let me pray
    you
To use all speed ; for so on needles' point
My wife's heart stands with haste of the revenge ;
Being, as you know, full of her brother's fire,
That she imagines I neglect my vow ;
Keeps off her kind embraces, and still [1] asks ;
" When, when, will this revenge come? when per-
    form'd
Will this dull vow be ?" and I vow to Heaven
So sternly, and so past her sex she urges
My vow's performance, that I almost fear
To see her, when I have awhile been absent,
Not showing her before I speak, the blood
She so much thirsts for, freckling hands and face.

Re. Get you the challenge writ, and look from me,
To hear your passage clear'd no long time after.

                     [*Exit* RENEL.

Ba. All restitution to your worthiest lordship,
Whose errand I must carry to the King,
As having sworn my service in the search
Of all such malcontents and their designs,
By seeming one affected with their faction,
And discontented humours 'gainst the state :
Nor doth my brother Clermont 'scape my counsel
Given to the King, about his Guisean greatness,
Which as I spice it, hath possess'd the King
(Knowing his daring spirit) of much danger
Charged in it to his person ; though my conscience
Dare swear him clear of any power to be
Infected with the least dishonesty :
Yet that sincerity, we politicians
Must say, grows out of envy, since it cannot

               [1] Always.

Aspire to policy's greatness : and the more
We work on all respects of kind and virtue,
The more our service to the King seems great,
In sparing no good that seems bad to him :
And the more bad we make the most of good,
The more our policy searcheth ; and our service
Is wonder'd at for wisdom and sincereness.
'Tis easy to make good suspected still,
Where good and God are made but cloaks for ill.
See Monsieur taking now his leave for Brabant ;

Enter HENRY, Monsieur, GUISE, CLERMONT, ESPER-
    NON, SOISSON. Monsieur *taking leave of the*
    King.

The Guise, and his dear minion, Clermont D'Ambois,
Whispering together, not of state affairs
I durst lay wagers (though the Guise be now
In chief heat of his faction) but of something
Savouring of that which all men else despise,
How to be truly noble, truly wise.

Mo. See how he hangs upon the ear of Guise,
Like to his jewel.

Es. He's now whispering in
Some doctrine of stability, and freedom,
Contempt of outward greatness, and the guises
That vulgar great ones make their pride and zeal,
Being only servile trains, and sumptuous houses,
High places, offices.

Mo. Contempt of these
Does he read to the Guise ? 'Tis passing needful.
And he, I think, makes show t'affect his doctrine.

Es. Commends, admires it.

Mo. And pursues another.
'Tis fine hypocrisy, and cheap, and vulgar,

Known for a covert practice, yet believed,
By those abused souls that they teach and govern,
No more than wives' adulteries by their husbands,
They bearing it with so unmoved aspects,
Hot coming from it, as 'twere not at all
Or made by custom nothing. This same D'Ambois
Hath gotten such opinion of his virtues,
Holding all learning but an art to live well,
And showing he hath learn'd it, in his life,
Being thereby strong in his persuading others;
That this ambitious Guise, embracing him,
Is thought t'embrace his virtues.

 Es. Yet in some
His virtues are held false for th'other's vices:
For 'tis more cunning held, and much more common,
To suspect truth than falsehood: and of both
Truth still fares worse; as hardly being believed,
As 'tis unusual, and rarely known.

 Mo. I'll part engendering virtue. Men affirm
Though this same Clermont hath a D'Ambois' spirit,
And breathes his brother's valour; yet his temper
Is so much past his, that you cannot move him:
I'll try that temper in. Come, you two
Devour each other with your virtue's zeal,
And leave, for other friends, no fragment of ye:
I wonder, Guise, you will thus ravish him
Out of my bosom that first gave the life
His manhood breathes, spirit, and means, and lustre.
What do men think of me, I pray thee, Clermont?
Once give me leave (for trial of that love
That from thy brother Bussy thou inherit'st)
T'unclasp thy bosom.

 Cl. As how, sir?

 Mo. Be a true glass to me, in which I may

Behold what thoughts the many-headed beast
And thou thyself breathes out conçerning me,
My ends, and new-upstarted state in Brabant,
For which I now am bound, my higher aims,
Imagined here in France : speak, man, and let
Thy words be born as naked as thy thoughts:
Oh, were brave Bussy living !

   Cl. Living, my lord?

   Mo. 'Tis true thou art his brother, but durst thou
Have braved the Guise, maugre [1] his presence, courted
His wedded lady, emptied even the dregs
Of his worst thoughts of me, even to my teeth ;
Discern'd not me, his rising sovereign,
From any common groom, but let me hear
My grossest faults, as gross-full as they were.
Durst thou do this ?

   Cl. I cannot tell : a man
Does never know the goodness of his stomach
Till he sees meat before him. Were I dared,
Perhaps, as he was, I durst do like him.

   Mo. Dare then to pour out here thy freest soul
Of what I am.

   Cl. 'Tis stale ; he told you it.

   Mo. He only jested, spake of spleen and envy ;
Thy soul, more learn'd, is more ingenuous,
Searching, judicial ; let me then from thee
Hear what I am.

   Cl. What but the sole support,
And most expectant hope of all our France,
The toward victor of the whole Low Countries?

   Mo. Tush, thou wilt sing encomions of my praise.
Is this like D'Ambois ? I must vex the Guise,
Or never look to hear free truth ; tell me,

<hr>

[1] In spite of.

For Bussy lives not ; he durst anger me,
Yet for my love, would not have fear'd to anger
The King himself.   Thou understand'st me, dost not?

Cl. I shall, my lord, with study.

Mo. Dost understand thyself?   I pray thee tell me,
Dost never search thy thoughts, what my design
Might be to entertain thee and thy brother?
What turn I meant to serve with you?

Cl. Even what you please to think.

Mo. But what think'st thou?
Had I no end in't, think'st?

Cl. I think you had.

Mo. When I took in such two as you two were,
A ragged couple of decay'd commanders,
When a French crown would plentifully serve
To buy you both to anything i'th' earth.

Cl. So it would you.

Mo. Nay, bought you both outright ;
You, and your trunks : I fear me, I offend thee.

Cl. No, not a jot.

Mo. The most renowned soldier,
Epaminondas, as good authors say,
Had no more suits than backs, but you two shared
But one suit 'twixt you both, when both your studies
Were not what meat to dine with ; if your partridge,
Your snipe, your woodcock, lark, or your red-herring,
But where to beg it ; whether at my house
Or at the Guise's (for you know you were
Ambitious beggars), or at some cook's-shop,
T'eternize the cook's trust, and score it up.
Dost not offend thee?

Cl. No, sir ; pray proceed.

Mo. As for thy gentry, I dare boldly take
Thy honourable oath ; and yet some say

Thou and thy most renowned noble brother,
Came to the Court first in a keel of sea-coal;
Dost not offend thee?

 Cl. Never doubt it, sir.

 Mo. Why do I love thee, then? why have I raked
  thee
Out of the dung-hill? cast my cast [1] wardrobe on thee?
Brought thee to Court too, as I did thy brother?
Made ye my saucy boon companions?
Taught ye to call our greatest noblemen
By the corruption of their names; Jack, Tom?
Have I blown both for nothing to this bubble?
Though thou art learn'd, th'ast no enchanting wit,
Or were thy wit good, am I therefore bound
To keep thee for my table? Well, sir, 'twere
A good knight's place. Many a proud dubb'd gallant
Seeks out a poor knight's living from such emrods. [2]
Or what use else should I design thee to?
Perhaps you'll answer me, to be my pander.

 Cl. Perhaps I shall.

 Mo. Or did the sly Guise put thee
Into my bosom, t'undermine my projects?
I fear thee not; for though I be not sure
I have thy heart, I know thy brain-pan yet
To be as empty a dull piece of wainscot
As ever arm'd the scalp of any courtier;
A fellow only that consists of sinews:
Mere Swisser, apt for any execution.

 Cl. But killing of the King.

 Mo. Right; now I see
Thou understand'st thyself.

 Cl. Ay, and you better:
You are a king's son born.

   [1] Cast-off.   [2] Emerods.

Mo. Right.

Cl. And a king's brother.

Mo. True.

Cl. And might not any fool have been so too,
As well as you?

Mo. A pox upon you!

Cl. You did no princely deeds
Ere you were born, I take it, to deserve it ;
Nor did you any since that I have heard ;
Nor will do ever any, as all think.

Mo. The devil take him !   I'll no more of him.

Gu. Nay : stay, my lord, and hear him answer you.

Mo. No more, I swear.   Farewell.

[*Exeunt* Monsieur, ESPERNON, SOISSON.

Gu. No more ! Ill fortune.
I would have given a million to have heard
His scoffs retorted, and the insolence
Of his high birth and greatness (which were never
Effects of his deserts, but of his fortune)
Made show to his dull eyes, beneath the worth
That men aspire to by their knowing virtues,
Without which greatness is a shade, a bubble.

Cl. But what one great man dreams of that, but
you?
All take their birth and birth-rights left to them
(Acquired by others) for their own worth's purchase,
When many a fool in both, is great as they :
And who would think they could win with their worths
Wealthy possessions, when won to their hands,
They neither can judge justly of their value
Nor know their use ; and therefore they are puff'd
With such proud tumours as this Monsieur is :
Enabled only by the goods they have,
To scorn all goodness : none great, fill their fortunes,

But as those men that make their houses greater,
Their households being less, so fortune raises
Huge heaps of outside in these mighty men,
And gives them nothing in them.

   Gu. True as truth :
And therefore they had rather drown their substance
In superfluities of bricks and stones
(Like Sisyphus, advancing of them ever,
And ever pulling down), than lay the cost
Of any sluttish corner, on a man,
Built with God's finger, and enstyled his Temple.

   Ba. 'Tis nobly said, my lord.

   Gu. I would have these things
Brought upon stages, to let mighty misers
See all their grave and serious miseries play'd,
As once they were in Athens and old Rome.

   Cl. Nay, we must now have nothing brought on
     stages,
But puppetry, and pied ridiculous antics ;
Men thither come to laugh, and feed fool-fat,
Check at all goodness there, as being profaned :
When wheresoever goodness comes she makes
The place still sacred, though with other feet
Never so much 'tis scandal'd and polluted.
Let me learn anything that fits a man,
In any stables shown, as well as stages.

   Ba. Why? is not all the world esteem'd a stage?

   Cl. Yes, and right worthily ; and stages too
Have a respect due to them, if but only
For what the good Greek moralist says of them :
" Is a man proud of greatness, or of riches?
Give me an expert actor, I'll show all
That can within his greatest glory fall.
Is a man fray'd with poverty and lowness?

Give me an actor, I'll show every eye
What he laments so, and so much doth fly,
The best and worst of both." If but for this then,
To make the proudest outside that most swells
With things without him, and above his worth,
See how small cause he has to be so blown up ;
And the most poor man to be grieved with poorness,
Both being so easily borne by expert actors.
The stage and actors are not so contemptful
As every innovating puritan,
And ignorant sweater out of zealous envy
Would have the world imagine. And besides,
That all things have been liken'd to the mirth
Used upon stages, and for stages fitted.
The splenative philosopher that ever
Laugh'd at them all, were worthy the enstaging ;
All objects, were they ne'er so full of tears,
He so conceited, that he could distil thence
Matter that still fed his ridiculous humour.
Heard he a lawyer, ne'er so vehement pleading,
He stood and laugh'd. Heard he a tradesman swear-
    ing
Never so thriftily, selling of his wares,
He stood and laugh'd. Heard he an holy brother,
For hollow ostentation at his prayers
Ne'er so impetuously, he stood and laugh'd.
Saw he a great man never so insulting,
Severely inflicting, gravely giving laws,
Not for their good, but his, he stood and laugh'd.
Saw he a youthful widow
Never so weeping, wringing of her hands
For her lost lord, still the philosopher laugh'd.
Now whether he supposed all these presentments
Were only maskeries, and wore false faces,

Q

Or else were simply vain, I take no care;
But still he laugh'd, how grave soe'er they were.

    Gu. And might right well, my Clermont; and for
        this
Virtuous digression, we will thank the scoffs
Of vicious Monsieur.   But now for the main point
Of your late resolution for revenge
Of your slain brother.

    Cl. I have here my challenge,
Which I will pray my brother Baligny
To bear the murderous earl.

    Ba. I have prepared
Means for access to him, through all his guard.

    Gu. About it then, my worthy Baligny,
And bring us the success.

    Ba. I will, my lord.   [*Exeunt.*

TAMYRA *sola.*

    Ta. Revenge, that ever red sitt'st in the eyes
Of injured ladies, till we crown thy brows
With bloody laurel, and receive from thee
Justice for all our honour's injury;
Whose wings none fly, that wrath or tyranny
Hath ruthless made, and bloody; enter here,
Enter, O enter; and, though length of time
Never lets any 'scape thy constant justice,
Yet now prevent that length.   Fly, fly, and here
Fix thy steel footsteps: here, O here, where still
Earth, moved with pity, yielded and embraced
My love's fair figure, drawn in his dear blood,
And mark'd the place, to show thee where was done
The cruell'st murder that e'er fled the sun.
O earth! why keep'st thou not as well his spirit,
To give his form life? No, that was not earthly;

That (rarefying the thin and yielding air)
Flew sparkling up into the sphere of fire,
Whence endless flames it sheds in my desire;
Here be my daily pallet; here all nights
That can be wrested from thy rival's arms,
O my dear Bussy, I will lie and kiss
Spirit into thy blood, or breathe out mine
In sighs and kisses, and sad tunes to thine.

　　　　　　　　　　　　　　　　[She sings.

　　　　　　Enter MONTSURRY.

　Mont. Still on this haunt? Still shall adulterous
　　　blood
Affect thy spirits? Think, for shame, but this,
This blood that cockatrice-like thus thou brood'st
Too dry is to breed any quench to thine.
And therefore now (if only for thy lust
A little cover'd with a veil of shame)
Look out for fresh life, rather than witch-like,
Learn to kiss horror, and with death engender.
Strange cross in nature, purest virgin shame
Lies in the blood, as lust lies; and together
Many times mix too; and in none more shameful
Than in the shamefaced. Who can then distinguish
'Twixt their affections; or tell when he meets
With one not common? Yet, as worthiest poets
Shun common and plebeian forms of speech;
Every illiberal and affected phrase
To clothe their matter; and together tie
Matter and form, with art and decency;
So worthiest women should shun vulgar guises,
And though they cannot but fly out for change,
Yet modesty, the matter of their lives,
Be it adulterate, should be painted true

With modest out-parts ; what they should do still,
Graced with good show, though deeds be ne'er so ill.

   Ta. That is so far from all ye seek of us,
That, though yourselves be common as the air,
We must not take the air, we must not fit
Our actions to our own affections :
But as geometricians, you still say,
Teach that no lines nor superficies
Do move themselves, but still accompany
The motions of their bodies ; so poor wives
Must not pursue, nor have their own affections ;
But to their husbands' earnests, and their jests,
To their austerities of looks, and laughters,
Though ne'er so foolish and injurious,
Like parasites and slaves, fit their disposures.

   Mont. I used thee as my soul, to move and rule me.

   Ta. So said you, when you woo'd. So soldiers
      tortured
With tedious sieges of some well-walled town
Propound conditions of most large contents,
Freedom of laws, all former government ;
But having once set foot within the walls,
And got the reins of power into their hands ;
Then do they tyrannize at their own rude swindges,
Seize all their goods, their liberties, and lives,
And make advantage and their lusts their laws.

   Mont. But love me, and perform a wife's part yet,
(With all my love before) I swear forgiveness.

   Ta. Forgiveness ! that grace you should seek of
      me ;
These tortured fingers and these stabb'd-through
      arms.
Keep that law in their wounds, yet, unobserved.
And ever shall.

Mont. Remember their deserts.

Ta. Those with fair warnings might have been
reform'd,
Not these unmanly rages.   You have heard
The fiction of the north-wind and the sun,
Both working on a traveller, and contending
Which had most power to take his cloak from him ;
Which when the wind attempted, he roar'd out
Outrageous blasts at him to force it off,
That wrapt it closer on.   When the calm sun
(The wind once leaving) charged him with still beams
Quiet and fervent, and therein was constant,
Which made him cast off both his cloak and coat ;
Like whom should men do.   If ye wish your wives
Should leave disliked things, seek it not with rage,
For that enrages ; what ye give, ye have ;
But use calm warnings, and kind manly means,
And that in wives most prostitute will win
Not only sure amends, but make us wives
Better than those that ne'er led faulty lives.

Enter a Soldier.

Sol. My lord.

Mont. How now ? would any speak with me ?

Sol. Ay, sir.

Mont. Perverse and traitorous miscreant,
Where are your other fellows of my guard ?
Have I not told you, I will speak with none
But Lord Renel ?

Sol. And 'tis he that stays you.

Mont. Oh, is it he ?   'Tis well ; attend him in :
I must be vigilant ; the furies haunt me.
Do you hear, dame ?

Enter RENEL *with the* Soldier.

Re. Be true now, for your lady's injured sake,
Whose bounty you have so much cause to honour ;
For her respect is chief in this design,
And therefore serve it ; call out of the way
All your confederate fellows of his guard,
Till Monsieur Baligny be enter'd here.

   Sol. Upon your honour, my lord shall be free
From any hurt, you say ?

   Re. Free as myself.   Watch then, and clear his
     entry.

   Sol. I will not fail, my lord.   [*Exit* Soldier.

   Re. God save your lordship.

   Mont. My noblest Lord Renel ! past all men
     welcome !
Wife, welcome his lordship.   [*Osculatur.*

   Re. I much joy in your return here.

   Ta. You do more than I.

   Mont. She's passionate still, to think we ever parted,
By my too stern injurious jealousy.

   Re. 'Tis well your lordship will confess your error
In so good time yet.

Enter BALIGNY *with a challenge.*

   Mont. Death !   Who have we here ?
Ho ! guard ! villains !

   Ba. Why exclaim you so ?

   Mont. Negligent traitors ! Murder, murder, murder !

   Ba. Y'are mad. Had mine intent been so like
     yours,
It had been done ere this.

   Re. Sir, your intent,
And action too, was rude to enter thus.

Ba. Y'are a decay'd lord to tell me of rudeness,
As much decay'd in manners as in means.

Re. You talk of manners, that thus rudely thrust
Upon a man that's busy with his wife.

Ba. And kept your lordship then the door?

Re. The door?

Mont. Sweet lord, forbear.   Show, show your
      purpose, sir,
To move such bold feet into others' roofs.[1]

Ba. This is my purpose, sir; from Clermont
      D'Ambois.
I bring this challenge.

Mont. Challenge! I'll touch none.

Ba. I'll leave it here then.

Re. Thou shalt leave thy life first.

Mont. Murder, murder!

Re. Retire, my lord; get off.
Hold, or thy death shall hold thee.   Hence, my lord.

Ba. There lie the challenge.

[*They all fight, and* BAL. *drives in* MONT.   *Exit*
      MONT.

Re. Was not this well handled!

Ba. Nobly, my lord.   All thanks.   [*Exit* BAL.

Ta. I'll make him read it.   [*Exit* TA.

Re. This was a sleight well mask'd. Oh, what is
      man,
Unless he be a politician?   [*Exit.*

---
[1] Houses.

ACT THE SECOND

SCENE I

HENRY, BALIGNY.

E. Come, Baligny, we now are private: say,
What service bring'st thou? make it short; the Guise,
Whose friend thou seem'st, is now in Court, and near,
And may observe us.

Ba. This, sir, then, in short:
The faction of the Guise (with which my policy,
For service to your highness seems to join)
Grows ripe, and must be gather'd into hold;
Of which my brother Clermont being a part
Exceeding capital, deserves to have
A capital eye on him. And as you may
With best advantage, and your speediest charge,
Command his apprehension; which (because
The Court, you know, is strong in his defence)
We must ask country swindge and open fields.
And, therefore, I have wrought him to go down
To Cambray with me (of which government
Your highness' bounty made me your Lieutenant)

Where, when I have him, I will leave my house,
And feign some service out about the confines;
When in the meantime, if you please to give
Command to my Lieutenant, by your letters,
To train him to some muster, where he may,
Much to his honour, see for him, your forces
Put into battle;[1] when he comes, he may
With some close stratagem be apprehended.
For otherwise your whole powers there will fail
To work his apprehension: and with that
My hand needs never be discern'd therein.

  He. Thanks, honest Baligny.

  Ba. Your highness knows
I will be honest; and betray for you
Brother and father: for, I know, my lord,
Treachery for kings is truest loyalty;
Nor is to bear the name of treachery,
But grave, deep policy.   All acts that seem
Ill in particular respects, are good
As they respect your universal rule.
As in the main sway of the universe
The supreme Rector's general decrees,
To guard the mighty globes of earth and heaven,
Since they make good that guard to preservation
Of both those in their order and first end,
No man's particular (as he thinks) wrong
Must hold him wrong'd; no, not though all men's
    reasons,
All law, all conscience, concludes it wrong.
Nor is comparison a flatterer
To liken you here to the King of kings;
Nor any man's particular offence
Against the world's sway, to offence at yours

           [1] Battle-array.

In any subject; who as little may
Grudge at their particular wrong, if so it seem
For th'universal right of your estate.
As (being a subject of the world's whole sway
As well as yours ; and being a righteous man
To whom Heaven promises defence, and blessing,
Brought to decay, disgrace, and quite defenceless)
He may complain of Heaven for wrong to him.

He. 'Tis true : the simile at all parts holds,
As all good subjects hold, that love our favour.

Ba. Which is our heaven here ; and a misery
Incomparable, and most truly hellish,
To live deprived of our king's grace and countenance,
Without which best conditions are most cursed :
Life of that nature, howsoever short,
Is a most lingering and tedious life ;
Or rather no life, but a languishing,
And an abuse of life.

He. 'Tis well conceited.

Ba. I thought it not amiss to yield your highness
A reason of my speeches ; lest perhaps
You might conceive I flatter'd ; which, I know,
Of all ills under heaven you most abhor.

He. Still thou art right, my virtuous Baligny,
For which I thank and love thee.   Thy advice
I'll not forget ; haste to thy government,
And carry D'Ambois with thee.   So farewell.   [*Exit.*

Ba. Your majesty fare ever like itself.

Enter GUISE.

Gu. My sure friend, Baligny !

Ba. Noblest of princes !

Gu. How stands the State of Cambray ?

Ba. Strong, my lord,

And fit for service : for whose readiness
Your creature Clermont D'Ambois, and myself
Ride shortly down.

   Gu. That Clermont is my love ;
France never bred a nobler gentleman
For all parts ; he exceeds his brother Bussy.

   Ba. Ay, my lord ?

   Gu. Far ; because, besides his valour,
He hath the crown of man, and all his parts,
Which learning is : and that so true and virtuous,
That it gives power to do as well as say
Whatever fits a most accomplish'd man ;
Which Bussy, for his valour's season, lack'd ;
And so was rapt with outrage oftentimes
Beyond decorum ; where this absolute Clermont,
Though, only for his natural zeal to right,
He will be fiery, when he sees it cross'd,
And in defence of it ; yet when he lists
He can contain that fire, as hid in embers.

   Ba. No question, he's a true, learn'd gentleman.

   Gu. He is as true as tides, or any star
Is in his motion ; and for his rare learning,
He is not, as all else are that seek knowledge,
Of taste so much depraved, that they had rather
Delight, and satisfy themselves to drink
Of the stream troubled, wandering ne'er so far
From the clear fount, than of the fount itself.
In all, Rome's Brutus is revived in him,
Whom he of industry doth imitate :
Or rather, as great Troy's Euphorbus was
After Pythagoras ; so is Brutus, Clermont.
And, were not Brutus a conspirator—

   Ba. Conspirator, my lord ? Doth that impair him ?
Cæsar began to tyrannize ; and when virtue

Nor the religion of the gods could serve
To curb the insolence of his proud laws,
Brutus would be the gods' just instrument.
What said the princess, sweet Antigone,
In the grave Greek tragedian, when the question
'Twixt her and Creon is, for laws of kings?
Which, when he urges, she replies on him;
Though his laws were a king's, they were not God's;
Nor would she value Creon's written laws
With God's unwrit edicts; since they last not
This day, and next, but every day and ever;
Where kings' laws alter every day and hour,
And in that change imply a bounded power.

Gu. Well, let us leave these vain disputings, what
Is to be done, and fall to doing something.
When are you for your government in Cambray?

Ba. When you command, my lord.

Gu. Nay, that's not fit.
Continue your designments with the King,
With all your service; only if I send,
Respect me as your friend, and love my Clermont.

Ba. Your highness knows my vows.

Gu. Ay, 'tis enough.

[*Exit* GUISE. *Manet* BALIGNY.

Ba. Thus, must we play on both sides, and thus hearten
In any ill those men whose good we hate.
Kings may do what they list; and for kings' subjects,
Either exempt from censure or exception;
For, as no man's worth can be justly judged
But when he shines in some authority;
So no authority should suffer censure
But by a man of more authority.[1]

---

[1] Ἀμήχανον δὲ παντὸς, &c. *Impossible est viri cognoscere mentem ac voluntatem, priusquam in Magistratibus apparet.*—Sopho. Antig. [Chap.]

Great vessels into less are emptied never,
There's a redundance past their continent ever.
These *virtuosi* are the poorest creatures ;
For look how spinners weave out of themselves
Webs, whose strange matter none before can see ;
So these, out of an unseen good in virtue,
Make arguments of right, and comfort in her,
That clothe them like the poor web of a spinner.

Enter CLERMONT.

Cl. Now, to my challenge. What's the place, the
weapon ?

Ba. Soft, sir ; let first your challenge be received ;
He would not touch, nor see it.

Cl. Possible !
How did you then ?

Ba. Left it in his despite,
But when he saw me enter so expectless.
To hear his base exclaims of murder, murder,
Made me think noblesse lost, in him quick [1] buried.

Cl. They are the breathing sepulchres of noblesse ;
No trulier noble men, than lion's pictures
Hung up for signs, are lions. Who knows not,
That lions the more soft kept, are more servile ? [2]
And look how lions close kept, fed by hand,
Lose quite th'innative fire of spirit and greatness
That lions free breathe, foraging for prey,
And grow so gross, that mastiffs, curs, and mongrels
Have spirit to cow them. So our soft French nobles
Chain'd up in ease and numb'd security,
Their spirits shrunk up like their covetous fists,
And never open'd but Domitian-like,

[1] Alive.
[2] *Quo mollius degunt, eo servilius.* Epict.   [Chap.]

And all his base obsequious minions
When they were catching, though it were but flies.
Besotted with their peasants' love of gain,
Rusting at home and on each other preying,
Are for their greatness but the greater slaves,
And none is noble but who scrapes and saves.

    Ba. 'Tis base, 'tis base! and yet they think them
      high.

    Cl. So children mounted on their hobby-horse
Think they are riding, when with wanton toil
They bear what should bear them. A man may well
Compare them to those foolish great-spleen'd camels,
That to their high heads, begg'd of Jove horns higher;
Whose most uncomely and ridiculous pride,
When he had satisfied, they could not use,
But where they went upright before, they stoop'd,
And bore their heads much lower for their horns.
As these high men do, low in all true grace,
Their height being privilege to all things base.
And as the foolish poet that still writ
All his most self-loved verse in paper royal,
Of parchment ruled with lead, smoothed with the
    pumice,
Bound richly up, and strung with crimson strings;
Never so blest as when he writ and read
The ape-loved issue of his brain, and never
But joying in himself, admiring ever:
Yet in his works behold him, and he show'd
Like to a ditcher. So these painted men,
All set on out-side, look upon within,
And not a peasant's entrails you shall find
More foul and measled, nor more sterved [1] of mind.

    Ba. That makes their bodies fat. I fain would know

---

    [1] Barren.

How many millions of our other nobles
Would make one Guise. There is a true tenth worthy,
Who (did not one act only blemish him)—

    Cl. One act? what one?

    Ba. One, that, though years past done,
Sticks by him still and will disdain [1] him ever.

    Cl. Good heaven! wherein? what one act can you
        name
Supposed his stain, that I'll not prove his lustre?

    Ba. To satisfy you, 'twas the massacre.

    Cl. The massacre? I thought 'twas some such
        blemish.

    Ba. Oh, it was heinous!

    Cl. To a brutish sense,
But not a manly reason. We so tender
The vile part in us, that the part divine
We see in hell, and shrink not. Who was first
Head of that massacre?

    Ba. The Guise.

    Cl. 'Tis nothing so.
Who was in fault for all the slaughters made
In Ilion, and about it? were the Greeks?
Was it not Paris ravishing the Queen
Of Lacedæmon? Breach of shame and faith?
And all the laws of hospitality?
This is the beastly slaughter made of men,
When truth is overthrown, his laws corrupted;
When souls are smother'd in the flatter'd flesh,
Slain bodies are no more than oxen slain.

    Ba. Differ not men from oxen?

    Cl. Who says so?
But see wherein; in the understanding rules
Of their opinions, lives, and actions;

        [1] Stain.

In their communities of faith and reason.
Was not the wolf that nourish'd Romulus
More humane than the men that did expose him ?

Ba. That makes against you.

Cl. Not, sir, if you note
That by that deed, the actions difference make
'Twixt men and beasts, and not their names nor forms.
Had faith, nor shame, all hospitable rights
Been broke by Troy, Greece had not made that
    slaughter.
Had that been saved (says a philosopher)
The Iliads and Odysseys had been lost ;
Had Faith and true Religion been preferr'd,
Religious Guise had never massacred.

Ba. Well, sir, I cannot when I meet with you
But thus digress a little, for my learning,
From any other business I intend.
But now the voyage we resolved for Cambray
I told the Guise begins, and we must haste.
And till the Lord Renel hath found some mean
Conspiring with the countess, to make sure
Your sworn wreak on her husband, though this fail'd
In my so brave command, we'll spend the time,
Sometimes in training out in skirmishes
And battles, all our troops and companies ;
And sometimes breathe your brave Scotch running
    horse,
That great Guise gave you, that all th' horse in France
Far overruns at every race and hunting
Both of the hare and deer. You shall be honour'd
Like the great Guise himself, above the King.
And (can you but appease your great-spleen'd sister
For our delay'd wreak of your brother's slaughter)
At all parts you'll be welcomed to your wonder.

Cl. I'll see my lord the Guise again before
We take our journey.

Ba. Oh, sir, by all means ;
You cannot be too careful of his love,
That ever takes occasion to be raising
Your virtues past the reaches of this age,
And ranks you with the best of th'ancient Romans.

Cl. That praise at no part moves me, but the worth
Of all he can give others sphered in him.

Ba. He yet is thought to entertain strange aims.

Cl. He may be well, yet not as you think strange.
His strange aims are to cross the common custom
Of servile nobles, in which he's so ravish'd,
That quite the earth he leaves, and up he leaps
On Atlas' shoulders, and from thence looks down,
Viewing how far off other high ones creep :
Rich, poor of reason, wander ; all pale looking,
And trembling but to think of their sure deaths,
Their lives so base are, and so rank their breaths.
Which I teach Guise to heighten, and make sweet
With life's dear odours, a good mind and name ;
For which he only loves me, and deserves
My love and life, which through all deaths I vow :
Resolving this, whatever change can be,
Thou hast created, thou hast ruin'd me. [*Exit*.

ACT THE THIRD

SCENE I

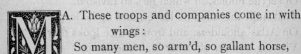

A march of Captains *over the stage.* MAILLARD,
CHALON, AUMALE, *following with* Soldiers.

Ma. These troops and companies come in with
    wings:
    So many men, so arm'd, so gallant horse,
    I think no other government in France
So soon could bring together. With such men
Methinks a man might pass th'insulting pillars
Of Bacchus and Alcides.

    Chal. I much wonder
Our lord-lieutenant brought his brother down
To feast and honour him, and yet now leaves him
At such an instance.

    Ma. 'Twas the King's command:
For whom he must leave brother, wife, friend, all
    things.

    Au. The confines of his government, whose view
Is the pretext of his command, hath need
Of no such sudden expedition.

    Ma. We must not argue that. The King's com-
    mand
Is need and right enough: and that he serves,
(As all true subjects should) without disputing.

Chal. But knows not he of your command to take
His brother Clermont?

Ma. No: the King's will is
Expressly to conceal his apprehension [1]
From my lord governor.   Observed ye not?
Again peruse the letters.   Both you are
Made my assistants, and have right and trust
In all the weighty secrets like myself.

Au. 'Tis strange a man that had, through his life
    past,
So sure a foot in virtue and true knowledge,
As Clermont D'Ambois, should be now found trip-
    ping,
And taken up thus, so to make his fall
More steep and headlong.

Ma. It is Virtue's fortune,
To keep her low, and in her proper place;
Height hath no room for her.   But as a man
That hath a fruitful wife, and every year
A child by her, hath every year a month
To breathe himself: where he that gets no child
Hath not a night's rest, if he will do well:
So, let one marry this same barren Virtue,
She never lets him rest; where fruitful Vice
Spares her rich drudge, gives him in labour breath:
Feeds him with bane, and makes him fat with death.

Chal. I see that good lives never can secure
Men from bad livers.   Worst men will have best
As ill as they, or heaven to hell they'll wrest.

Au. There was a merit for this, in the fault
That Bussy made, for which he, doing penance,
Proves that these foul adulterous guilts will run
Through the whole blood, which not the clear can shun.

_____
[1] Capture.

Ma. I'll therefore take heed of the bastarding
Whole innocent races; 'tis a fearful thing.
And as I am a true bachelor, I swear,
To touch no woman, to the coupling ends,
Unless it be mine own wife, or my friend's.
I may make bold with him.

    Au. 'Tis safe and common.
The more your friend dares trust, the more deceive him.
And as, through dewy vapours, the sun's form
Makes the gay rainbow girdle to a storm,
So in hearts hollow, friendship (even the sun
To all good growing in society)
Makes his so glorious and divine name hold
Colours for all the ill that can be told.

    Ma. Hark, our last troops are come.

                           [*Trumpets within.*

    Chal. Hark, our last foot.   [*Drums beat.*

    Ma. Come, let us put all quickly into battle,
And send for Clermont, in whose honour all
This martial preparation we pretend.

    Chal. We must bethink us, ere we apprehend him,
(Besides our main strength), of some stratagem
To make good our severe command on him,
As well to save blood, as to make him sure:
For if he come on his Scotch horse, all France
Put at the heels of him, will fail to take him.

    Ma. What think you, if we should disguise a brace
Of our best soldiers in fair lackeys' coats,
And send them for him, running by his side,
Till they have brought him in some ambuscado
We close may lodge for him, and suddenly
Lay sure hand on him, plucking him from horse.

    Au. It must be sure and strong hand; for if once
He feels the touch of such a stratagem,

'Tis not the choicest brace of all our bands
Can manacle or quench his fiery hands.

Ma. When they have seized him, the ambush shall
make in.

Au. Do as you please ; his blameless spirit deserves,
I dare engage my life, of all this, nothing.

Chal. Why should all this stir be, then ?

Au. Who knows not
The bombast polity thrust into his giant,
To make his wisdom seem of size as huge,
And all for slight encounter of a shade,
So he be touch'd, he would have heinous made ?

Ma. It may be once so, but so ever, never :
Ambition is abroad, on foot, on horse ;
Faction chokes every corner, street, the Court ;
Whose faction 'tis you know, and who is held
The fautor's right hand ; how high his aims reach
Nought but a crown can measure. This must fall
Past shadows' weights, and is most capital.

Chal. No question ; for since he is come to Cambray,
The malcontent, decay'd Marquis Renel
Is come, and new arrived, and made partaker
Of all the entertaining shows and feasts
That welcomed Clermont to the brave virago,
His manly sister. Such we are esteem'd
As are our consorts. Marquess Malcontent
Comes where he knows his vein hath safest vent.

Ma. Let him come at his will, and go as free ;
Let us ply Clermont, our whole charge is he. [*Exeunt.*

Enter a Gentleman Usher, *before* CLERMONT, RENEL,
CHARLOTTE, *with two* women attendants, *with
others : shows having passed within.*

Ch. This for your lordship's welcome into Cambray.

Re. Noblest of ladies, 'tis beyond all power,
Were my estate at first full, in my means
To quit or merit.

Cl. You come something later
From Court, my lord, than I ; and since news there
Is every day increasing with th'affairs,
Must I not ask now, what the news is there ?
Where the Court lies ? what stir ? change ? what
    advice
From England ? Italy ?

Re. You must do so,
If you'll be call'd a gentleman well qualified,
And wear your time and wits in those discourses.

Cl. The Locrian Princes therefore were brave rulers ;
For whosoever there came new from country
And in the city ask'd, what news ? was punish'd ;
Since commonly such brains are most delighted
With innovations, gossips' tales, and mischiefs ;
But as of lions it is said and eagles,
That when they go, they draw their seres [1] and talons
Close up, to shun rebating of their sharpness ;
So our wit's sharpness, which we should employ
In noblest knowledge, we should never waste
In vile and vulgar admirations.

Re. 'Tis right ; but who, save only you, performs it,
And your great brother ?   Madam, where is he ?

Ch. Gone a day since, into the country's confines,
To see their strength, and readiness for service.

Re. 'Tis well ; his favour with the King hath made
    him
Most worthily great, and live right royally.

Cl. Ay, would he would not do so !   Honour never
Should be esteem'd with wise men, as the price

---

[1] Claws.

And value of their virtuous services,
But as their sign or badge; for that bewrays
More glory in the outward grace of goodness,
Than in the good itself; and then 'tis said
Who more joy takes, that men his good advance,
Than in the good itself, does it by chance.

   Ch. My brother speaks all principle; what man
Is moved with your soul, or hath such a thought
In any rate of goodness?

   Cl. 'Tis their fault:
We have examples of it, clear and many.
Demetrius Phalerius, an orator,
And (which not oft meet) a philosopher,
So great in Athens grew, that he erected
Three hundred statues of him; of all which,
No rust nor length of time corrupted one;
But in his lifetime, all were overthrown.
And Demades (that pass'd Demosthenes
For all extemporal orations)
Erected many statues, which, he living,
Were broke, and melted into chamber-pots.
Many such ends have fall'n on such proud honours,
No more because the men on whom they fell
Grew insolent and left their virtue's state;
Than for their hugeness, that procured their hate;
And therefore little pomp in men most great,
Makes mightily and strongly to the guard
Of what they win by chance, or just reward.
Great and immodest braveries again,
Like statutes, much too high made for their bases,
Are overturn'd as soon as given their places.

       Enter a Messenger *with a Letter.*
   Me. Here is a letter, sir, deliver'd me,

Now at the fore-gate by a gentleman.

 Cl. What gentleman?

 Me. He would not tell his name;
He said, he had not time enough to tell it,
And say the little rest he had to say.

 Cl. That was a merry saying; he took measure
Of his dear time like a most thrifty husband.

 Ch. What news?

 Cl. Strange ones, and fit for a novation [1];
Weighty, unheard of, mischievous enough.

 Re. Heaven shield! what are they?

 Cl. Read them, good my lord.

 Re. "You are betrayed into this country."
   Monstrous!

 Ch, How's that?

 Cl. Read on.

 Re. "Millard, your brother's lieutenant, that yesterday invited you to see his musters, hath letters and strict charge from the King to apprehend you."

 Ch. To apprehend him?

 Re. "Your brother absents himself of purpose."

 Cl. That's a sound one.

 Ch. That's a lie.

 Re. "Get on your Scotch horse, and retire to your strength; you know where it is, and there it expects you; believe this as your best friend had sworn it. Fare well, if you will.   ANONYMOS." What's that?

 Cl. Without a name.

 Ch. And all his notice too without all truth.

 Cl. So I conceive it, sister; I'll not wrong
My well-known brother for Anonymos.

 Ch. Some fool hath put this trick on you, yet more
T"uncover your defect of spirit and valour,

<hr>

[1] Innovation.

First shown in lingering my dear brother's wreak.
See what it is to give the envious world
Advantage to diminish eminent virtue.
Send him a challenge?   Take a noble course
To wreak a murder, done so like a villain?

   Cl. Shall we revenge a villany with villany?

   Ch. Is it not equal?

   Cl. Shall we equal be with villains?
Is that your reason?

   Ch. Cowardice evermore
Flies to the shield of reason.

   Cl. Nought that is
Approved by reason can be cowardice.

   Ch. Dispute when you should fight.   Wrong,
             wreakless sleeping,
Makes men die honourless; one borne, another
Leaps on our shoulders.

   Cl. We must wreak our wrongs
So as we take not more.

   Ch. One wreak'd in time
Prevents all other.   Then shines virtue most
When time is found for facts; and found, not lost.

   Cl. No time occurs to kings, much less to virtue;
Nor can we call it virtue that proceeds
From vicious fury.   I repent that ever
(By any instigation in th'appearance
My brother's spirit made, as I imagined)
That e'er I yielded to revenge his murder.
All worthy men should ever bring their blood
To bear all ill, not to be wreak'd with good:
Do ill for no ill; never private cause
Should take on it the part of public laws.

   Ch. A D'Ambois bear in wrong so tame a spirit!

   Re. Madam, be sure there will be time enough

For all the vengeance your great spirit can wish.
The course yet taken is allow'd [1] by all,
Which, being noble, and refused by th'earl,
Now makes him worthy of your worst advantage;
And I have cast a project with the countess
To watch a time when all his wariest guards
Shall not exempt him.　Therefore give him breath;
Sure death delay'd is a redoubled death.

Cl. Good sister, trouble not yourself with this;
Take other ladies' care; practise your face.
There's the chaste matron, Madam Perigot,
Dwells not far hence; I'll ride and send her to you.
She did live by retailing maidenheads
In her minority; but now she deals
In wholesale altogether for the Court.
I tell you, she's the only fashion-monger,
For your complexion, powdering of your hair,
Shadows, rebatoes,[2] wires, tires, and such tricks,
That Cambray, or I think, the Court affords;
She shall attend you, sister, and with these
Womanly practices employ your spirit;
This other suits you not, nor fits the fashion.
Though she be dear, lay't on, spare for no cost,
Ladies in these have all their bounties lost.

Re. Madam, you see his spirit will not check
At any single danger; when it stands
Thus merrily firm against a host of men,
Threaten'd to be in arms for his surprise.

Ch. That's a mere bugbear, an impossible mock.
If he, and him I bound by nuptial faith
Had not been dull and drossy in performing
Wreak of the dear blood of my matchless brother,
What prince, what king, which of the desperatest ruffians

<hr />

[1] Approved.　　[2] Ruffs.

Outlaws in Arden, durst have tempted thus
One of our blood and name, be't true or false?

Cl. This is not caused by that; 'twill be as sure
As yet it is not, though this should be true.

Ch. True? 'tis past thought false.

Cl. I suppose the worst,
Which far I am from thinking; and despise
The army now in battle that should act it.

Ch. I would not let my blood up to that thought,
But it should cost the dearest blood in France.

Cl. Sweet sister, [*osculatur*] far be both off as the fact
Of my feign'd apprehension.

Ch. I would once
Strip off my shame with my attire, and try
If a poor woman, votist of revenge,
Would not perform it with a precedent
To all you bungling, foggy-spirited men;
But for our birthright's honour, do not mention
One syllable of any word may go
To the begetting of an act so tender
And full of sulphur as this letter's truth;
It comprehends so black a circumstance
Not to be named, that but to form one thought,
It is or can be so, would make me mad;
Come, my lord, you and I will fight this dream
Out at the chess.

Re. Most gladly, worthiest lady.

[*Exit* CHARLOTTE *and* RENEL.

Enter a Messenger.

Me. Sir, my Lord Governor's Lieutenant prays
Access to you.

Cl. Himself alone?

Me. Alone, sir.

Cl. Attend him in. [*Exit* Mess.] Now comes this
    plot to trial.
I shall discern, if it be true as rare,
Some sparks will fly from his dissembling eyes.
I'll sound his depth.

Enter MAILLARD *with the* Messenger.

Ma. Honour, and all things noble!
    Cl. As much to you, good Captain. What's th'
    affair?
    Ma. Sir, the poor honour we can add to all
Your studied welcome to this martial place,
In presentation of what strength consists.
My lord, your brother's government is ready.
I have made all his troops and companies
Advance, and put themselves ranged in battalia,
That you may see, both how well-arm'd they are;
How strong is every troop and company;
How ready, and how well prepared for service.
    Cl. And must they take me?
    Ma. Take you, sir? O heaven!
    Me. Believe it, sir; his countenance changed in
    turning.
    Ma. What do you mean, sir?
    Cl. If you have charged them,
You being charged yourself, to apprehend me,
Turn not your face; throw not your looks about so.
    Ma. Pardon me, sir. You amaze me to conceive
From whence our wills to honour you should turn
To such dishonour of my lord your brother.
Dare I, without him, undertake your taking?
    Cl. Why not? by your direct charge from the
    King?
    Ma. By my charge from the King? would he so much

Disgrace my lord, his own lieutenant here,
To give me his command without his forfeit?

Cl. Acts that are done by kings are not ask'd why:
I'll not dispute the case, but I will search you.

Ma. Search me? for what?

Cl. For letters.

Ma. I beseech you
Do not admit one thought of such a shame
To a commander.

Cl. Go to; I must do't.
Stand and be search'd; you know me.

Ma. You forget
What 'tis to be a captain, and yourself.

Cl. Stand! or I vow to heaven, I'll make you lie,
Never to rise more.

Ma. If a man be mad
Reason must bear him.

Cl. So coy to be search'd?

Ma. 'Sdeath, sir! use a captain like a carrier?

Cl. Come, be not furious; when I have done
You shall make such a carrier of me,
If't be your pleasure; you're my friend, I know,
And so am bold with you.

Ma. You'll nothing find
Where nothing is.

Cl. Swear you have nothing.

Ma. Nothing you seek, I swear, I beseech you;
Know I desired this out of great affection,
To th'end my lord may know out of your witness
His forces are not in so bad estate
As he esteem'd them lately in your hearing:
For which he would not trust me with the confines;
But went himself to witness their estate.

Cl. I heard him make that reason, and am sorry

I had no thought of it before I made
Thus bold with you ; since 'tis such rhubarb to you,
I'll therefore search no more.   If you are charged
By letters from the King, or otherwise,
To apprehend me ; never spice it more
With forced terms of your love ; but say ; I yield ;
Hold ; take my sword ; here ; I forgive thee freely ;
Take ; do thine office.

    Ma. 'Sfoot, you make me a hangman ;
By all my faith to you, there's no such thing.

    Cl. Your faith to me ?

    Ma. My faith to God ; all's one,
Who hath no faith to men, to God hath none.

    Cl. In that sense I accept your oath, and thank
        you :
I gave my word to go, and I will go.   [*Exit* CLER.

    Ma. I'll watch you whither.   [*Exit* MAIL.

    Me. If he goes, he proves
How vain are men's foreknowledges of things,
When heaven strikes blind their powers of note and
      use ;
And makes their way to ruin seem more right
Than that which safety opens to their sight.
Cassandra's prophecy had no more profit
With Troy's blind citizens, when she foretold
Troy's ruin ; which, succeeding, made her use
This sacred inclamation : " God " (said she)
" Would have me utter things uncredited :
" For which now they approve what I presaged ;
" They count me wise, that said before I raged."

      Enter CHALON *with two* Soldiers.

    Chal. Come, soldiers, you are downwards fit for
      lackeys ;

Give me your pieces, and take you these coats,
To make you complete footmen, in whose forms,
You must be complete soldiers ; you two only
Stand for our army.

    1st. That were much.

    Chal. 'Tis true,
You two must do, or enter, what our army
Is now in field for.

    2nd. I see then our guerdon
Must be the deed itself, 'twill be such honour.

    Chal. What fight soldiers most for ?

    1st. Honour only.

    Chal. Yet here are crowns beside.

    1st. We thank you, captain.

    2nd. Now, sir, how show we ?

    Chal. As you should at all parts.
Go now to Clermont D'Ambois, and inform him—
Two battles [1] are set ready in his honour,
And stay his presence only for their signal,
When they shall join ; and that t'attend him hither,
Like one we so much honour, we have sent him——

    1st. Us two in person.

    Chal. Well, sir, say it so.
And having brought him to the field, when I
Fall in with him, saluting, get you both
Of one side of his horse, and pluck him down,
And I with th'ambush laid, will second you.

    1st. Nay, we shall lay on hands of too much strength
To need your secondings.

    2nd. I hope we shall.
Two are enough to encounter Hercules.

    Chal. 'Tis well said, worthy soldiers : haste, and
      haste him.   [*Exeunt.*

           [1] Armies.

Enter CLERMONT, MAILLARD *close following him.*

Cl. My Scotch horse to their army.

Ma. Please you, sir ?

Cl. 'Sdeath, you're passing diligent.

Ma. Of my soul

'Tis only in my love to honour you

With what would grace the King ; but since I see

You still sustain a jealous eye on me,

I'll go before.

    Cl. 'Tis well ; I'll come ; my hand.

    Ma. Your hand, sir ? Come, your word, your
choice be used.   [*Exit.*

CLERMONT *solus.*

Cl. I had an aversion [1] to this voyage,

When first my brother moved it ; and have found

That native power in me was never vain ;

Yet now neglected it : I wonder much

At my inconstancy in these decrees,

I every hour set down to guide my life.

When Homer made Achilles passionate,

Wrathful, revengeful, and insatiate

In his affections ; what man will deny,

He did compose it all of industry,

To let men see, that men of most renown,

Strong'st, noblest, fairest, if they set not down

Decrees within them, for disposing these,

Of judgment, resolution, uprightness,

And certain knowledge of their use and ends,

Mishap and misery no less extends

To their destruction, with all that they prized,

Than to the poorest, and the most despised.

               [1] Aversion.

Enter RENEL.

Re. Why, how now, friend? retired? take heed you
    prove not
Dismay'd with this strange fortune; all observe you:
Your government's as much mark'd as the King's.
What said a friend to Pompey?

Cl. What?

Re. The people
Will never know, unless in death thou try,
That thou know'st how to bear adversity.

Cl. I shall approve how vile I value fear
Of death at all times; but to be too rash,
Without both will and care to shun the worst
(It being in power to do, well and with cheer),
Is stupid negligence, and worse than fear.

Re. Suppose this true now.

Cl. No, I cannot do't.
My sister truly said, there hung a tail
Of circumstance so black on that supposure,
That to sustain it thus, abhorr'd our metal.
And I can shun it, too, in spite of all:
Not going to field, and there, too, being so mounted
As I will, since I go.

Re. You will then go?

Cl. I am engaged, both in my word and hand;
But this is it that makes me thus retired,
To call myself t'account how this affair
Is to be managed if the worst should chance;
With which I note, how dangerous it is
For any man to praise [1] beyond the place
To which his birth, or means, or knowledge ties him;
For my part, though of noble birth, my birthright

[1] Press.

S

Had little left it, and I know 'tis better
To live with little, and to keep within
A man's own strength still, and in man's true end,
Than run a mix'd course.   Good and bad hold never
Anything common ; you can never find
Things outward care, but you neglect your mind.
God hath the whole world perfect made, and free,
His parts to th'use of th'all ; men then that are
Parts of that all, must, as the general sway
Of that importeth, willingly obey
In everything without their power to change.
He that, unpleased to hold his place, will range,
Can in no other be contain'd that's fit,
And so resisting th'All, is crush'd with it,
But he, that knowing how divine a frame
The whole world is ; and of it all, can name,
Without self-flattery, no part so divine
As he himself, and therefore will confine
Freely, his whole powers, in his proper part,
Goes on most God-like.   He that strives t'invert
The Universal's course with his poor way,
Not only dust-like shivers with the sway,
But, crossing God in his great work, all earth
Bears not so cursed and so damn'd a birth.

   Re. Go on ; I'll take no care what comes of you ;
Heaven will not see it ill, howe'er it show :
But the pretext to see these battles ranged
Is much your honour.

   Cl. As the world esteems it.
But to decide that, you make me remember
An accident of high and noble note,
And fits the subject of my late discourse
Of holding on our free and proper way.
I overtook, coming from Italy,

In Germany, a great and famous earl
Of England, the most goodly-fashion'd man
I ever saw; from head to foot in form
Rare and most absolute; he had a face
Like one of the most ancient honour'd Romans,
From whence his noblest family was derived;
He was beside of spirit passing great,
Valiant, and learn'd, and liberal as the sun,
Spoke and writ sweetly, or of learned subjects,
Or of the discipline of public weals;
And 'twas the Earl of Oxford; and being offer'd
At that time, by Duke Cassimere, the view
Of his right royal army then in field;
Refused it, and no foot was moved, to stir
Out of his own free fore-determined course:
I, wondering at it, ask'd for it his reason,
It being an offer so much for his honour.
He, all acknowledging, said, 'twas not fit
To take those honours that one cannot quit.[1]

   Re. 'Twas answer'd like the man you have described.

   Cl. And yet he cast it only in the way,
To stay and serve the world. Nor did it fit
His own true estimate how much it weighed,
For he despised it; and esteem'd it freër
To keep his own way straight; and swore that he
Had rather make away his whole estate
In things that cross'd the vulgar, than he would
Be frozen up, stiff, like a Sir John Smith,
His countryman, in common nobles' fashions;
Affecting, as the end of noblesse were
Those servile observations.

   Re. It was strange.

   Cl. Oh, 'tis a vexing sight to see a man

---

[1] Repay.

Out of his way, stalk proud as he were in ;
Out of his way to be officious,
Observant, wary, serious, and grave,
Fearful and passionate, insulting, raging.
Labour with iron flails, to thresh down feathers
Flitting in air.

    Re. What one considers this,
Of all that are thus out ? or once endeavours,
Erring to enter, on man's right-hand path ;

    Cl. These are too grave for brave wits; give them
        toys ;
Labour bestow'd on these is harsh and thriftless.
If you would consul be, says one, of Rome,
You must be watching, starting out of sleeps ;
Every way whisking ; glorifying plebeians.
Kissing patricians' hands, rot at their doors ;
Speak and do basely ; every day bestow
Gifts and observance upon one or other ;
And what's th'event of all ?   Twelve rods before thee ;
Three or four times sit for the whole tribunal ;
Exhibit Circean games ; make public feasts ;
And for these idle outward things (says he)
Would'st thou lay on such cost, toil, spend thy spirits,
And to be void of perturbation
For constancy, sleep when thou would'st have sleep,
Wake when thou would'st wake, fear nought, vex for
       nought,
No pains wilt thou bestow ? no cost, no thought ?

    Re. What should I say ?   As good consort with you
As with an angel ; I could hear you ever.

    Cl. Well ; in, my lord, and spend time with my
        sister,
And keep her from the field with all endeavour ;
The soldiers love her so and she so madly

Would take my apprehension,[1] if it chance,
That blood would flow in rivers.

    Re. Heaven forbid;
And all with honour your arrival speed.   [*Exit.*

    Enter Messenger *with two* Soldiers *like lackeys.*

    Me. Here are two lackeys, sir, have message to you.
    Cl. What is your message; and from whom, my
        friend?
    1st. From the lieutenant-colonel, and the captains;
Who sent us to inform you that the battles
Stand ready ranged; expecting but your presence,
To be their honour'd signal when to join,
And we are charged to run by, and attend you.
    Cl. I come. I pray you see my running horse
Brought to the back-gate to me.
    Me. Instantly.   [*Exit* Mess.
    Cl. Chance what can chance me, well or ill is equal
In my acceptance, since I joy in neither;
But go with sway of all the world together.
In all successes, fortune and the day
To me alike are; I am fix'd, be she
Never so fickle; and will there repose,
Far past the reach of any die she throws.
                    [*Exit, cum Pediss.*

        [1] Capture.

ACT THE FOURTH

SCENE I

Alarum within ; Excursions over the Stage.

The Lackeys *running,* MAILLARD *following them.*

A. Villains ! not hold him when ye had him
    down ?

   1st. Who can hold lightning ? 'Sdeath, a
    man as well
Might catch a cannon-bullet in his mouth,
And spit it in your hands, as take and hold him.

   Ma. Pursue, enclose him ; stand, or fall on him.
And ye may take him. 'Sdeath ! they make him,
   guards.   [*Exit.*

Alarum still, and enter CHALON.

   Chal. Stand, cowards, stand ; strike, send your
    bullets at him.
   1st. We came to entertain him, sir, for honour.
   2nd. Did ye not say so ?
   Chal. Slaves, he is a traitor !
Command the horse-troops to over-run the traitor.

                                       [*Exit.*

Shouts within.   Alarum still, and chambers shot off.
Then enter AUMALE.

Au. What spirit breathes thus, in this more than
  man,
Turns flesh to air possess'd, and in a storm,
Tears men about the field like autumn leaves?
He turn'd wild lightning in the lackeys' hands,
Who, though their sudden violent twitch unhorsed him
Yet when he bore himself, their saucy fingers
Flew as too hot off, as he had been fire.
The ambush then made in, through all whose force,
He drave as if a fierce and fire-given cannon
Had spit his iron vomit out amongst them.
The battles then in two half-moons enclosed him,
In which he show'd as if he were the light,
And they but earth, who wondering what he was,
Shrunk their steel horns, and gave him glorious pass;
And as a great shot from a town besieged,
At foes before it, flies forth black and roaring,
But they too far, and that with weight oppress'd
(As if disdaining earth) doth only graze,
Strike earth, and up again into the air;
Again sinks to it, and again doth rise,
And keeps such strength that when it softliest moves
It piecemeal shivers any let[1] it proves;
So flew brave Clermont forth, till breath forsook him;
His spirit's convulsions made him bound again,
Past all their reaches; till all motion spent,
His fix'd eyes cast a blaze of such disdain,
All stood and stared, and untouch'd let him lie,
As something sacred fall'n out of the sky.

         [*A cry within.*

O now some rude hand hath laid hold on him!

    [1] Hindrance.

Enter MAILLARD, CHALON *leading* CLERMONT, Captains
and Soldiers *following.*

See, prisoner led, with his bands [1] honour'd more
Than all the freedom he enjoy'd before.

  Ma. At length we have you, sir.

  Cl. You have much joy too ;
I made you sport yet, but I pray you tell me,
Are not you perjured?

  Ma. No ; I swore for the King.

  Cl. Yet perjury I hope is perjury.

  Ma. But thus forswearing is not perjury ;
You are no politician ; not a fault,
How foul soever, done for private ends,
Is fault in us sworn to the public good ;
We never can be of the damned crew,
We may impolitic ourselves (as 'twere)
Into the kingdom's body politic,
Whereof indeed we're members ; you miss terms.

  Cl. The things are yet the same.

  Ma. 'Tis nothing so ; the property is alter'd ;
You are no lawyer.   Or say that oath and oath
Are still the same in number, yet their species
Differ extremely, as for flat example,
When politic widows try men for their turn,
Before they wed them, they are harlots then,
But when they wed them, they are honest women ;
So private men, when they forswear, betray,
Are perjured treachers, but being public once,
That is, sworn, married to the public good—

  Cl. Are married women public?

  Ma. Public good ;
For marriage makes them, being the public good,

[1] Bonds.

And could not be without them. So I say
Men public, that is, being sworn or married
To the good public, being one body made
With the realm's body politic, are no more
Private, nor can be perjured, though forsworn,
More than a widow married, for the act
Of generation is for that an harlot,
Because for that she was so, being unmarried ;
An argument *a paribus.*

   Chal. 'Tis a shrewd one.

   Cl. "Who hath no faith to men, to God hath none ;"
Retain you that, sir ?   Who said so ?

   Mail. 'Twas I.

   Cl. Thy own tongue damn thine infidelity.
But captains all, you know me nobly born,
Use ye t'assault such men as I with lackeys ?

   Chal. They are no lackeys, sir, but soldiers
Disguised in lackeys' coats.

   1st. Sir, we have seen the enemy.

   Cl. Avaunt, ye rascals, hence !

   Ma. Now leave your coats.

   Cl. Let me not see them more.

   Au. I grieve that virtue lives so undistinguish'd
From vice in any ill, and though the crown
Of sovereign law, she should be yet her footstool,
Subject to censure, all the shame and pain
Of all her rigour.

   Cl. Yet false policy
Would cover all, being like offenders hid,
That (after notice taken where they hide)
The more they crouch and stir, the more are spied.

   Au. I wonder how this chanced you.

   Cl. Some informer,
Bloodhound to mischief, usher to the hangman,

Thirsty of honour for some huge state act,
Perceiving me great with the worthy Guise ;
And he (I know not why) held dangerous,
Made me the desperate organ of his danger,
Only with that poor colour ; 'tis the common
And more than whore-like trick of treachery,
And vermin bred to rapine and to ruin ;
For which this fault is still to be accused,
Since good acts fail, crafts and deceits are used
If it be other, never pity me.

 Au. Sir, we are glad, believe it, and have hope,
The King will so conceit it.

 Cl. At his pleasure.
In meantime, what's your will, lord-lieutenant ?

 Ma. To leave your own horse, and to mount the
   trumpets.

 Cl. It shall be done ; this heavily prevents
My purposed recreation in these parts ;
Which now I think on, let me beg you, sir,
To lend me some one captain of your troops
To bear the message of my hapless service
And misery, to my most noble mistress,
Countess of Cambray ; to whose house this night
I promised my repair, and know most truly,
With all the ceremonies of her favour,
She sure expects me.

 Ma. Think you now on that ?

 Cl. On that, sir ? ay, and that so worthily,
That if the King, in spite of your great service,
Would send me instant promise of enlargement,
Condition I would set this message by,
I would not take it, but had rather die.

 Au. Your message shall be done, sir ; I myself
Will be for you a messenger of ill.

Cl. I thank you, sir, and doubt not yet to live
To quite your kindness.

Au. Mean space, use your spirit
And knowledge for the cheerful patience
Of this so strange and sudden consequence.

Cl. Good sir, believe that no particular torture
Can force me from my glad obedience
To any thing the high and general Cause,
To match with his whole fabric, hath ordain'd :
And know ye all (though far from all your aims,
Yet worth them all, and all men's endless studies)
That in this one thing, all the discipline
Of manners and of manhood is contain'd ;
A man to join himself with th'Universe
In his main sway, and make in all things fit)
One with that All, and go on, round as it ;
Not plucking from the whole his wretched part,
And into straits, or into nought revert,
Wishing the complete Universe might be
Subject to such a rag of it as he ;
But to consider great Necessity,
All things as well refract as voluntary
Reduceth to the prime celestial cause,
Which he that yields to with a man's applause,
And cheek by cheek goes, crossing it no breath,
But, like God's image, follows to the death,
That man is truly wise, and everything,
(Each cause, and every part distinguishing),
In nature, with enough art understands,
And that full glory merits at all hands,
That doth the whole world at all parts adorn,
And appertains to one celestial born. [*Exeunt omnes.*

Enter BALIGNY, RENEL.

Ba. So foul a scandal never man sustain'd,
Which caused by th'King, is rude and tyrannous :
Give me a place, and my lieutenant make
The filler of it !

Re. I should never look
For better of him ; never trust a man
For any justice, that is rapt with pleasure ;
To order arms well, that makes smocks his ensigns,
And his whole government's sails : you heard of late,
He had the four and twenty ways of venery
Done all before him.

Ba. 'Twas abhorr'd and beastly.

Re. 'Tis more than nature's mighty hand can do
To make one humane and a lecher too.
Look how a wolf doth like a dog appear,
So like a friend is an adulterer :
Voluptuaries, and these belly-gods,
No more true men are than so many toads.
A good man happy, is a common good ;
Vile men advanced live of the common blood.

Ba. Give and then take like children.

Re. Bounties are
As soon repented as they happen rare.

Ba. What should kings do, and men of eminent places,
But as they gather, sow gifts to the graces ?
And where they have given, rather give again,
(Being given for virtue) than like babes and fools,
Take and repent gifts ; why are wealth and power ?

Re. Power and wealth move to tyranny, not bounty :
The merchant for his wealth is swoln in mind,
When yet the chief lord of it is the wind.

Ba. That may so chance to our state-merchants too

Something perform'd, that hath not far to go.

  Re. That's the main point, my lord ; insist on that.

  Ba. But doth this fire rage further? hath it taken
The tender tinder of my wife's sere blood?
Is she so passionate?

  Re. So wild, so mad,
She cannot live, and this unwreak'd sustain.
The woes are bloody that in women reign.
The Sicile gulf keeps fear in less degree ;
There is no tiger not more tame than she.

  Ba. There is no looking home then?

  Re. Home! Medea
With all her herbs, charms, thunders, lightnings,
Made not her presence and black haunts more
    dreadful.

  Ba. Come to the King ; if he reform not all,
Mark the event, none stand where that must fall.

                         [*Exeunt.*

    Enter Countess, RIOVA, *and an* Usher.

  Us. Madam, a captain come from Clermont
    D'Ambois
Desires access to you.

  Co. And not himself?

  Us. No, madam.

  Co. That's not well. Attend him in. [*Exit* Usher.
The last hour of his promise now run out
And he break? some brack's [1] in the frame of nature
That forceth his breach.

      Enter Usher *and* AUMALE.

  Au. Save your ladyship.

  Co. All welcome! Come you from my worthy
    servant ?

               [1] Flaw.

Au. Ay, madam ; and confer such news from him.

Co. Such news ?   What news ?

Au. News that I wish some other had the charge of.

Co. Oh ! what charge ?   What news ?

Au. Your ladyship must use some patience
Or else I cannot do him that desire
He urged with such affection to your graces.

Co. Do it ; for heaven's love do it, if you serve
His kind desires, I will have patience.
Is he in health ?

Au. He is ?

Co. Why, that's the ground
Of all the good estate we hold in earth ;
All our ill built upon that, is no more
Than we may bear, and should ; express it all.

Au. Madam, 'tis only this ; his liberty.

Co. His liberty !   Without that health is nothing.
Why live I, but to ask in doubt of that,
Is that bereft him ?

Au. You'll again prevent me.

Co. No more, I swear ; I must hear, and together
Come all my misery.   I'll hold though I burst.

Au. Then, madam, thus it fares.   He was invited,
By way of honour to him, to take view
Of all the powers his brother Baligny
Hath in his government ; which ranged in battles,
Maillard, lieutenant to the governor,
Having received strict letters from the King
To train him to the musters, and betray him,
To their surprise, which, with Chalon in chief,
And other captains (all the field put hard
By his incredible valour for his 'scape)
They haplessly and guiltlessly perform'd,
And to Bastile he's now led prisoner.

Co. What change is here! how are my hopes
 prevented!
O my most faithful servant; thou betray'd!
Will kings make treason lawful? Is society
(To keep which only kings were first ordain'd)
Less broke in breaking faith 'twixt friend and friend;
Than 'twixt the king and subject? Let them fear,
Kings' precedents in licence lack no danger.
Kings are compared to gods, and should be like them,
Full in all right, in nought superfluous;
Nor nothing straining past right, for their right;
Reign justly, and reign safely. Policy
Is but a guard corrupted, and a way
Ventured in deserts, without guide or path.
Kings punish subjects' errors with their own.
Kings are like archers, and their subjects, shafts;
For as when archers let their arrows fly,
They call to them, and bid them fly or fall,
As if 'twere in the free power of the shaft
To fly or fall, when only 'tis the strength,
Straight shooting, compass given it by the archer,
That makes it hit or miss; and doing either,
He's to be praised or blamed, and not the shaft:
So kings to subjects crying, "Do, do not this;"
Must to them by their own examples' strength,
The straightness of their acts, and equal compass,
Give subjects power t'obey them in the like;
Not shoot them forth with faulty aim and strength,
And lay the fault in them for flying amiss.

 Au. But for your servant, I dare swear him guiltless.

 Co. He would not for his kingdom traitor be;
His laws are not so true to him as he.
Oh knew I how to free him, by way forced
Through all their army, I would fly, and do it;

And had I, of my courage and resolve,
But ten such more, they should not all retain him ;
But I will never die before I give
Maillard an hundred slashes with a sword,
Chalon an hundred breaches with a pistol.
They could not all have taken Clermont D'Ambois
Without their treachery ; he had bought his bands out
With their slave bloods ; but he was credulous ;
He would believe, since he would be believed ;
Your noblest natures are most credulous.
Who gives no trust, all trust is apt to break ;
Hate like hell-mouth who think not what they speak.

 Au. Well, madam, I must tender my attendance
On him again. Will't please you to return
No service to him by me ?

 Co. Fetch me straight
My little cabinet. [*Exit* ANCIL.] 'Tis little, tell him,
And much too little for his matchless love.
But as in him the worths of many men
Are close contracted [*Intr.* ANCIL], so in this are
  jewels
Worth many cabinets. Here, with this, good sir,
Commend my kindest service to my servant,
Thank him, with all my comforts ; and, in them
With all my life for them : all sent from him
In his remembrance of me, and true love ;
And look you tell him, tell him how I lie
      [*She kneels down at his feet.*
Prostrate at feet of his accursed misfortune,
Pouring my tears out, which shall ever fall
Till I have pour'd for him out eyes and all.

 Au. O madam, this will kill him : comfort you
With full assurance of his quick acquittal :
Be not so passionate : rise, cease your tears.

Co. Then must my life cease. Tears are all the
    vent
My life hath to 'scape death. Tears please me better
Than all life's comforts, being the natural seed
Of hearty sorrow. As a tree fruit bears,
So doth an undissembled sorrow, tears.
            [*He raises her, and leads her out. Exeunt.*
Us. This might have been before, and saved much
    charge.   [*Exit.*

Enter HENRY, GUISE, BALIGNY, ESPERNON, SOISSON,
    PERICOT *with pen, ink, and paper.*

Gu. Now, sir, I hope your much abused eyes see
In my word for my Clermont, what a villain
He was that whisper'd in your jealous ear
His own black treason in suggesting Clermont's ;
Colour'd with nothing but being great with me.
Sign then this writ for his delivery ;
Your hand was never urged with worthier boldness :
Come pray, sir, sign it : why should kings be pray'd
To act of justice ? 'Tis a reverence
Makes them despised, and shows they stick and tire
In what their free powers should be hot as fire.
   He. Well, take your will, sir, I'll have mine ere
    long.   [*Aversus.*
But wherein is this Clermont such a rare one ?
   Gu. In his most gentle and unwearied mind,
Rightly to virtue framed ; in very nature ;
In his most firm inexorable spirit,
To be removed from anything he chooseth
For worthiness ; or bear the best persuasion
To what is base, or fitteth not his object ;
In his contempt of riches and of greatness ;
In estimation of th'idolatrous vulgar ;

T

His scorn of all things servile and ignoble,
Though they could gain him never such advance-
    ment ;
His liberal kind of speaking what is truth
In spite of temporizing ; the great rising
And learning of his soul, so much the more
Against ill fortune, as she set herself
Sharp against him, or would present most hard,
To shun the malice of her deadliest charge ;
His detestation of his special friends
When he perceived their tyrannous will to do,
Or their abjection basely to sustain
Any injustice that they could revenge ;
The flexibility of his most anger,
Even in the main career and fury of it,
When any object of desertful pity
Offers itself to him ; his sweet disposure
As much abhorring to behold, as do
Any unnatural and bloody action ;
His just contempt of jesters, parasites,
Servile observers, and polluted tongues :
In short, this Senecal man is found in him,
He may with heaven's immortal powers compare,
To whom the day and fortune equal are ;
Come fair or foul, whatever chance can fall,
Fix'd in himself, he still is one to all.

    He. Shows he to others thus ?

    Omnes. To all that know him.

    He. And apprehend I this man for a traitor ?

    Gu. These are your Machiavellian villains,
Your bastard Teucers that, their mischiefs done,
Run to your shield for shelter : Caucuses
That cut their too large murderous thieveries
To their dens' length still : woe be to that state

Where treachery guards, and ruin makes men great.

He. Go, take my letters for him, and release him.

Omnes. Thanks to your highness; ever live your
highness !   [*Exeunt.*

Ba. Better a man were buried quick,[1] than live
A property for state and spoil to thrive   [*Exit.*

Enter CLERMONT, MAILLARD, CHALON, *with* Soldiers.

Ma. We joy you take a chance so ill, so well.

Cl. Who ever saw me differ in acceptance
Of either fortune ?

Chal. What, love bad like good ?
How should one learn that ?

Cl. To love nothing outward,
Or not within our own powers to command ;
And so being sure of everything we love,
Who cares to lose the rest ?   If any man
Would neither live nor die in his free choice,
But as he sees necessity will have it
(Which if he would resist, he strives in vain),
What can come near him, that he doth not well,
And if in worst events his will be done,
How can the best be better ?   All is one.

Ma. Methinks 'tis pretty.

Cl. Put no difference
If you have this, or not this ; but as children
Playing at quoits, ever regard their game,
And care not for their quoits ; so let a man
The things themselves that touch him not esteem,
But his free power in all disposing them.

Chal. Pretty from toys !

Cl. Methinks this double distich

[1] Alive.

Seems prettily too to stay superfluous longings :
" Not to have want, what riches doth exceed ?
Not to be subject, what superior thing ?
He that to nought aspires, doth nothing need ;
Who breaks no law is subject to no king."

Ma. This goes to mine ear well, I promise you.

Chal. Oh, but 'tis passing hard to stay one thus.

Cl. 'Tis so ; rank custom wraps men so beyond it ;
And as 'tis hard so well men's doors to bar
To keep the cat out, and th'adulterer ;
So 'tis as hard to curb affections so,
We let in nought to make them overflow.
And as of Homer's verses many critics
On those stand, of which Time's old moth hath eaten
The first or last feet, and the perfect parts
Of his unmatched poem sink beneath,
With upright gasping and sloth dull as death :
So the unprofitable things of life,
And those we cannot compass, we affect,
All that doth profit and we have, neglect ;
Like covetous and basely-getting men,
That gathering much, use never what they keep,
But for the least they lose, extremely weep.

Ma. This pretty talking and our horses walking
Down this steep hill, spends time with equal profit.

Cl. 'Tis well bestow'd on ye, meat and men sick
Agree like this, and you ; and yet even this
Is th'end of all skill, power, wealth, all that is.

Chal. I long to hear, sir, how your mistress takes this.

Enter AUMALE *with a cabinet.*

Ma. We soon shall know it ; see Aumale return'd.

Au. Ease to your bands, sir.

Cl. Welcome, worthy friend.

Chal. How took his noblest mistress your sad
    message?

Au. As great rich men take sudden poverty:
I never witness'd a more noble love,
Nor a more ruthful sorrow: I well wish'd
Some other had been master of my message.

Ma. You're happy, sir, in all things, but this one
Of your unhappy apprehension.

Cl. This is to me, compared with her much moan,
As one tear is to her whole passion.[1]

Au. Sir, she commends her kindest service to you,
And this rich cabinet.

Chal. O happy man!
This may enough hold to redeem your bands.

Cl. These clouds, I doubt not, will be soon blown
    over.

Enter BALIGNY *with his discharge*, RENEL, *and others.*

Au. Your hope is just and happy; see, sir, both,
In both the looks of these.

Ba. Here's a discharge
For this your prisoner, my good lord lieutenant.

Ma. Alas! sir, I usurp'd that style enforced,
And hope you know it was not my aspiring.

Ba. Well, sir, my wrong aspired past all men's
    hopes.

Ma. I sorrow for it, sir.

Re. You see, sir, there
Your prisoner's discharge authentical.

Ma. It is, sir, and I yield it him with gladness.

---

[1] Sorrow.

Ba. Brother, I brought you down to much good
  purpose.

Cl. Repeat not that, sir; the amends makes all.

Re. I joy in it, my best and worthiest friend :
O y'have a princely fautor of the Guise.

Ba. I think I did my part too.

Re. Well, sir, all
Is in the issue well : and, worthiest friend,
Here's from your friend the Guise ; here from the
  Countess,
Your brother's mistress, the contents whereof
I know, and must prepare you now to please
Th' unrested spirit of your slaughter'd brother,
If it be true, as you imagined once,
His apparition show'd it ; the complot
Is now laid sure betwixt us ; therefore haste
Both to your great friend (who hath some use weighty
For your repair to him) and to the Countess,
Whose satisfaction is no less important.

Cl. I see all, and will haste as it importeth ;
And, good friend, since I must delay a little
My wish'd attendance on my noblest mistress,
Excuse me to her, with return of this,
And endless protestation of my service ;
And now become as glad a messenger
As you were late a woful.

Au. Happy change !
I ever will salute thee with my service.   [*Exit.*

Ba. Yet more news, brother ; the late jesting
  Monsieur
Makes now your brother's dying prophecy equal
At all parts, being dead as he presaged.

Re. Heaven shield the Guise from seconding that
  truth,

With what he likewise prophesied on him.

　Cl. It hath enough, 'twas graced with truth in one,
To th'other falsehood and confusion.
Lead to the Court, sir.

　Ba. You I'll lead no more,
It was too ominous and foul before.　　　*[Exeunt.*

ACT THE FIFTH

SCENE I

Ascendit UMBRA BUSSY.

M. Up from the chaos of eternal night,
(To which the whole digestion of the world
Is now returning) once more I ascend,
And bide the cold damp of this piercing air,
To urge the justice whose almighty word
Measures the bloody acts of impious men
With equal penance, who in th'act itself
Includes th'infliction, which like chained shot
Batter together still; though (as the thunder
Seems by men's duller hearing than their sight,
To break a great time after lightning forth,
Yet both at one time tear the labouring cloud),
So men think penance of their ills is slow,
Though th'ill and penance still together go.
Reform, ye ignorant men, your manless lives,
Whose laws ye think are nothing but your lusts
When leaving but for supposition' sake
The body of felicity, religion,

296

Set in the 'midst of Christendom, and her head
Cleft to her bosom ; one half one way swaying,
Another th'other ; all the Christian world
And all her laws, whose observation
Stands upon faith, above the power of reason ;
Leaving, I say, all these, this might suffice
To fray ye from your vicious swindge in ill,
And set you more on fire to do more good ;
That since the world (as which of you denies?)
Stands by proportion, all may thence conclude,
That all the joints and nerves sustaining nature,
As well may break, and yet the world abide,
As any one good unrewarded die,
Or any one ill 'scape his penalty.

[*The* Ghost *stands close.*[1]

Enter GUISE, CLERMONT.

Gu. Thus, friend, thou seest how all good men would
    thrive,
Did not the good thou prompt'st me with prevent
The jealous ill pursuing them in others.
But now thy dangers are dispatch'd, note mine ;
Hast thou not heard of that admired voice
That at the barricadoes spake to me,
No person seen, "let's lead, my lord, to Rheims"?
  Cl. Nor could you learn the person?
  Gu. By no means.
  Cl. 'Twas but your fancy then, a waking dream ;
For as in sleep, which binds both th'outward senses,
And the sense common too ; th'imagining power
(Stirr'd up by forms hid in the memory's store,
Or by the vapours of o'erflowing humours
In bodies full and foul, and mix'd with spirits)

               [1] Hidden.

Feigns many strange, miraculous images,
In which act it so painfully applies
Itself to those forms, that the common sense
It actuates with his motion ; and thereby
Those fictions true seem, and have real act ;
So, in the strength of our conceits awake
The cause alike, doth of like fictions make.

Gu. Be what it will, 'twas a presage of something
Weighty and secret, which th'advertisements
I have received from all parts, both without
And in this kingdom, as from Rome and Spain,
Soccaine and Savoy, gives me cause to think ;
All writing that our plot's catastrophe,
For propagation of the Catholic cause,
Will bloody prove, dissolving all our counsels.

Cl. Retire, then, from them all.

Gu. I must not do so.
The Archbishop of Lyons tells me plain
I shall be said then to abandon France
In so important an occasion ;
And that mine enemies (their profit making
Of my faint absence) soon would let that fall,
That all my pains did to this height exhale.

Cl. Let all fall that would rise unlawfully :
Make not your forward spirit in virtue's right
A property for vice, by thrusting on
Further than all your powers can fetch you off.
It is enough, your will is infinite
To all things virtuous and religious,
Which, within limits kept, may, without danger,
Let virtue some good from your graces gather ;
Avarice of all is ever nothing's father.

Um. Danger, the spur of all great minds, is ever
The curb to your tame spirits ; you respect not,

With all your holiness of life and learning,
More than the present, like illiterate vulgars.
Your mind, you say, kept in your flesh's bounds,
Shows that man's will must ruled be by his power,
When, by true doctrine, you are taught to live
Rather without the body, than within,
And rather to your God still than yourself;
To live to Him, is to do all things fitting
His image, in which, like Himself, we live;
To be His image, is to do those things
That make us deathless, which by death is only;
Doing those deeds that fit eternity;
And those deeds are the perfecting that justice
That makes the world last, which proportion is
Of punishment and wreak for every wrong,
As well as for right a reward as strong.
Away, then; use the means thou hast to right
The wrong I suffer'd. What corrupted law
Leaves unperform'd in kings, do thou supply,
And be above them all in dignity. [*Exit.*

   Gu. Why stand'st thou still thus, and apply'st thine
     ears
And eyes to nothing?
   Cl. Saw you nothing here?
   Gu. Thou dream'st awake now; what was here to
     see?
   Cl. My brother's spirit, urging his revenge.
   Gu. Thy brother's spirit! Pray thee, mock me not.
   Cl. No, by my love and service.
   Gu. Would he rise,
And not be thundering threats against the Guise?
   Cl. You make amends for enmity to him
With ten parts more love, and desert of me;
And as you make your hate to him no let

Of any love to me, no more bears he
(Since you to me supply it) hate to you ;
Which reason and which justice is perform'd
In spirits ten parts more than fleshy men ;
To whose fore-sights our acts and thoughts lie open ;
And therefore, since he saw the treachery
Late practised by my brother Baligny,
He would not honour his hand with the justice
(As he esteems it) of his blood's revenge,
To which my sister needs would have him sworn,
Before she would consent to marry him.

   Gu. Oh, Baligny, who would·believe there were
A man, that (only since his looks are raised
Upwards, and have but sacred heaven in sight)
Could bear a mind so more than devilish ?
As for the painted glory of the countenance,
Flitting in kings, doth good for nought esteem,
And the more ill he does, the better seem.

   Cl. We easily may believe it, since we see
In this world's practice few men better be.
Justice to live doth nought but justice need,
But policy must still on mischief feed.
Untruth for all his ends, truth's name doth sue in ;
None safely live but those that study ruin.
A good man happy is a common good ;
Ill men advanced live of the common blood.

   Gu. But this thy brother's spirit startles me :
These spirits seld' or never haunting men,
But some mishap ensues.

   Cl. Ensue what can ;
Tyrants may kill, but never hurt a man ;
All to his good makes, spite of death and hell.

Enter AUMALE.

Au. All the desert of good, renown your highness !

Gu. Welcome, Aumale.

Cl. My good friend, friendly welcome.
How took my noblest mistress the changed news ?

Au. It came too late, sir, for those loveliest eyes
(Through which a soul look'd so divinely loving,
Tears nothing uttering her distress enough)
She wept quite out, and like two falling stars
Their dearest sights quite vanish'd with her tears.

Cl. All good forbid it !

Gu. What events are these ?

Cl. All must be borne, my lord : and yet this chance
Would willing enforce a man to cast off
All power to bear with comfort, since he sees
In this, our comforts made our miseries.

Gu. How strangely thou art loved of both the
    sexes ;
Yet thou lovest neither but the good of both.

Cl. In love of women my affection first
Takes fire out of the frail parts of my blood :
Which till I have enjoy'd, is passionate,
Like other lovers' : but, fruition past,
I then love out of judgment ; the desert
Of her I love still sticking in my heart,
Though the desire and delight be gone,
Which must chance still, since the comparison
Made upon trial 'twixt what reason loves,
And what affection, makes in me the best
Ever preferr'd ; what most love, valuing lest.[1]

Gu. Thy love being judgment then, and of the
    mind,
Marry thy worthiest mistress now being blind.

[1] Least.

Cl. If there were love in marriage, so I would :
But I deny that any man doth love,
Affecting wives, maids, widows, any women :
For neither flies love milk, although they drown
In greedy search thereof ; nor doth the bee
Love honey, though the labour of her life
Is spent in gathering it ; nor those that fat
On beasts, or fowls, do anything therein
For any love : for as when only nature
Moves men to meat, as far as her power rules,
She doth it with a temperate appetite,
The too much men devour, abhorring nature ;
And in our most health, is our most disease ;
So, when humanity rules men and women,
'Tis for society confined in reason.
But what excites the bed's desire in blood,
By no means justly can be construed love ;
For when love kindles any knowing spirit,
It ends in virtue and effects divine,
And is in friendship chaste and masculine.

    Gu. Thou shalt my mistress be ; methinks my blood
Is taken up to all love with thy virtues.
And howsoever other men despise
These paradoxes strange, and too precise ;
Since they hold on the right way of our reason,
I could attend them ever.   Come, away ;
Perform thy brother's thus importuned wreak ;
And I will see what great affairs the King
Hath to employ my counsel, which he seems
Much to desire, and more and more esteems.[*Exeunt.*

    Enter HENRY, BALIGNY, *with six of the* Guard.

    He. Saw you his saucy forcing of my hand
To D'Ambois' freedom ?

Ba. Saw, and through mine eyes
Let fire into my heart, that burn'd to bear
An insolence so giantly austere.

He. The more kings bear at subjects' hands, the
    more
Their lingering justice gathers ; that resembles
The weighty and the goodly-bodied eagle,
Who, being on earth, before her shady wings
Can raise her into air, a mighty way
Close by the ground she runs; but being aloft
All she commands, she flies at ; and the more
Death in her seres bears, the more time she stays
Her thundery stoop from that on which she preys.

Ba. You must be then more secret in the weight
Of these your shady counsels ; who will else
Bear where such sparks fly as the Guise and D'Ambois
Powder about them. Counsels, as your entrails,
Should be unpierced and sound kept ; for not those,
Whom you discover, you neglect : but ope
A ruinous passage to your own best hope.

He. We have spies set on us, as we on others ;
And therefore they that serve us must excuse us,
If what we most hold in our hearts, take wind ;
Deceit hath eyes that see into the mind.
But this plot shall be quicker than their twinkling,
On whose lids Fate, with her dead weight shall lie,
And Confidence that lightens ere she die.
Friends of my guard, as ye gave oath to be
True to your sovereign, keep it manfully ;
Your eyes have witness'd oft th'ambition
That never made access to me in Guise
But treason ever sparkled in his eyes ;
Which if you free us of, our safety shall
You not our subjects, but our patrons call.

Omnes. Our duties bind us ; he is now but dead.

He. We trust in it, and thank ye. Baligny,
Go lodge their ambush, and thou God that art
Fautor of princes, thunder from the skies,
Beneath his hill of pride this giant Guise.   [*Exeunt.*

  Enter TAMYRA *with a letter,* CHARLOTTE *in
    man's attire.*

Ta. I see y'are servant, sir, to my dear sister,
The lady of her loved Baligny.

Ch. Madam, I am bound to her virtuous bounties,
For that life which I offer in her virtuous service,
To the revenge of her renowned brother.

Ta. She writes to me as much, and much desires,
That you may be the man, whose spirit she knows
Will cut short off these long and dull delays,
Hitherto bribing the eternal Justice ;
Which I believe, since her unmatched spirit
Can judge of spirits, that have her sulphur in them ;
But I must tell you, that I make no doubt,
Her living brother will revenge her dead,
On whom the dead imposed the task, and he,
I know, will come t'effect it instantly.

Ch. They are but words in him ; believe them not.

Ta. See ; this is the vault, where he must enter ;
Where now I think he is.

  Enter RENEL *at the vault, with the* Countess,
    being blind.

Re. God save you, lady.
What gentleman is this, with whom you trust
The deadly weighty secret of this hour ?

Ta. One that yourself will say, I well may trust.

Re. Then come up, madam.

       [*He helps the* Countess *up.*

See here, honour'd lady,
A Countess, that in love's mishap doth equal
At all parts your wrong'd self; and is the mistress
Of your slain servant's brother; in whose love
For his late treacherous apprehension,
She wept her fair eyes from her ivory brows,
And would have wept her soul out, had not I
Promised to bring her to this mortal quarry,
That by her lost eyes for her servant's love,
She might conjure him from this stern attempt,
In which (by a most ominous dream she had)
She knows his death fix'd, and that never more
Out of this place the sun shall see him live.

   Ch. I am provided then to take his place
And undertaking on me.

   Re. You, sir! why?

   Ch. Since I am charged so by my mistress,
His mournful sister.

   Ta. See her letter, sir.   [*He reads.*
Good madam, I rue your fate, more than mine,
And know not how to order these affairs,
They stand on such occurrents.

   Re. This, indeed,
I know to be your lady mistress' hand,
And know besides, his brother will and must
Endure no hand in this revenge but his.

Enter UMBRA BUSSY.

   Um. Away, dispute no more; get up and see,
Clermont must author this just tragedy.

   Countess. Who's that?

   Re. The spirit of Bussy.

   Ta. O my servant [1]: let us embrace.

              [1] Lover.

U

Um. Forbear !   The air in which
My figure's likeness is impressed, will blast ;
Let my revenge for all loves satisfy,
In which, dame, fear not, Clermont shall not die :
No word dispute more, up, and see th'event.

                             [*Exeunt* Ladies.

Make the guard sure, Renel, and then the doors
Command to make fast when the Earl is in.

                             [*Exit* RENEL.

The black soft-footed hour is now on wing,
Which, for my just wreak, ghosts shall celebrate
With dances dire and of infernal state.   [*Exit.*

Enter GUISE.

Gu. Who says that death is natural, when nature
Is with the only thought of it dismay'd ?
I have had lotteries set up for my death,
And I have drawn beneath my trencher one,
Knit in my handkerchief another lot,
The word being, " Y'are a dead man if you enter " ;
And these words, this imperfect blood and flesh,
Shrink at in spite of me, their solidest part
Melting like snow within me, with cold fire :
I hate myself, that seeking to rule kings,
I cannot curb my slave.   Would any spirit,
Free, manly, princely, wish to live to be
Commanded by this mass of slavery,
Since reason, judgment, resolution,
And scorn of what we fear, will yield to fear ?
While this same sink of sensuality swells,
Who would live sinking in it, and not spring
Up to the stars, and leave this carrion here
For wolves, and vultures, and for dogs to tear ?
O, Clermont D'Ambois, wert thou here to chide

This softness from my flesh, far as my reason,
Far as my resolution, not to stir
One foot out of the way, for death and hell.
Let my false man by falsehood perish here,
There's no way else to set my true man clear.

Enter Messenger.

Me. The King desires your grace to come to council.
Gu. I come.   It cannot be : he will not dare
To touch me with a treachery so profane.
Would Clermont now were here, to try how he
Would lay about him, if this plot should be :
Here would be tossing souls into the sky.
Who ever knew blood saved by treachery ?
Well, I must on, and will ; what should I fear ?
Not against two Alcides : against two,
And Hercules to friend, the Guise will go.

*He takes up the arras, and the Guard enters upon
him : he draws.*

Gu. Hold, murderers !   So then, this is confidence
                    [*They strike him down.*
In greatness, not in goodness : where is the King ?

The King *comes in sight with* ESPERNON, SOISSONS,
and others.

Let him appear to justify his deed,
In spite of my betray'd wounds ; ere my soul
Take her flight through them, and my tongue hath
    strength
To urge his tyranny.
    He. See, sir, I am come
To justify it before men, and God,
Who knows with what wounds in my heart for woe

Of your so wounded faith, I made these wounds,
Forced to it by an insolence of force
To stir a stone, nor as a rock opposed
To all the billows of the churlish sea,
More beat, and eaten with them, than was I
With your ambitious mad idolatry;
And this blood I shed, is to save the blood
Of many thousands.

    Gu. That's your white pretext,
But you will find one drop of blood shed lawless
Will be the fountain to a purple sea :
The present lust and shift made for kings' lives
Against the pure form and just power of law,
Will thrive like shifters' purchases ; there hangs
A black star in the skies, to which the sun
Gives yet no light, will rain a poison'd shower
Into your entrails, that will make you feel
How little safety lies in treacherous steel.

    He. Well, sir, I'll bear it ; ye have a brother too,
Bursts with like threats, the scarlet Cardinal :
Seek, and lay hands on him ; and take this hence,
Their bloods, for all you, on my conscience.   [*Exit.*

    Gu. So, sir, your full swindge take ; mine, death hath
      curb'd.
Clermont, farewell : Oh, didst thou see but this !
But it is better, see by this the ice
Broke to thine own blood, which thou wilt despise,
When thou hear'st mine shed. Is there no friend here
Will bear my love to him ?

    Au. I will, my lord.

    Gu. Thanks with my last breath : recommend me
      then
To the most worthy of the race of men.

                  [*Dies. Exeunt.*

Enter MONTSURRY *and* TAMYRA.

Mont. Who have you let into my house?

Ta. I, none.

Mont. 'Tis false; I savour the rank blood of foes
In every corner.

Ta. That you may do well,
It is the blood you lately shed, you smell.

Mont. 'Sdeath, the vault opes.   [*The gulf opens.*

Ta. What vault? Hold your sword.

                    [CLERMONT *ascends.*

Cl. No, let him use it.

Mont. Treason, murder, murder!

Cl. Exclaim not; 'tis in vain, and base in you,
Being one to only one.

Mont. O bloody strumpet!

Cl. With what blood charge you her? it may be
       mine
As well as yours; there shall not any else
Enter or touch you; I confer no guards,
Nor imitate the murderous course you took;
But, single here, will have my former challenge
Now answer'd single; not a minute more
My brother's blood shall stay for his revenge,
If I can act it; if not, mine shall add
A double conquest to you, that alone
Put it to fortune now, and use no odds;
Storm not, nor beat yourself thus 'gainst the doors
Like to a savage vermin in a trap;
All doors are sure made, and you cannot 'scape
But by your valour.

Mont. No, no; come and kill me.

Cl. If you will die so like a beast, you shall;
But when the spirit of a man may save you,
Do not so shame man, and a noble man.

Mont. I do not show this baseness that I fear thee,
But to prevent and shame thy victory,
Which of one base is base, and so I'll die.

Cl. Here, then.

Mont. Stay, hold ; one thought hath harden'd me ;

　　　　　　　　　　　　　　　　[He starts up.

And since I must afford thee victory,
It shall be great and brave, if one request
Thou wilt admit me.

Cl. What's that ?

Mont. Give me leave
To fetch and use the sword thy brother gave me
When he was bravely giving up his life.

Cl. No, I'll not fight against my brother's sword ;
Not that I fear it, but since 'tis a trick
For you to show your back.

Mont. By all truth, no :
Take but my honourable oath, I will not.

Cl. Your honourable oath ? Plain truth no place
　　has
Where oaths are honourable.

Ta. Trust not his oath.
He will lie like a lapwing, when she flies
Far from her sought nest, still " here 'tis," she cries.

Mont. Out on thee, dam of devils ; I will quite
Disgrace thy brave's conquest, die, not fight.

　　　　　　　　　　　　　　　　[Lies down.

Ta. Out on my fortune, to wed such an abject.
Now is the people's voice the voice of God ;
He that to wound a woman vaunts so much
(As he did me), a man dares never touch.

Cl. Revenge your wounds now, madam ; I resign
　　him
Up to your full will, since he will not fight.

First you shall torture him (as he did you,
And Justice wills), and then pay I my vow.
Here, take this poniard.

 Mont. Sink earth, open heaven,
And let fall vengeance.

 Ta. Come, sir, good sir, hold him.

 Mont. O shame of women, whither art thou fled?

 Cl. Why, good my lord, is it a greater shame
For her than you? Come, I will be the bands [1]
You used to her, profaning her fair hands.

 Mont. No, sir; I'll fight now, and the terror be
Of all you champions to such as she.
I did but thus far dally: now observe,
O all you aching foreheads, that have robb'd
Your hands of weapons, and your hearts of valour,
Join in me all your rages and rebutters,
And into dust ram this same race of furies,
In this one relic of the Ambois gall,
In his one purple soul shed, drown it all. [*Fight.*

 Mont. Now give me breath a while.

 Cl. Receive it freely.

 Mont. What think y'a this now?

 Cl. It is very noble;
Had it been free, at least, and of yourself,
And thus we see (where valour most doth vaunt)
What 'tis to make a coward valiant.

 Mont. Now I shall grace your conquest.

 Cl. That you shall.

 Mont. If you obtain it.

 Cl. True, sir, 'tis in fortune.

 Mont. If you were not a D'Ambois, I would scarce
Change lives with you, I feel so great a change
In my tall spirits; breathed, I think, with the breath

<hr>

[1] Bonds.

A D'Ambois breathes here, and necessity
(With whose point now prick'd on, and so, whose help
My hands may challenge, that doth all men conquer,
If she except not you, of all men only)
May change the case here.

 Cl. True, as you are changed,
Her power in me urged, makes y'another man
Than yet you ever were.

 Mont. Well, I must on.

 Cl. Your lordship must, by all means.

 Mont. Then at all.

[*Fights, and* D'AMBOIS *hurts him.*

RENEL, Countess, *and* CHARLOTTE *above.*

 Ch. Death of my father! what a shame is this,
Stick in his hands thus?

 Re. Gentle sir, forbear.

 Co. Is he not slain yet?   [*She gets down*

 Re. No, madam, but hurt in divers parts of him.

 Mont. Y'have given it me,
And yet I feel life for another veney.[1]

Enter CHARLOTTE.

 Cl. What would you, sir?

 Ch. I would perform this combat.

 Cl. Against which of us?

 Ch. I care not much if 'twere
Against thyself: thy sister would have shamed
To have thy brother's wreak with any man,
In single combat, stick so in her fingers.

 Cl. My sister? know you her?

 Ta. Ay, sir, she sent him
With this kind letter, to perform the wreak
Of my dear servant.

[1] Bout.

Cl. Now, alas! good sir,
Think you you could do more?

Ch. Alas! I do,
And were't not, I, fresh, sound, should charge a man
Weary and wounded, I would long ere this
Have proved what I presume on.

Cl. Y'have a mind
Like to my sister, but have patience now,
If next charge speed not, I'll resign to you.

Mont. Pray thee let him decide it.

Cl. No, my lord,
I am the man in fate, and since so bravely
Your lordship stands me, 'scape but one more charge,
And on my life, I'll set your life at large.

Mont. Said like a D'Ambois, and if now I die,
Sit joy and all good on thy victory.

                              [*Fights and falls down.*
Farewell, I heartily forgive thee, wife,
And thee, let penitence spend thy rest of life.

            [*He gives his hand to* CLERMONT *and his* Wife.

Cl. Noble and Christian!

Ta. Oh, it breaks my heart!

Cl. And should; for all faults found in him before,
These words, this end, makes full amends and more.
Rest, worthy soul, and with it the dear spirit
Of my loved brother, rest in endless peace;
Soft lie thy bones, Heaven be your soul's abode,
And to your ashes be the earth no load.

Music, and the Ghost of BUSSY *enters, leading the Ghost
     of the* GUISE, *Monsieur, Cardinal* GUISE, *and*
     CHATILLON; *they dance about the dead body, and
     Exeunt.*

Cl. How strange is this! the Guise amongt these spirits,

And his great brother Cardinal, both yet living,
And that the rest with them, with joy thus celebrate
This our revenge !   This certainly presages
Some instant death both to the Guise and Cardinal.
That the Chatillon's ghost too should thus join
In celebration of this just revenge,
With Guise, that bore a chief stroke in his death,
It seems that now he doth approve the act,
And these true shadows of the Guise and Cardinal,
Fore-running thus their bodies, may approve
That all things to be done, as here we live,
Are done before all times in th'other life.
That spirits should rise in these times yet are fables ;
Though learned'st men hold that our sensive spirits
A little time abide about the graves
Of their deceased bodies ; and can take
In cold condensed air the same forms they had,
When they were shut up in this body's shade.

Enter AUMALE.

Au. Oh, sir, the Guise is slain !

Cl. Avert it, heaven !

Au. Sent for to council, by the King, an ambush
(Lodged for the purpose) rush'd on him, and took
His princely life ; who sent, in dying then,
His love to you, as to the best of men.

Cl. The worst, and most accursed of things creeping
On earth's sad bosom.   Let me pray ye all
A little to forbear, and let me use
Freely mine own mind in lamenting him.
I'll call ye straight again.

Au. We will forbear, and leave you free, sir.

[*Exeunt.*

Cl. Shall I live, and he

Dead, that alone gave means of life to me?
There's no disputing with the acts of kings,
Revenge is impious on their sacred persons:
And could I play the worldling (no man loving
Longer than gain is reapt, or grace from him)
I should survive, and shall be wonder'd at
Though in mine own hands being, I end with him:
But friendship is the cement of two minds,
As of one man the soul and body is,
Of which one cannot sever, but the other
Suffers a needful separation.

[*Descend* REN. *and* Coun.

Re. I fear your servant, madam; let's descend.
Cl. Since I could skill of man, I never lived
To please men worldly, and shall I in death,
Respect their pleasures, making such a jar
Betwixt my death and life, when death should make
The consort sweetest; th'end being proof and crown
To all the skill and worth we truly own?
Guise, O my lord, how shall I cast from me
The bands and coverts hindering me from thee?
The garment or the cover of the mind,
The humane soul is; of the soul, the spirit
The proper robe is; of the spirit, the blood;
And of the blood, the body is the shroud.
With that must I begin then to unclothe,
And come at th'other.   Now then as a ship,
Touching at strange and far-removed shores;
Her men ashore go, for their several ends,
Fresh water, victuals, precious stones, and pearl,
All yet intentive (when the master calls,
The ship to put off ready) to leave all
Their greediest labours, lest they there be left
To thieves, or beasts, or be the country's slaves:

So, now my master calls, my ship, my venture,
All in one bottom put, all quite put off,
Gone under sail, and I left negligent,
To all the horrors of the vicious time,
The far-removed shores to all virtuous aims,
None favouring goodness ; none but he respecting
Piety or manhood ; shall I here survive,
Not cast me after him into the sea,
Rather than here live, ready every hour
To feed thieves, beasts, and be the slave of power?
I come, my lord, Clermont thy creature comes.

[*He kills himself.*

Enter AUMALE, TAMYRA, CHARLOTTE.

Au. What ! lie and languish, Clermont ?   Cursed
man,
To leave him here thus : he hath slain himself.

Ta. Misery on misery !   O me, wretched dame
Of all that breathe, all heaven turn all his eyes,
In hearty envy thus on one poor dame.

Ch. Well done, my brother ; I did love thee ever,
But now adore thee ; loss of such a friend
None should survive, of such a brother ;
With my false husband live, and both these slain ?
Ere I return to him, I'll turn to earth.

Enter RENEL, *leading the* Countess.

Re. Horror   of   human   eyes !   O   Clermont
D'Ambois !
Madam, we stay'd too long ; your servant's slain.

Co. It must be so ; he lived but in the Guise,
As I in him.   O follow, life, mine eyes.

Ta. Hide, hide thy snaky head ; to cloisters fly,
In penance pine, too easy 'tis to die.

Ch. It is.   In cloisters then let's all survive:
Madam, since wrath nor grief can help these fortunes,
Let us forsake the world in which they reign,
And for their wish'd amends to God complain.

Co. 'Tis fit and only needful: lead me on,
In heaven's course comfort seek, in earth is none.

[Exeunt.

Enter Henry, Espernon, Soissons, *and others.*

He. We came indeed too late, which much I rue,
And would have kept this Clermont as my crown:
Take in the dead, and make this fatal room,
The house shut up, the famous D'Ambois tomb.

[Exeunt.

THE CONSPIRACY OF CHARLES, DUKE OF BYRON

THE two *Byron* plays may properly be considered
as one. They were published in 1608, but had
been acted as early as 1605. The French
ambassador was offended at certain portions,
and for a time the performances were prohibited.
When the two plays were published, the passages that had
caused trouble were suppressed : this partly accounts for
the absence of the second act in *Byron's Tragedy*.

The material for these plays was largely taken from De
Thou.

TO

MY HONOURABLE AND CONSTANT FRIEND,

SIR THOMAS WALSINGHAM, KNIGHT;

AND TO

MY MUCH LOVED FROM HIS BIRTH, THE RIGHT TOWARD

AND WORTHY GENTLEMAN HIS SON,

THOMAS WALSINGHAM, ESQUIRE.

SIR,—

THOUGH I know you ever stood little affected to these unprofitable rites of Dedication (which disposition in you hath made me hitherto dispense with your right in my other impressions), yet, lest the world may repute it a neglect in me of so ancient and worthy a friend, having heard your approbation of these in their presentment, I could not but prescribe them with your name; and that my affection may extend to your posterity, I have entitled to it, herein, your hope and comfort in your generous son; whom I doubt not that most reverenced mother of manly sciences, to whose instruction your virtuous care commits him, will so profitably initiate in her learned labours, that they will make him flourish in his riper life, over the idle lives of our ignorant gentlemen, and enable him to supply the honourable places of your name; extending your years and his right noble mother's, in the true comforts of his virtues, to the sight of much and most happy progeny; which most affectionately wishing, and dividing these poor dismembered poems betwixt you, I desire to live still in your graceful loves, and ever

The most assured at your commandments,

GEORGE CHAPMAN.

PROLOGUS

WHEN the uncivil civil wars of France
     Had pour'd upon the country's beaten breast
     Her batter'd cities ; press'd her under hills
     Of slaughter'd carcases ; set her in the mouths
Of murderous breaches, and made pale Despair
Leave her to Ruin ; through them all, Byron
Stept to her rescue, took her by the hand ;
Pluck'd her from under her unnatural press,
And set her shining in the height of peace.
And now new cleansed from dust, from sweat, and
     blood,
And dignified with title of a Duke ;
As when in wealthy Autumn, his bright star,
Wash'd in the lofty ocean, thence ariseth,
Illustrates heaven, and all his other fires
Out-shines and darkens : so admired Byron
All France exempted from comparison.
He touch'd heaven with his lance ; nor yet was
     touch'd
With hellish treachery ; his country's love
He yet thirsts, not the fair shades of himself ;
Of which empoison'd spring, when policy drinks,
He bursts in growing great ; and rising, sinks :
Which now behold in our Conspirator,
And see in his revolt how honour's flood
Ebbs into air, when men are great, not good.

DRAMATIS PERSONÆ [1]

HENRY IV., King of France.
ALBERT, Arch-duke of Austria.
DUKE OF SAVOY.
DUKE BYRON.
D'AUVERGNE.
NEMOURS.
SOISSONS.
BELIEURE.
BRULART.
D'AUMALE.
ORENGE.
D'AUMONT.
CREQUIE.
RONCAS,
ROCHETTE,   } attendants of Savoy.
BRETON,
ROISEAU.
PICOTÉ.
LA FIN.
EPERNON.
VITRY.
JANIN.
MANSFIELD, a Count.
LA BROSSE, a Magician.
Three Ladies.

[1] Now first printed.

THE CONSPIRACY OF CHARLES, DUKE OF BYRON

ACT THE FIRST

SCENE I

Enter SAVOY, RONCAS, ROCHETTE, BRETON.

A. I would not for half Savoy, but have
bound
France to some favour, by my personal
presence
More than your self, my lord ambassador,
Could have obtain'd; for all ambassadors,
You know, have chiefly these instructions:
To note the state and chief sway of the Court
To which they are employ'd; to penetrate
The heart and marrow of the king's designs,
And to observe the countenances and spirits
Of such as are impatient of rest,
And wring beneath some private discontent.
But, past all these, there are a number more
Of these state criticisms that our personal view

325

May profitably make, which cannot fall
Within the powers of our instruction
To make you comprehend ; I will do more
With my mere shadow than you with your persons.
All you can say against my coming here
Is that which I confess may for the time
Breed strange affections in my brother Spain ;
But when I shall have time to make my cannons
The long-tongued heralds of my hidden drifts,
Our reconcilement will be made with triumphs.

 Ron. If not, your highness hath small cause to care,
Having such worthy reason to complain
Of Spain's cold friendship, and his lingering succours,
Who only entertains your griefs with hope,
To make your medicine desperate.

 Roc. My lord knows
The Spanish gloss too well ; his form, stuff, lasting,
And the most dangerous conditions
He lays on them with whom he is in league.
Th'injustice in the most unequal dower,
Given with th'Infanta, whom my lord espoused,
Compared with that her elder sister had,
May tell him how much Spain's love weighs to him ;
When of so many globes and sceptres held
By the great king, he only would bestow
A portion but of six-score thousand crowns
In yearly pension, with his highness' wife,
When the Infanta, wedded by the Archduke,
Had the Franch County, and Low Provinces.

 Br. We should not set these passages of spleen
'Twixt Spain and Savoy, to the weaker part ;
More good by sufferance grows than deeds of heart ;
The nearer princes are, the further off
In rites of friendship ; my advice had never

Consented to this voyage of my lord,
In which he doth endanger Spain's whole loss,
For hope of some poor fragment here in France.

   Sa. My hope in France you know not, though my
      counsel,
And for my loss of Spain, it is agreed
That I should slight it ; ofttimes princes' rules
Are like the chymical philosophers' ;
Leave me then to mine own projection,
In this our thrifty alchemy of state ;
Yet help me thus far, you that have been here
Our lord ambassador ; and, in short, inform me,
What spirits here are fit for our designs.

   Ron. The new-created Duke Byron is fit,
Were there no other reason for your presence,
To make it worthy ; for he is a man
Of matchless valour, and was ever happy
In all encounters, which were still made good
With an unwearied sense of any toil,
Having continued fourteen days together
Upon his horse ; his blood is not voluptuous,
Nor much inclined to women ; his desires
Are higher than his state, and his deserts
Not much short of the most he can desire,
If they be weigh'd with what France feels by them.
He is past measure glorious ;[1] and that humour
Is fit to feed his spirits, whom it possesseth
With faith in any error, chiefly where
Men blow it up with praise of his perfections,
The taste whereof in him so soothes his palate,
And takes up all his appetite, that ofttimes
He will refuse his meat and company
To feast alone with their most strong conceit ;

          [1] Boastful.

Ambition also cheek by cheek doth march
With that excess of glory, both sustain'd
With an unlimited fancy, that the King,
Nor France itself, without him can subsist,

   Sa. He is the man, my lord, I come to win ;
And that supreme intention of my presence
Saw never light till now, which yet I fear
The politic King, suspecting, is the cause,
That he hath sent him so far from my reach,
And made him chief in the commission
Of his ambassage to my brother Archduke,
With whom he is now ; and, as I am told,
So entertain'd and fitted in his humour,
That ere I part, I hope he will return
Prepared, and made the more fit for the physic
That I intend to minister.

   Ron. My lord,
There is another discontented spirit
Now here in Court, that for his brain and aptness
To any course that may recover him
In his declined and litigious state
Will serve Byron, as he were made for him
In giving vent to his ambitious vein,
And that is, de La Fin.

   Sa. You tell me true,
And him I think you have prepared for me.

   Ron. I have, my lord, and doubt not he will prove
Of the yet taintless fortress of Byron
A quick expugner, and a strong abider.

   Sa. Perhaps the battery will be brought before him
In this ambassage, for I am assured
They set high price of him, and are inform'd
Of all the passages, and means for mines
That may be thought on, to his taking in.

Enter HENRY *and* LA FIN.

The King comes, and La Fin ; the King's aspect
Folded in clouds.

   He. I will not have my train,
Made a retreat for bankrouts,[1] nor my Court
A hive for drones ; proud beggars, and true thieves,
That with a forced truth they swear to me,
Rob my poor subjects, shall give up their arts,
And henceforth learn to live by their desarts ;
Though I am grown, by right of birth and arms
Into a greater kingdom, I will spread
With no more shade than may admit that kingdom
Her proper, natural, and wonted fruits ;
Navarre shall be Navarre, and France still France :
If one may be the better for the other
By mutual rites, so neither shall be worse.
Thou art in law, in quarrels, and in debt,
Which thou wouldst quit with countenance[2] ; borrowing
With thee is purchase,[3] and thou seekest by me,
In my supportance, now our old wars cease
To wage worse battles, with the arms of peace.

   La. Peace must not make men cowards, nor keep
      calm
Her pursy regiment[4] with men's smother'd breaths ;
I must confess my fortunes are declined,
But neither my deservings, nor my mind :
I seek but to sustain the right I found,
When I was rich, in keeping what is left,
And making good my honour as at best,
Though it be hard ; man's right to everything
Wanes with his wealth, wealth is his surest king ;
Yet Justice should be still indifferent.

<hr>

[1] Bankrupts.   [2] Assurance.   [3] Robbery.   [4] Rule.

The overplus of kings, in all their might,
Is but to piece out the defects of right :
And this I sue for, nor shall frowns and taunts,
The common scarecrows of all poor men's suits,
Nor misconstruction that doth colour still
Licentiary justice, punishing good for ill,
Keep my free throat from knocking at the sky,
If thunder chid me for my equity.

   He. Thy equity is to be ever banish'd
From Court, and all society of noblesse,
Amongst whom thou throw'st balls of all dissension ;
Thou art at peace with nothing but with war,
Hast no heart but to hurt, and eat'st thy heart,
If it but think of doing any good :
Thou witchest with thy smiles, suck'st blood with praises,
Mock'st all humanity ; society poison'st,
Cozen'st with virtue ; with religion
Betray'st and massacrest ; so vile thyself,
That thou suspect'st perfection in others :
A man must think of all the villanies
He knows in all men, to decipher thee,
That art the centre to impiety :
Away, and tempt me not.

   La. But you tempt me,
To what, thou Sun to judge, and make him see.

                                 [*Exit.*

   Sa. Now by my dearest Marquisate of Salusses,
Your Majesty hath with the greatest life
Described a wicked man ; or rather thrust
Your arm down through him to his very feet,
And pluck'd his inside out, that ever yet
My ears did witness ; or turn'd ears to eyes ;
And those strange characters, writ in his face,
Which at first sight were hard for me to read,

The doctrine of your speech hath made so plain,
That I run through them like my natural language :
Nor do I like that man's aspect, methinks,
Of all looks where the beams of stars have carved
Their powerful influences ; and (O rare)
What an heroic, more than royal spirit
Bewray'd you in your first speech, that defies
Protection of vile drones, that eat the honey
Sweat from laborious virtue, and denies
To give those of Navarre, though bred with you,
The benefits and dignities of France.
When little rivers by their greedy currents,
Far far extended from their mother springs,
Drink up the foreign brooks still as they run,
And force their greatness, when they come to sea,
And justle with the ocean for a room,
Oh, how he roars, and takes them in his mouth,
Digesting them so to his proper streams
That they are no more seen, he nothing raised
Above his usual bounds, yet they devour'd
That of themselves were pleasant, goodly floods.

He. I would do best for both, yet shall not be secure
Till in some absolute heirs my crown be settled ;
There is so little now betwixt aspirers
And their great object in my only self,
That all the strength they gather under me
Tempts combat with mine own : I therefore make
Means for some issue by my marriage,
Which with the great duke's niece is now concluded,
And she is coming ; I have trust in heaven
I am not yet so old, but I may spring,
And then I hope all traitors' hopes will fade.

Sa. Else may their whole estates fly, rooted up,
To ignominy and oblivion :

And (being your neighbour, servant, and poor kinsman)
I wish your mighty race might multiply,
Even to the period of all empery.

  He. Thanks to my princely cousin : this your love
And honour shown me in your personal presence,
I wish to welcome to your full content :
The peace I now make with your brother Archduke,
By Duke Byron, our lord ambassador,
I wish may happily extend to you,
And that at his return we may conclude it.

  Sa. It shall be to my heart the happiest day
Of all my life, and that life all employ'd
To celebrate the honour of that day.   [*Exeunt.*

Enter ROISEAU.

  Ro. The wondrous honour done our Duke Byron
In his ambassage here, in th'Archduke's court,
I fear will taint his loyalty to our King.
I will observe how they observe his humour,
And glorify his valour : and how he
Accepts and stands attractive to their ends,
That so I may not seem an idle spot
In train of this embassage, but return
Able to give our King some note of all,
Worth my attendance ; and see, here's the man,
Who (though a Frenchman, and in Orleans born
Serving the Archduke) I do most suspect,
Is set to be the tempter of our Duke ;
I'll go where I may see, although not hear.

Enter PICOTÉ *with two others, spreading a carpet.*

  Pi. Spread here this history of Catiline,
That earth may seem to bring forth Roman spirits,
Even to his genial feet ; and her dark breast

Be made the clear glass of his shining graces.
We'll make his feet so tender, they shall gall
In all paths but to empire; and therein
I'll make the sweet steps of his state begin. [*Exit.*

Loud music; and enter BYRON.

By. What place is this? what air? what region?
In which a man may hear the harmony
Of all things moving? Hymen marries here
Their ends and uses, and makes me his temple.
Hath any man been blessed, and yet lived?
The blood turns in my veins, I stand on change,
And shall dissolve in changing; 'tis so full
Of pleasure not to be contain'd in flesh.
To fear a violent good, abuseth goodness;
'Tis immortality to die aspiring,
As if a man were taken quick [1] to heaven;
What will not hold perfection, let it burst;
What force hath any cannon, not being charged,
Or being not discharged? To have stuff and form,
And to lie idle, fearful, and unused,
Nor form nor stuff shows; happy Semele,
That died compress'd with glory! Happiness
Denies comparison of less or more,
And not at most, is nothing; like the shaft
Shot at the sun by angry Hercules,
And into shivers by the thunder broken,
Will I be if I burst; and in my heart
This shall be written: " Yet 'twas high and right."
[*Music again.*

Here too! they follow all my steps with music,
As if my feet were numerous, and trod sounds
Out of the centre,[2] with Apollo's virtue,

---

[1] Alive.   [2] Centre of the earth.

That out of every thing his ech-part[1] touch'd,
Struck musical accents ; wheresoe'er I go,
They hide the earth from me with coverings rich,
To make me think that I am here in heaven.

Enter PICOTÉ *in haste.*

Pi. This way, your highness.
By. Come they ?
Pi. Ay, my lord.   [*Exeunt.*

Enter the other Commissioners *of France,* BELIEURE,
BRULART, D'AUMALE, ORENGE.

Be. My Lord D'Aumale, I am exceeding sorry
That your own obstinacy to hold out
Your mortal enmity against the King,
When Duke Du Maine, and all the faction yielded,
Should force his wrath to use the rites of treason
Upon the members of your senseless statue,
Your name and house, when he had lost your person,
Your love and duty.
Br. That which men enforce
By their own wilfulness, they must endure
With willing patience and without complaint.
D'A. I use not much impatience nor complaint,
Though it offend me much to have my name
So blotted with addition[2] of a traitor,
And my whole memory with such despite
Mark'd and begun to be so rooted out.
Br. It was despite that held you out so long,
Whose penance in the King was needful justice.
Be. Come, let us seek our Duke, and take our
leaves
Of th' Archduke's grace.   [*Exeunt.*

        [1] Each part.   [2] Title.

Enter BYRON *and* PICOTÉ.

By. Here we may safely breathe.

Pi. No doubt, my lord, no stranger knows this way;
Only the Archduke, and your friend Count Mansfield
Perhaps may make their general scapes to you,
To utter some part of their private loves,
Ere your departure.

By. Then I well perceive
To what th'intention of his highness tends;
For whose, and others here, most worthy lords,
I will become, with all my worth, their servant,
In any office but disloyalty;
But that hath ever show'd so foul a monster
To all my ancestors, and my former life,
That now to entertain it I must wholly
Give up my habit, in his contrary,
And strive to grow out of privation.

Pi. My lord, to wear your loyal habit still,
When it is out of fashion, and hath done
Service enough, were rustic misery;
The habit of a servile loyalty
Is reckon'd now amongst privations,
With blindness, dumbness, deafness, silence, death,
All which are neither natures by themselves
Nor substances, but mere decays of form,
And absolute decessions [1] of nature;
And so 'tis nothing, what shall you then lose?
Your highness hath a habit in perfection,
And in desert of highest dignities,
Which carve yourself, and be your own rewarder.
No true power doth admit privation
Adverse to him; or suffers any fellow

[1] Death.

Join'd in his subject; you, superiors;
It is the nature of things absolute
One to destroy another; be your highness
Like those steep hills that will admit no clouds,
No dews, nor least fumes bound about their brows;
Because their tops pierce into purest air,
Expert of humour; or like air itself
That quickly changeth, and receives the sun
Soon as he riseth, everywhere dispersing
His royal splendour, girds it in his beams,
And makes itself the body of the light;
Hot, shining, swift, light, and aspiring things,
Are of immortal and celestial nature;
Cold, dark, dull, heavy, of infernal fortunes,
And never aim at any happiness;
Your excellency knows that simple loyalty,
Faith, love, sincerity, are but words, no things;
Merely devised for form; and as the legate,
Sent from his Holiness, to frame a peace
'Twixt Spain and Savoy, labour'd fervently,
For common ends, not for the Duke's particular,[1]
To have him sign it; he again endeavours,
Not for the legate's pains, but his own pleasure,
To gratify him; and being at last encounter'd,
Where the flood Ticin enters into Po,
They made a kind contention, which of them
Should enter th'other's boat, one thrust the other;
One leg was over, and another in;
And with a fiery courtesy, at last
Savoy leaps out, into the legate's arms,
And here ends all his love, and th'other's labour.
So shall these terms and impositions
Express'd before, hold nothing in themselves

[1] For the Duke himself.

Really good, but flourishes of form ;
And further than they make to private ends
None wise, or free, their proper use intends.

   By. Oh, 'tis a dangerous and a dreadful thing
To steal prey from a lion ; or to hide
A head distrustful, in his open'd jaws ;
To trust our blood in other's veins ; and hang
'Twixt heaven and earth, in vapours of their breaths ;
To leave a sure pace on continuate earth,
And force a gate in jumps, from tower to tower,
As they do that aspire from height to height.
The bounds of loyalty are made of glass,
Soon broke, but can in no date be repair'd ;
And as the Duke D'Aumale, now here in Court,
Flying his country, had his statue torn
Piece-meal with horses, all his goods confiscate,
His arms of honour kick'd about the streets,
His goodly house at Annet razed to th'earth,
And, for a strange reproach of his foul treason,
His trees about it, cut off by their waists ;
So, when men fly the natural clime of truth,
And turn themselves loose, out of all the bounds
Of justice, and the straight way to their ends ;
Forsaking all the sure force in themselves
To seek without them that which is not theirs,
The forms of all their comforts are distracted,
The riches of their freedoms forfeited,
Their human noblesse shamed ; the mansions
Of their cold spirits eaten down with cares ;
And all their ornaments of wit and valour,
Learning, and judgment, cut from all their fruits.

Enter ALBERT.

   Al. Oh, here were now the richest prize in Europe,

  Y

Were he but taken in affection.
Would we might grow together, and be twins
Of either's fortune ; or that still embraced
I were but ring to such a precious stone.

   By. Your highness' honours, and high bounty shown
     me,
Have won from me my voluntary power ;
And I must now move by your eminent will
To what particular objects, if I know
By this man's intercession, he shall bring
My utmost answer, and perform betwixt us
Reciprocal and full intelligence.

   Al. Even for your own deserved royal good,
'Tis joyfully accepted ; use the loves
And worthy admirations of your friends,
That beget vows of all things you can wish,
And be what I wish : danger says, no more.   [*Exit.*

     Enter MANSFIELD, *at another door.*
        Exit PICOTÉ.

   Ma. Your highness makes the light of this Court
     stoop
With your so near departure ; I was forced
To tender to your excellence, in brief,
This private wish, in taking of my leave,
That in some army royal, old Count Mansfield
Might be commanded by your matchless valour
To the supremest point of victory ;
Who vows for that renown all prayer and service :
No more, lest I may wrong you.   [*Exit* MANSFIELD.

   By. Thank your lordship.

     Enter D'AUMALE *and* ORENGE.

   D'A. All majesty be added to your highness,

Of which I would not wish your breast to bear
More modest apprehension than may tread
The high gait of your spirit; and be known
To be a fit bound for your boundless valour.

Or. So Orenge wisheth, and to the deserts
Of your great actions their most royal crown.

Enter PICOTÉ.

Pi. Away, my lord, the lords inquire for you.

[*Exit* BYRON.

Manet ORENGE, D'AUMALE, ROISEAU.

Or. Would we might win his valour to our part.

D'A. 'Tis well prepared in his entreaty here,
With all state's highest observations;
And to their form and words are added gifts.
He was presented with two goodly horses,
One of which two was the brave beast Pastrana,
With plate of gold, and a much prized jewel,
Girdle and hangers, set with wealthy stones,
All which were valued at ten thousand crowns.
The other lords had suits of tapestry,
And chains of gold; and every gentleman
A pair of Spanish gloves, and rapier blades:
And here ends their entreaty, which I hope
Is the beginning of more good to us
Than twenty thousand times their gifts to them.

Enter ALBERT, BYRON, BELIEURE, MANSFIELD,
ROISEAU, *with others.*

Al. My lord, I grieve that all the setting forth
Of our best welcome made you more retired;
Your chamber hath been more loved than our honours,
And therefore we are glad your time of parting
Is come, to set you in the air you love.

Commend my service to his Majesty,
And tell him that this day of peace with him
Is held as holy.   All your pains, my lords,
I shall be always glad to gratify
With any love and honour your own hearts
Shall do me grace to wish express'd to you.

    Ro. Here hath been strange demeanour, which shall
        fly
To the great author of this ambassy.

ACT THE SECOND

SCENE I

Enter Savoy, La Fin, Roncas, Rochette, Breton.

SA. Admit no entry, I will speak with none.
    Good signior de La Fin your worth shall
        find
    That I will make a jewel for my cabinet
    Of that the King, in surfeit of his store,
Hath cast out, as the sweepings of his hall.
I told him, having threaten'd you away,
That I did wonder this small time of peace
Could make him cast his armour so securely
In such as you, and, as 'twere, set the head
Of one so great in counsels, on his foot,
And pitch him from him with such guardlike strength.

    La. He may, perhaps, find he hath pitch'd away
The axle-tree that kept him on his wheels.

    Sa. I told him so, I swear, in other terms,
And not with too much note of our close loves,
Lest so he might have smoked our practices.[1]

    La. To choose his time, and spit his poison on me,
Through th'ears and eyes of strangers.

    Sa. So I told him,
And more than that, which now I will not tell you :

[1] Plots.

341

It rests now then, noble and worthy friend,
That to our friendship we draw Duke Byron,
To whose attraction there is no such chain
As you can forge, and shake out of your brain.

   La. I have devised the fashion and the weight ;
To valours hard to draw, we use retreats ;
And, to pull shafts home, with a good bow-arm,
We thrust hard from us ; since he came from Flanders
He heard how I was threaten'd with the King,
And hath been much inquisitive to know
The truth of all, and seeks to speak with me ;
The means he used, I answered doubtfully,
And with an intimation that I shunn'd him,
Which will, I know, put more spur to his charge ;
And if his haughty stomach be prepared
With will to any act, for the aspiring
Of his ambitious aims, I make no doubt
But I shall work him to your highness' wish.

   Sa. But undertake it, and I rest assured :
You are reported to have skill in magic,
And the events of things, at which they reach
They are in nature apt to overreach,
Whom the whole circle of the present time,
In present pleasures, fortunes, knowledges,
Cannot contain ; those men, as broken loose
From human limits, in all violent ends
Would fain aspire the faculties of fiends,
And in such air breathe his unbounded spirits,
Which therefore well will fit such conjurations.
Attempt him then by flying ; close with him,
And bring him home to us, and take my dukedom.

   La. My best in that, and all things, vows your service.

   Sa. Thanks to my dear friend, and the French
    Ulysses.   [*Exit* SAVOY.

Enter BYRON.

By. Here is the man : my honour'd friend, La Fin,
Alone, and heavy countenanced ! On what terms
Stood th'insultation of the King upon you?

La. Why do you ask ?

By. Since I would know the truth.

La. And when you know it, what ?

By. I'll judge betwixt you.
And, as I may, make even th'excess of either.

La. Alas ! my lord, not all your loyalty,
Which is in you more than hereditary,
Nor all your valour (which is more than humane)
Can do the service you may hope on me
In sounding my displeased integrity.
Stand for the King, as much in policy
As you have stirr'd for him in deeds of arms,
And make yourself his glory, and your country's,
Till you be suck'd as dry and wrought as lean,
As my flea'd carcass ; you shall never close
With me, as you imagine.

By. You much wrong me
To think me an intelligencing instrument.[1]

La. I know not how your so affected zeal
To be reputed a true-hearted subject,
May stretch or turn you ; I am desperate ;
If I offend you, I am in your power ;
I care not how I tempt your conquering fury,
I am predestined to too base an end
To have the honour of your wrath destroy me,
And be a worthy object for your sword.
I lay my hand and head too at your feet,
As I have ever, here I hold it still ;
End me directly, do not go about.

---

[1] Spy.

By. How strange is this ! the shame of his disgrace
Hath made him lunatic.

La. Since the King hath wrong'd me
He thinks I'll hurt myself; no, no, my lord;
I know that all the kings in Christendom,
If they should join in my revenge, would prove
Weak foes to him, still having you to friend ;
If you were gone (I care not if you tell him)
I might be tempted then to right myself.   [*Exit.*

By. He has a will to me, and dares not show it ;
His state decay'd, and he disgraced, distracts him.

Redit LA FIN.

La. Change not my words, my lord ; I only said,
" I might be tempted then to right myself ; "
Temptation to treason, is no treason ;
And that word tempted was conditional too ;
" If you were gone ; " I pray inform the truth.

[*Exiturus.*

By. Stay, injured man, and know I am your friend,
Far from these base and mercenary reaches ;
I am, I swear to you.

La. You may be so ;
And yet you'll give me leave to be La Fin,
A poor and expuate [1] humour of the Court ;
But what good blood came out with me, what veins
And sinews of the triumph, now it makes,
I list [2] not vaunt ; yet will I now confess,
And dare assume it ; I have power to add
To all his greatness ; and make yet more fix'd
His bold security ; tell him this, my lord,
And this, if all the spirits of earth and air
Be able to enforce, I can make good ;

[1] Ejected.   [2] Wish to.

If knowledge of the sure events of things,
Even from the rise of subjects into kings,
And falls of kings to subjects, hold a power
Of strength to work it, I can make it good ;
And tell him this too : if in midst of winter
To make black groves grow green, to still the thunder,
And cast out able flashes from mine eyes
To beat the lightning back into the skies,
Prove power to do it, I can make it good ;
And tell him this too ; if to lift the sea
Up to the stars, when all the winds are still,
And keep it calm, when they are most enraged ;
To make earth's driest palms sweat humorous springs,
To make fix'd rocks walk, and loose shadows stand,
To make the dead speak, midnight see the sun,
Mid-day turn midnight, to dissolve all laws
Of nature and of order, argue power
Able to work all, I can make all good :
And all this tell the King.

    By. 'Tis more than strange,
To see you stand thus at the rapier's point
With one so kind and sure a friend as I.

    La. Who cannot friend himself is foe to any,
And to be fear'd of all, and that is it
Makes me so scorn'd ; but make me what you can,
Never so wicked, and so full of fiends,
I never yet was traitor to my friends :
The laws of friendship I have ever held
As my religion ; and for other laws
He is a fool that keeps them with more care
Than they keep him safe, rich, and popular.
For riches, and for popular respects
Take them amongst ye, minions ; but for safety,
You shall not find the least flaw in my arms

To pierce or taint me ; what will great men be
To please the King, and bear authority !   [*Exit.*

   By. How fit a sort were this to hansel [1] fortune !
And I will win it though I lose my self ;
Though he prove harder than Egyptian marble,
I'll make him malleable as th' Ophir gold ;
I am put off from this dull shore of East,
Into industrious and high-going seas ;
Where, like Pelides in Scamander's flood,
Up to the ears in surges I will fight,
And pluck French Ilion underneath the waves.
If to be highest still, be to be best,
All works to that end are the worthiest :
Truth is a golden ball, cast in our way,
To make us stript by falsehood : and as Spain
When the hot scuffles of barbarian arms
Smother'd the life of Don Sebastian,
To gild the leaden rumour of his death
Gave for a slaughter'd body, held for his,
A hundred thousand crowns ; caused all the state
Of superstitious Portugal to mourn
And celebrate his solemn funerals ;
The Moors to conquest thankful feasts prefer,
And all made with the carcass of a Switzer :
So in the giantlike and politic wars
Of barbarous greatness, raging still in peace,
Shows to aspire just objects are laid on
With cost, with labour, and with form enough,
Which only makes our best acts brook the light,
And their ends had, we think we have their right,
So worst works are made good, with good success,
And so for kings, pay subjects carcasses.   [*Exit.*

             [1] Experiment with.

Enter HENRY, ROISEAU.

He. Was he so courted?

Ro. As a city dame,
Brought by her jealous husband to the Court,
Some elder courtiers entertaining him,
While others snatch a favour from his wife :
One starts from this door ; from that nook another,
With gifts and junkets, and with printed phrase,
Steal her employment, shifting place by place
Still as her husband comes ; so Duke Byron
Was woo'd and worshipp'd in the Archduke's Court ;
And as th'assistants that your Majesty
Join'd in commission with him, or myself,
Or any other doubted eye appear'd,
He ever vanish'd ; and as such a dame,
As we compared with him before, being won
To break faith to her husband, lose her fame,
Stain both their progenies, and coming fresh
From underneath the burthen of her shame,
Visits her husband with as chaste a brow
As temperate and confirm'd behaviour,
As she came quitted from confession :
So from his scapes would he present a presence ;
The practice of his state adultery,
And guilt that should a graceful bosom strike
Drown'd in the set lake of a hopeless cheek.

He. It may be he dissembled, or suppose
He be a little tainted : men whom virtue
Forms with the stuff of fortune, great and gracious
Must needs partake with fortune in her humour
Of instability ; and are like to shafts
Grown crook'd with standing, which to rectify
Must twice as much be bow'd another way.

He that hath borne wounds for his worthy parts,
Must for his worst be borne with : we must fit
Our government to men, as men to it :
In old time they that hunted savage beasts
Are said to clothe themselves in savage skins ;
They that were fowlers when they went on fowling,
Wore garments made with wings resembling fowls ;
To bulls we must not show ourselves in red,
Nor to the warlike elephant in white.
In all things govern'd their infirmities
Must not be stirr'd, nor wrought on ; Duke Byron
Flows with adust and melancholy choler,
And melancholy spirits are venomous,
Not to be touch'd, but as they may be cured.
I therefore mean to make him change the air,
And send him further from those Spanish vapours,
That still bear fighting sulphur in their breasts,
To breathe a while in temperate English air,
Where lips are spiced with free and loyal counsels,
Where policies are not ruinous, but saving ;
Wisdom is simple, valour righteous,
Humane, and hating facts of brutish forces ;
And whose grave natures scorn the scoffs of France,
The empty compliments of Italy,
The any-way encroaching pride of Spain,
And love men modest, hearty, just, and plain.

SAVOY, *whispering with* LA FIN.

Sa. I'll sound him for Byron ; and what I find
In the King's depth, I'll draw up, and inform
In excitations to the Duke's revolt,
When next I meet with him.

　　La. It must be done
With praising of the Duke ; from whom the King

Will take to give himself; which told the Duke,
Will take his heart up into all ambition.

  Sa. I know it, politic friend, and 'tis my purpose.

                            [*Exit* LA FIN.

Your Majesty hath miss'd a royal sight:
The Duke Byron, on his brave beast Pastrana,
Who sits him like a full-sail'd argosy,
Danced with a lofty billow, and as snug
Plies to his bearer, both their motions mix'd;
And being consider'd in their site together,
They do the best present the state of man
In his first royalty ruling, and of beasts
In their first loyalty serving; one commanding,
And no way being moved; the other serving,
And no way being compell'd; of all the sights
That ever my eyes witness'd; and they make
A doctrinal and witty hieroglyphic
Of a blest kingdom: to express and teach,
Kings to command as they could serve, and subjects
To serve as if they had power to command.

  He. You are a good old horseman, I perceive,
And still[1] out all the use of that good part;
Your wit is of the true Pierean spring,
That can make anything of anything.

  Sa. So brave a subject as the Duke, no king
Seated on earth can vaunt of but your highness,
So valiant, loyal, and so great in service.

  He. No question he sets valour in his height,
And hath done service to an equal pitch,
Fortune attending him with fit events,
To all his venturous and well-laid attempts.

  Sa. Fortune to him was Juno to Alcides;
For when or where did she but open way

                   [1] Distill.

To any act of his? what stone took he
With her help, or without his own lost blood?
What fort won he by her? or was not forced?
What victory but 'gainst odds? on what commander,
Sleepy or negligent, did he ever charge?
What summer ever made she fair to him?
What winter, not of one continued storm?
Fortune is so far from his creditress
That she owes him much; for in him, her looks
Are lovely, modest, and magnanimous,
Constant, victorious; and in his achievements
Her cheeks are drawn out with a virtuous redness,
Out of his eager spirit to victory,
And chaste contention to convince with honour;
And, I have heard, his spirits have flow'd so high
In all his conflicts against any odds,
That, in his charge, his lips have bled with fervour.
How served he at your famous siege of Dreux?
Where the enemy, assured of victory,
Drew out a body of four thousand horse,
And twice six thousand foot, and like a crescent,
Stood for the signal, you, that show'd yourself
A sound old soldier, thinking it not fit
To give your enemy the odds, and honour
Of the first stroke, commanded de la Guiche
To let fly all his cannons, that did pierce
The adverse thickest squadrons, and had shot
Nine volleys ere the foe had once given fire;
Your troop was charged, and when your duke's old
        father
Met with th'assailants, and their grove of ritters [1]
Repulsed so fiercely, made them turn their beards
And rally up themselves behind their troops;

        [1] Knights.

Fresh forces, seeing your troops a little sever'd
From that part first assaulted, gave it charge,
Which then, this duke made good, seconds his father,
Beats through and through . the enemy's greatest
    strength,
And breaks the rest like billows 'gainst a rock,
And there the heart of that huge battle broke.

    He. The heart but now came on, in that strong
    body
Of twice two thousand horse, led by du Maine;
Which, if I would be glorious,[1] I could say
I first encounter'd.

    Sa. How did he take in,
Beaune in view of that invincible army
Led by the Lord Great Constable of Castile,
Autun and Nuis, in Burgundy, chased away
Viscount Tavannes' troops before Dijon,
And puts himself in, and there that was won.

    He. If you would only give me leave, my lord,
I would do right to him, yet must not give.

    Sa. A league from Fontaine Françoise, when you
    sent him
To make discovery of the Castile army,
When he discern'd 'twas it, with wondrous wisdom
Join'd to his spirit, he seem'd to make retreat,
But when they press'd him, and the Baron of Lux,
Set on their charge so hotly, that his horse
Was slain, and he most dangerously engaged,
Then turn'd your brave duke head, and, with such
    ease
As doth an echo beat back violent sounds
With their own forces, he, as if a wall
Start suddenly before them, pash'd[2] them all

        [1] Boastful.   [2] Crushed.

Flat as the earth, and there was that field won.

He. Y'are all the field wide.

Sa. Oh, I ask you pardon,

The strength of that field yet lay in his back,
Upon the foe's part ; and what is to come
Of this your Marshal, now your worthy duke,
Is much beyond the rest ; for now he sees
A sort of horse troops issue from the woods,
In number near twelve hundred ; and retiring
To tell you that the entire army follow'd,
Before he could relate it, he was forced
To turn head, and receive the main assault
Of five horse troops ; only with twenty horse ;
The first he met, he tumbled to the earth,
And brake through all, not daunted with two wounds,
One on his head, another on his breast,
The blood of which drown'd all the field in doubt ;
Your Majesty himself was then engaged,
Your power not yet arrived, and up you brought
The little strength you had ; a cloud of foes,
Ready to burst in storms about your ears ;
Three squadrons rush'd against you, and the first
You took so fiercely, that you beat their thoughts
Out of their bosoms, from the urged fight ;
The second all amazed [1] you overthrew,
The third dispersed, with five and twenty horse
Left of the fourscore that pursued the chase ;
And this brave conquest, now your marshal seconds
Against two squadrons, but with fifty horse
One after other he defeats them both,
And made them run, like men whose heels were
          tripp'd,
And pitch their heads in their great general's lap ;

          [1] Confused.

And him he sets on, as he had been shot
Out of a cannon; beats him into rout,
And as a little brook being overrun
With a black torrent, that bears all things down,
His fury overtakes, his foamy back,
Loaded with cattle and with stacks of corn,
And makes the miserable plowman mourn;
So was du Maine surcharged, and so Byron
Flow'd over all his forces; every drop
Of his lost blood, bought with a worthy man;
And only with a hundred gentlemen
He won the place from fifteen hundred horse.

 He. He won the place?
 Sa. On my word, so 'tis said.
 He. Fie, you have been extremely misinform'd.
 Sa. I only tell your highness what I heard;
I was not there; and though I have been rude
With wonder of his valour, and presumed
To keep his merit in his full career,
Not hearing you, when yours made such a thunder;
Pardon my fault, since 'twas t'extol your servant.
But is it not most true, that 'twixt ye both,
So few achieved the conquest of so many?
 He. It is a truth must make me ever thankful,
But not perform'd by him; was not I there?
Commanded him, and in the main assault
Made him but second?
 Sa. He's the capital soldier
That lives this day in holy Christendom,
Except your highness, always except Plato.
 He. We must not give to one to take from many:
For (not to praise our countrymen) here served
The general, Mylor Norris, sent from England;
As great a captain as the world affords,

 z

One fit to lead, and fight for Christendom ;
Of more experience, and of stronger brain ;
As valiant for abiding in command,
On any sudden ; upon any ground,
And in the form of all occasions
As ready, and as profitably dauntless ;
And here was then another, Colonel Williams,
A worthy captain ; and more like the duke,
Because he was less temperate than the general ;
And being familiar with the man you praise,
(Because he knew him haughty and incapable
Of all comparison) would compare with him,
And hold his swelling valour to the mark
Justice had set in him, and not his will ;
And as in open vessels fill'd with water,
And on men's shoulders borne, they put treene [1] cups
To keep the wild and slippery element
From washing over ; follow all his sways
And tickle aptness to exceed his bounds,
And at the brim contain him ; so this knight
Swum in Byron, and held him, but to right.
But leave these hot comparisons ; he's mine own,
And than what I possess, I'll more be known.
    Sa. All this shall to the duke ; I fish'd for this.

[*Exeunt.*

[1] Wooden.

ACT THE THIRD

SCENE I

Enter LA FIN, BYRON *following, unseen.*

A. A feigned passion in his hearing now
        (Which he thinks I perceive not), making
                conscience,
        Of the revolt that he hath urged to me,
(Which now he means to prosecute) would sound,
How deep he stands affected with that scruple.
As when the moon hath comforted the night,
And set the world in silver of her light,
The planets, asterisms,[1] and whole state of heaven,
In beams of gold descending; all the winds,
Bound up in caves, charged not to drive abroad
Their cloudy heads; an universal peace
Proclaim'd in silence, of the quiet earth:
Soon as her hot and dry fumes are let loose,
Storms and clouds mixing suddenly put out
The eyes of all those glories; the creation
Turn'd into chaos, and we then desire,
For all our joy of life, the death of sleep:
So when the glories of our lives, men's loves,
Clear consciences, our fames, and loyalties,

[1] Constellations.

That did us worthy comfort, are eclipsed,
Grief and disgrace invade us; and for all
Our night of life besides, our misery craves
Dark earth would ope and hide us in our graves.

   By. How strange is this!

   La. What! did your highness hear?

   By. Both heard and wonder'd that your wit and
      spirit,

And profit in experience of the slaveries
Imposed on us in those mere politic terms
Of love, fame, loyalty, can be carried up
To such a height of ignorant conscience,
Of cowardice, and dissolution,
In all the free-born powers of royal man.
You that have made way through all the guards
Of jealous state; and seen on both your sides
The pikes' points charging heaven to let you pass,
Will you, in flying with a scrupulous wing,
Above those pikes to heavenward, fall on them?
This is like men, that, spirited with wine,
Pass dangerous places safe; and die for fear
With only thought of them, being simply sober;
We must, in passing to our wished ends,
Through things call'd good and bad, be like the air
That evenly interposed betwixt the seas
And the opposed element of fire,
At either toucheth, but partakes with neither;
Is neither hot nor cold, but with a slight
And harmless temper mix'd of both th'extremes

   La. 'Tis shrewd.

   By. There is no truth of any good
To be discern'd on earth: and by conversion,
Nought therefore simply bad: but as the stuff
Prepared for Arras pictures, is no picture

Till it be form'd, and man hath cast the beams
Of his imaginous fancy through it,
In forming ancient kings and conquerors,
As he conceives they look'd and were attired,
Though they were nothing so : so all things here
Have all their price set down, from men's concepts,
Which make all terms and actions good or bad,
And are but pliant and well-colour'd threads
Put into feigned images of truth :
To which, to yield and kneel as truth pure kings,
That pull'd us down with clear truth of their Gospel,
Were superstition to be hiss'd to hell.

   La. Believe it, this is reason.

   By. 'Tis the faith
Of reason and of wisdom.

   La. You persuade,
As if you could create : what man can shun
The searches and compressions of your graces ?

   By. We must have these lures when we hawk for
       friends,
And wind about them like a subtle river,
That, seeming only to run on its course,
Doth search yet as he runs, and still finds out
The easiest parts of entry on the shore ;
Gliding so slyly by, as scarce it touch'd,
Yet still eats something in it : so must those
That have large fields and currents to dispose.
Come, let us join our streams, we must run far,
And have but little time : the Duke of Savoy
Is shortly to be gone, and I must needs
Make you well known to him.

   La. But hath your highness
Some enterprise of value join'd with him ?

   By. With him and greater persons.

La. I will creep
Upon my bosom in your princely service;
Vouchsafe to make me known. I hear there lives not
So kind, so bountiful, and wise a prince
But in your own excepted excellence.

    By. He shall both know and love you: are you
        mine?

    La. I take the honour of it, on my knee,
And hope to quite it with your Majesty.   [*Exeunt.*

    Enter SAVOY, RONCAS, ROCHETTE, BRETON.

    Sa. La Fin is in the right, and will obtain;
He draweth with his weight, and like a plummet
That sways a door, with falling off, pulls after.

    Ron. Thus will La Fin be brought a stranger to you
By him he leads; he conquers that is conquer'd,
That's fought, as hard to win, that sues to be won.

    Sa. But is my painter warn'd to take his picture,
When he shall see me, and present La Fin?

    Roc. He is, my lord, and, as your highness will'd,
All we will press about him, and admire
The royal promise of his rare aspect,
As if he heard not.

    Sa. 'Twill inflame him:
Such tricks the Archduke used t'extol his greatness,
Which compliments though plain men hold absurd,
And a mere remedy for desire of greatness,
Yet great men use them as their state potatoes,[1]
High coolisses,[2] and potions to excite
The lust of their ambition: and this duke
You know is noted in his natural garb
Extremely glorious; who will therefore bring

      [1] The potato was considered a strong provocative.
      [2] Strong broths.

An appetite expecting such a bait :
He comes ; go instantly, and fetch the painter.

Enter BYRON, LA FIN.

By. All honour to your highness.

Sa. 'Tis most true.
All honours flow to me, in you their ocean ;
As welcome, worthiest duke, as if my marquisate
Were circled with you in these amorous arms.

By. I sorrow, sir, I could not bring it with me,
That I might so supply the fruitless compliment
Of only visiting your excellence,
With which the King now sends me t'entertain you ;
Which, notwithstanding, doth confer this good
That it hath given me some small time to show
My gratitude for the many secret bounties
I have, by this your lord ambassador,
Felt from your highness ; and in short, t'assure you,
That all my most deserts are at your service.

Sa. Had the King sent me by you half his kingdom,
It were not half so welcome.

By. For defect
Of whatsoever in myself, my lord,
I here commend to your most princely service
This honour'd friend of mine.

Sa. Your name, I pray you, sir ?

La. La Fin, my lord.

Sa. La Fin ? Is this the man,
That you so recommended to my love ?

Ron. The same, my lord.

Sa. Y'are, next my lord the duke,
The most desired of all men. O my lord,
The King and I have had a mighty conflict
About your conflicts, and your matchless worth

In military virtues; which I put
In balance with the continent of France,
In all the peace and safety it enjoys,
And made even weight with all he could put in
Of all men's else, and of his own deserts.

 By. Of all men's else? would he weigh other men's
With my deservings?

 Sa. Ay, upon my life,
The English General, the Mylor Norris,
That served amongst you here, he parallel'd
With you, at all parts, and in some preferr'd him,
And Colonel Williams, a Welsh Colonel,
He made a man, that at your most contain'd you;
Which the Welsh herald of their praise, the cuckoo,
Would scarce have put, in his monology, [1]
In jest, and said with reverence to his merits.

 By. With reverence? Reverence scorns him: by
  the spoil
Of all her merits in me, he shall rue it.
Did ever Curtian Gulf play such a part?
Had Curtius been so used, if he had brook'd
That ravenous whirlpool, pour'd his solid spirits
Through earth-dissolved sinews, stopp'd her veins,
And rose with saved Rome, upon his back.
As I swum pools of fire, and gulfs of brass,
To save my country, thrust this venturous arm
Beneath her ruins; took her on my neck,
And set her safe on her appeased shore:
And opes the King a fouler bog than this,
In his so rotten bosom, to devour
Him that devour'd what else had swallow'd him
In a detraction, so with spite embrued
And drown such good in such ingratitude?

     [1] Soliloquy.

My spirit as yet, but stooping to his rest,
Shines hotly in him, as the sun in clouds
Purpled and made proud with a peaceful even :
But when I throughly set to him, his cheeks,
Will, like those clouds, forego their colour quite,
And his whole blaze smoke into endless night.

   Sa. Nay, nay, we must have no such gall, my lord,
O'erflow our friendly livers ; my relation
Only delivers my inflamed zeal
To your religious merits ; which methinks
Should make your highness canonized a saint.

   By. What had his armies been, without my arm,
That with his motion made the whole field move ?
And this held up, we still had victory.
When overcharged with number, his few friends,
Retired amazed, I set them on assured,
And what rude ruin seized on I confirm'd ;
When I left leading, all his army reel'd,
One fell on other foul, and as the Cyclop
That having lost his eye, struck every way,
His blows directed to no certain scope :
Or as the soul departed from the body,
The body wants coherence in his parts,
Cannot consist, but sever, and dissolve :
So I removed once, all his armies shook,
Panted, and fainted, and were ever flying,
Like wandering pulses 'spersed through bodies dying.

   Sa. It cannot be denied, 'tis all so true
That what seems arrogance, is desert in you.

   By. What monstrous humours feed a prince's blood,
Being bad to good men, and to bad men good ?

   Sa. Well, let these contradictions pass, my lord,
Till they be reconciled, or put in form,
By power given to your will, and you present

The fashion of a perfect government :
In mean space but a word ; we have small time
To spend in private, which I wish may be
With all advantage taken : Lord La Fin—

   Ron. Is't not a face of excellent presentment ?
Though not so amorous with pure white and red,
Yet is the whole proportion singular.

   Roc. That ever I beheld

   Br. It hath good lines,
And tracts drawn through it ; the purfle,[1] rare.

   Ron. I heard the famous and right learned earl,
And archbishop of Lyons, Pierce Pinac,
Who was reported to have wondrous judgment
In men's events and natures, by their looks,
Upon his death-bed, visited by this duke,
He told his sister, when his grace was gone,
That he had never yet observed a face
Of worse presage than this ; and I will swear
That, something seen in physiognomy,
I do not find in all the rules it gives
One slenderest blemish tending to mishap,
But, on the opposite part, as we may see
On trees late-blossom'd, when all frosts are past,
How they are taken, and what will be fruit :
So on this tree of sceptres, I discern
How it is loaden with appearances,[2]
Rules answering rules ; and glances crown'd with
    glances.   [*He snatches away the picture.*

   By. What! does he take my picture ?

   Sa. Ay, my lord.

   By. Your highness will excuse me ; I will give you
My likeness put in statue, not in picture ;
And by a statuary of mine own,

       [1] Adornment.   [2] Preparations.

That can in brass express the wit of man,
And in his form make all men see his virtues;
Others that with much strictness imitate
The something-stooping carriage of my neck,
The voluble and mild radiance of mine eyes,
Never observe my masculine aspect
And lion-like instinct, it shadoweth;
Which envy cannot say, is flattery;
And I will have my image promised you,
Cut in such matter as shall ever last;
Where it shall stand, fix'd with eternal roots,
And with a most unmoved gravity;
For I will have the famous mountain Oros,
That looks out of the duchy where I govern
Into your highness' dukedom, first made yours,
And then with such inimitable art
Express'd and handled; chiefly from the place
Where most conspicuously he shows his face,
That though it keep the true form of that hill
In all his longitudes and latitudes,
His height, his distances, and full proportion,
Yet shall it clearly bear my counterfeit,
Both in my face and all my lineaments;
And every man shall say, This is Byron.
Within my left hand I will hold a city,
Which is the city Amiens; at whose siege
I served so memorably; from my right,
I'll pour an endless flood into a sea
Raging beneath me; which shall intimate
My ceaseless service, drunk up by the King
As th'ocean drinks up rivers, and makes all
Bear his proud title; ivory, brass, and gold,
That thieves may purchase, and be bought and sold,
Shall not be used about me; lasting worth

Shall only set the Duke of Byron forth.

   Sa. O that your statuary could express you
With any nearness to your own instructions ;
That statue would I prize past all the jewels
Within my cabinet of Beatrice,
The memory of my grandame Portugal.
Most royal duke, we cannot long endure
To be thus private ; let us then conclude
With this great resolution, that your wisdom
Will not forget to pass a pleasing veil
Over your anger, that may hide each glance
Of any notice taken of your wrong,
And show yourself the more obsequious.
'Tis but the virtue of a little patience ;
There are so oft attempts made 'gainst his person,
That sometimes they may speed, for they are plants
That spring the more for cutting, and at last
Will cast their wished shadow : mark ere long.

         Enter NEMOURS, SOISSONS.

See who comes here, my lord, as now no more,
Now must we turn our stream another way :
My lord, I humbly thank his Majesty
That he would grace my idle time spent here
With entertainment of your princely person ;
Which, worthily, he keeps for his own bosom,
My lord the Duke Nemours, and Count Soissons,
Your honours have been bountifully done me
In often visitation : let me pray you
To see some jewels now, and help my choice
In making up a present for the King.

   Ne. Your highness shall much grace us.

   Sa. I am doubtful
That I have much incensed the Duke Byron

With praising the King's worthiness in arms
So much past all men.

    So. He deserves it highly.

                            [*Exit: manet* BYRON, LA FIN.

    By. What wrongs are these, laid on me by the King,
To equal others' worths in war with mine ;
Endure this, and be turn'd into his moil [1]
To bear his sumptures [2] ; honour'd friend, be true,
And we will turn these torrents hence.

                   [*Enter the* King.   *Exit* LA FIN.

Enter HENRY, EPERNON, VITRY, JANIN.

    He. Why suffer you that ill-aboding vermin
To breed so near your bosom ? be assured
His haunts are ominous ; not the throats of ravens
Spent on infected houses, howls of dogs,
When no sound stirs, at midnight ; apparitions
And strokes of spirits, clad in black men's shapes,
Or ugly women's ; the adverse decrees
Of constellations, nor security
In vicious peace, are surer fatal ushers
Of femall [3] mischiefs and mortalities
Than this prodigious fiend is, where he fawns :
Lafiend, and not La Fin, he should be call'd.

    By. Be what he will, men in themselves entire,
March safe with naked feet on coals of fire :
I build not outward, nor depend on props,
Nor choose my consort by the common ear,
Nor by the moonshine, in the grace of kings ;
So rare are true deservers loved or known,
That men loved vulgarly are ever none :
Nor men graced servilely, for being spots

           [1] Drudge.   [2] Burdens.
        [3] Female ; mischief brought on by the Fates.

In princes' trains, though borne even with their crowns;
The stallion power hath such a besom tail
That it sweeps all from justice, and such filth
He bears out in it that men mere exempt
Are merely clearest; men will shortly buy
Friends from the prison or the pillory
Rather than honour's markets.   I fear none
But foul ingratitude and detraction
In all the brood of villany.

    He. No? not treason?

Be circumspect, for to a credulous eye
He comes invisible, veil'd with flattery,
And flatterers look like friends, as wolves like dogs.
And as a glorious poem fronted well
With many a goodly herald of his praise,
So far from hate of praises to his face,
That he prays men to praise him, and they ride
Before, with trumpets in their mouths, proclaiming
Life to the holy fury of his lines;
All drawn, as if with one eye he had leer'd
On his loved hand, and led it by a rule;
That his plumes only imp the muses' wings,
He sleeps with them, his head is napt with bays,
His lips break out with nectar, his tuned feet
Are of the great last, the perpetual motion,
And he puff'd with their empty breath believes
Full merit eased those passions of wind,
Which yet serve but to praise, and cannot merit,
And so his fury in their air expires:
So de La Fin, and such corrupted heralds,
Hired to encourage and to glorify,
May force what breath they will into their cheeks
Fitter to blow up bladders than full men;
Yet may puff men too, with persuasions

That they are gods in worth, and may rise kings
With treading on their noises; yet the worthiest,
From only his own worth receives his spirit,
And right is worthy bound to any merit;
Which right shall you have ever; leave him then,
He follows none but mark'd and wretched men.
And now for England you shall go, my lord,
Our Lord Ambassador to that matchless Queen.
You never had a voyage of such pleasure,
Honour, and worthy objects; there's a Queen
Where nature keeps her state, and state her Court,
Wisdom her study, continence her fort,
Where magnanimity, humanity,
Firmness in counsel and integrity;
Grace to her poorest subjects; majesty
To awe the greatest, have respects divine,
And in her each part, all the virtues shine.

> [*Exit* HEN. *and* SAV. : *manet* BYRON.

By. Enjoy your will awhile, I may have mine.
Wherefore, before I part to this ambassage,
I'll be resolved [1] by a magician
That dwells hereby, to whom I'll go disguised,
And show him my birth's figure, set before
By one of his profession, of the which
I'll crave his judgment, feigning I am sent
From some great personage, whose nativity
He wisheth should be censured [2] by his skill:
But on go my plots, be it good or ill. [*Exit.*

Enter LA BROSSE.

La. This hour by all rules of astrology
Is dangerous to my person, if not deadly.
How hapless is our knowledge to foretell,

---

[1] Informed.   [2] Judged.

And not be able to prevent a mischief.
O the strange difference 'twixt us and the stars ;
They work with inclinations strong and fatal
And nothing know ; and we know all their working
And nought can do, or nothing can prevent.
Rude ignorance is beastly, knowledge wretched,
The heavenly powers envy what they enjoin ;
We are commanded t'imitate their natures,
In making all our ends eternity ;
And in that imitation we are plagued,
And worse than they esteem'd that have no souls
But in their nostrils, and like beasts expire ;
As they do that are ignorant of arts,
By drowning their eternal parts in sense
And sensual affections : while we live
Our good parts take away, the more they give.

BYRON *solus, disguised like a carrier of letters.*

By. The forts that favourites hold in princes' hearts,
In common subjects' loves, and their own strengths
Are not so sure and unexpugnable
But that the more they are presumed upon,
The more they fail ; daily and hourly proof
Tells us prosperity is at highest degree
The fount and handle of calamity :
Like dust before a whirlwind those men fly
That prostrate on the grounds of fortune lie ;
And being great, like trees that broadest sprout,
Their own top-heavy state grubs up their root.
These apprehensions startle all my powers,
And arm them with suspicion 'gainst themselves.
In my late projects, I have cast myself
Into the arms of others, and will see
If they will let me fall, or toss me up

Into th'affected compass of a throne.
God save you, sir.

    La. Y'are welcome, friend : what would you ?

    By. I would entreat you, for some crowns I bring,
To give your judgment of this figure cast,
To know, by his nativity there seen,
What sort of end the person shall endure,
Who sent me to you, and whose birth it is.

    La. I'll herein do my best in your desire ;
The man is raised out of a good descent,
And nothing older than yourself, I think ;
Is it not you ?

    By. I will not tell you that :
But tell me on what end he shall arrive.

    La. My son, I see that he whose end is cast
In this set figure, is of noble parts,
And by his military valour raised
To princely honours, and may be a king ;
But that I see a *caput algol* here,
That hinders it, I fear.

    By. A *caput algol* ?
What's that, I pray ?

    La. Forbear to ask me, son ;
You bid me speak what fear bids me conceal.

    By. You have no cause to fear, and therefore speak.

    La. You'll rather wish you had been ignorant,
Than be instructed in a thing so ill.

    By. Ignorance is an idle salve for ill ;
And therefore do not urge me to enforce
What I would freely know ; for by the skill
Shown in thy aged hairs, I'll lay thy brain
Here scatter'd at my feet, and seek in that
What safely thou may'st utter with thy tongue,
If thou deny it.

2 A

La. Will you not allow me
To hold my peace ?   What less can I desire ?
If not, be pleased with my constrained speech.

By. Was ever man yet punish'd for expressing
What he was charged ?   Be free, and speak the worst.

La. Then briefly this : the man hath lately done
An action that will make him lose his head.

By. Cursed be thy throat and soul, raven, screech-
        owl, hag !

La. Oh, hold ; for heaven's sake, hold !

By. Hold on, I will.
Vault, and contractor of all horrid sounds,
Trumpet of all the miseries in hell,
Of my confusions ; of the shameful end
Of all my services ; witch, fiend, accursed
For ever be the poison of thy tongue,
And let the black fume of thy venom'd breath
Infect the air, shrink heaven, put out the stars,
And rain so fell and blue a plague on earth,
That all the world may falter with my fall.

La. Pity my age, my lord.

By. Out, prodigy,
Remedy of pity, mine of flint,
Whence with my nails and feet I'll dig enough
Horror and savage cruelty to build
Temples to massacre : dam of devils take thee !
Hadst thou no better end to crown my parts ?
The bulls of Colchos, nor his triple neck,
That howls out earthquakes : the most mortal vapours
That ever stifled and struck dead the fowls,
That flew at never such a sightly pitch,
Could not have burnt my blood so.

La. I told truth ;
And could have flatter'd you.

By. O that thou hadst !
Would I had given thee twenty thousand crowns
That thou hadst flatter'd me ; there's no joy on earth,
Never so rational, so pure, and holy,
But is a jester, parasite, a whore
In the most worthy parts, with which they please
A drunkenness of soul and a disease.

    La. I knew you not.

    By. Peace, dog of Pluto, peace,
Thou knew'st my end to come, not me here present :
Pox of your halting humane knowledges ;
O death ! how far off hast thou kill'd ! how soon
A man may know too much, though never nothing.
Spite of the stars, and all astrology,
I will not lose my head ; or if I do
A hundred thousand heads shall off before.
I am a nobler substance than the stars,
And shall the baser overrule the better ?
Or are they better, since they are the bigger ?
I have a will, and faculties of choice,
To do, or not to do : and reason why,
I do, or not do this ; the stars have none.
They know not why they shine more than this taper,
Nor how they work, nor what ; I'll change my course.
I'll piece-meal pull the frame of all my thoughts,
And cast my will into another mould :
And where are all your *Caput Algols* then ?
Your planets all, being underneath the earth
At my nativity : what can they do ?
Malignant in aspects ? in bloody houses ?
Wild fire consume them ! one poor cup of wine,
More than I use, that my weak brain will bear,
Shall make them drunk and reel out of their spheres
For any certain act they can enforce.

O that mine arms were wings, that I might fly,
And pluck out of their hearts my destiny !
I'll wear those golden spurs upon my heels,
And kick at fate ; be free, all worthy spirits,
And stretch yourselves, for greatness and for height :
Untruss your slaveries : you have height enough
Beneath this steep heaven to use all your reaches ;
'Tis too far off to let [1] you or respect you.
Give me a spirit that on this life's rough sea
Love's t'have his sails fill'd with a lusty wind,
Even till his sail-yards tremble, his masts crack,
And his rapt ship run on her side so low
That she drinks water, and her keel plows air.
There is no danger to a man that knows
What life and death is ; there's not any law
Exceeds his knowledge ; neither is it lawful
That he should stoop to any other law.
He goes before them, and commands them all,
That to himself is a law rational.   [*Exit.*

[1] Hinder.

ACT THE FOURTH

SCENE I

Enter D'AUMONT, *with* CREQUIE.

D'AU. The Duke of Byron is return'd from
England,
 And, as they say, was princely entertain'd,
 School'd by the matchless queen there,
who, I hear,
Spake most divinely; and would gladly hear
Her speech reported.
 Cr. I can serve your turn,
As one that speaks from others, not from her,
And thus it is reported at his parting.
" Thus, Monsieur Du Byron, you have beheld
Our Court proportion'd to our little kingdom
In every entertainment; yet our mind,
To do you all the rites of your repair,
Is as unbounded as the ample air.
What idle pains have you bestow'd to see
A poor old woman; who in nothing lives
More than in true affections borne your king,
And in the perfect knowledge she hath learn'd
Of his good knights, and servants of your sort.

373

We thank him that he keeps the memory
Of us and all our kindness ; but must say
That it is only kept, and not laid out
To such affectionate profit as we wish ;
Being so much set on fire with his deserts
That they consume us ; not to be restored
By your presentment of him, but his person :
And we had thought that he whose virtues fly
So beyond wonder and the reach of thought,
Should check at eight hours' sail, and his high spirit
That stoops to fear, less than the poles of heaven,
Should doubt an under-billow of the sea,
And, being a sea, be sparing of his streams :
And I must blame all you that may advise him ;
That, having helped him through all martial dangers,
You let him stick at the kind rites of peace,
Considering all the forces I have sent,
To set his martial seas up in firm walls,
On both his sides for him to pass at pleasure ;
Did plainly open him a guarded way
And led in Nature to this friendly shore.
But here is nothing worth his personal sight,
Here are no walled cities ; for that crystal
Sheds with his light, his hardness, and his height,
About our thankful person and our realm ;
Whose only aid we ever yet desired ;
And now I see the help we sent to him,
Which should have swum to him in our own blood,
Had it been needful (our affections
Being more given to his blood than he himself),
Ends in the actual right it did his state,
And ours is slighted ; all our worth is made
The common stock and bank ; from whence are served
All men's occasions ; yet, thanks to heaven,

Their gratitudes are drawn dry, not our bounties.
And you shall tell your King that he neglects
Old friends for new, and sets his soothed ease
Above his honour; marshals' policy
In rank before his justice; and his profit
Before his royalty; his humanity gone,
To make me no repayment of mine own."

   D'A. What answered the duke?

   Cr. In this sort.

" Your highness' sweet speech hath no sharper end
Than he would wish his life, if he neglected
The least grace you have named; but to his wish
Much power is wanting: the green roots of war
Not yet so close cut up, but he may dash
Against their relics to his utter ruin,
Without more near eyes, fix'd upon his feet,
Than those that look out of his country's soil.
And this may well excuse his personal presence,
Which yet he oft hath long'd to set by yours;
That he might imitate the majesty
Which so long peace hath practised, and made full,
In your admired appearance; to illustrate
And rectify his habit in rude war.
And his will to be here must needs be great,
Since heaven hath throned so true a royalty here,
That he thinks no king absolutely crowned
Whose temples have not stood beneath this sky,
And whose height is not harden'd with these stars,
Whose influences for this altitude,
Distill'd, and wrought in with this temperate air
And this division of the element,
Have with your reign brought forth more worthy
    spirits
For counsel, valour, height of wit, and art,

Than any other region of the earth,
Or were brought forth to all your ancestors.
And as a cunning orator reserves
His fairest similes, best adorning figures,
Chief matter, and most moving arguments
For his conclusion; and doth then supply
His ground-streams laid before, glides over them,
Makes his full depth seen through; and so takes up
His audience in applauses past the clouds.
So in your government, conclusive nature
(Willing to end her excellence in earth
When your foot shall be set upon the stars)
Shows all her sovereign beauties, ornaments,
Virtues, and raptures; overtakes her works
In former empires, makes them but your foils,
Swells to her full sea, and again doth drown
The world in admiration of your crown."

D'A. He did her, at all parts, confessed right.

Cr. She took it yet but as a part of courtship,
And said "he was the subtle orator
To whom he did too gloriously resemble
Nature in her, and in her government."
He said "he was no orator, but a soldier,
More than this air in which you breathe hath made me,
My studious love of your rare government
And simple truth, which is most eloquent.
Your empire is so amply absolute
That even your theatres show more comely rule,
True noblesse, royalty, and happiness
Than others' courts: you make all state before
Utterly obsolete; all to come, twice sod.
And therefore doth my royal sovereign wish
Your years may prove as vital as your virtues,
That (standing on his turrets this way turn'd,

Ordering and fixing his affairs by yours)
He may at last, on firm grounds, pass your seas,
And see that maiden-sea of majesty,
In whose chaste arms so many kingdoms lie."

   D'A. When came she to her touch of his ambition?

   Cr. In this speech following, which I thus re-
       member:

"If I hold any merit worth his presence,
Or any part of that your courtship gives me,
My subjects have bestow'd it; some in counsel,
In action some, and in obedience all;
For none knows with such proof as you, my lord,
How much a subject may renown his prince,
And how much princes of their subjects hold.
In all the services that ever subject
Did for his sovereign, he that best deserved
Must, in comparison, except Byron;
And to win this prize clear, without the maims
Commonly given men by ambition,
When all their parts lie open to his view,
Shows continence, past their other excellence;
But for a subject to affect a kingdom,
Is like the camel that of Jove begg'd horns.
And such mad-hungry men as well may eat
Hot coals of fire to feed their natural heat,
For, to aspire to competence with your King,
What subject is so gross and giantly?
He having now a dauphin born to him,
Whose birth, ten days before, was dreadfully
Usher'd with earthquakes in most parts of Europe;
And that gives all men cause enough to fear
All thought of competition with him.
Commend us, good my lord, and tell our brother
How much we joy in that his royal issue,

And in what prayers we raise our heart to heaven,
That in more terror to his foes, and wonder
He may drink earthquakes, and devour the thunder.
So we admire your valour and your virtues,
And ever will contend to win their honour."
Then spake she to Crequie, and Prince D'Auvergne,
And gave all gracious farewells ; when Byron
Was thus encounter'd by a councillor
Of great and eminent name and matchless merit :
" I think, my lord, your princely Dauphin bears
Arion on his cradle through your kingdom,
In the sweet music joy strikes from his birth.
He answer'd : " And good right ; the cause commands
    it."
"But," said the other, " had we a fifth Henry
To claim his old right, and one man to friend,
Whom you well know, my lord, that for his friend-
    ship
Were promised the vice-royalty of France,
We would not doubt of conquest, in despite
Of all those windy earthquakes."   He replied :
" Treason was never guide to English conquests,
And therefore that doubt shall not fright our Dauphin ;
Nor would I be the friend to such a foe
For all the royalties in Christendom."
" Fix there your foot," said he, " I only give
False fire, and would be loth to shoot you off :
He that wins empire with the loss of faith
Out-buys it, and will bank-rout ; you have laid
A brave foundation, by the hand of virtue,
Put not the roof to fortune : foolish statuaries,
That under little saints suppose great bases
Make less to sense the saints ; and so, where Fortune
Advanceth vile minds to states great and noble,

She much the more exposeth them to shame,
Not able to make good and fill their bases
With a conformed structure : I have found
(Thanks to the Blesser of my search), that counsels
Held to the line of justice still produce
The surest states and greatest, being sure ;
Without which fit assurance, in the greatest,
As you may see a mighty promontory
More digg'd and under-eaten than may warrant
A safe supportance to his hanging brows ;
All passengers avoid him, shun all ground
That lies within his shadow, and bear still
A flying eye upon him : so great men,
Corrupted in their ground, and building out
Too swelling fronts for their foundations ;
When most they should be propt are most forsaken ;
And men will rather thrust into the storms
Of better-grounded states than take a shelter
Beneath their ruinous and fearful weight ;
Yet they so oversee their faulty bases,
That they remain securer in conceit :
And that security doth worse presage
Their near destruction than their eaten grounds ;
And therefore heaven itself is made to us
A perfect hieroglyphic to express
The idleness of such security,
And the grave labour of a wise distrust,
In both sorts of the all-inclining stars,
Where all men note this difference in their shining,
As plain as they distinguish either hand ;
The fix'd stars waver, and the erring stand."
    D'A. How took he this so worthy admonition?
    Cr. "Gravely applied," said he, "and like the
        man,

Whom all the world says overrules the stars ;
Which are divine books to us ; and are read
By understanders only, the true objects
And chief companions of the truest men ;
And, though I need it not, I thank your counsel,
That never yet was idle, but, spherelike,
Still moves about, and is the continent
To this blest isle."

ACT THE FIFTH

SCENE I

Enter Byron, D'Auvergne, La Fin.

BY. The circle of this ambassy is closed,
    For which I long have long'd, for mine
      own ends;
    To see my faithful, and leave courtly
      friends,
To whom I came, methought, with such a spirit
As you have seen a lusty courser show,
That hath been long time at his manger tied;
High fed, alone, and when, his headstall broken,
He runs his prison, like a trumpet neighs,
Cuts air in high curvets, and shakes his head,
With wanton stoppings 'twixt his forelegs, mocking
The heavy centre; spreads his flying crest,
Like to an ensign hedge and ditches leaping,
Till in the fresh meat, at his natural food,
He sees free fellows, and hath met them free.
And now, good friend, I would be fain inform'd
What our right princely lord, the Duke of Savoy
Hath thought on, to employ my coming home.
   La. To try the king's trust in you, and withal
How hot he trails on our conspiracy,
He first would have you beg the government

Of the important citadel of Bourg;
Or to place in it any you shall name;
Which will be wondrous fit to march before
His other purposes; and is a fort
He rates in love above his patrimony;
To make which fortress worthy of your suit,
He vows, if you obtain it, to bestow
His third fair daughter on your excellence,
And hopes the king will not deny [1] it you.

 By. Deny it me? deny me such a suit?
Who will he grant it, he deny it me?

 La. He'll find some politic shift to do't, I fear.

 By. What shift, or what evasion can he find?
What one patch is there in all policy's shop,
The botcher-up of kingdoms, that can mend
The brack [2] betwixt us, any way denying?

 D'A. That's at your peril.

 By. Come, he dares not do't.

 D'A. Dares not? presume not so; you know, good
  duke,
That all things he thinks fit to do, he dares.

 By. By heaven, I wonder at you; I will ask it,
As sternly, and secure of all repulse,
As th'ancient Persians did when they implored
Their idol fire to grant them any boon;
With which they would descend into a flood,
And threaten there to quench it, if they fail'd
Of that they ask'd it.

 La. Said like your king's king;
Cold hath no act in depth, nor are suits wrought,
Of any high price, that are coldly sought;
I'll haste, and with your courage comfort Savoy.

         [*Exit* LA FIN.

---

   [1] Refuse.   [2] Breach.

D'A. I am your friend, my lord, and will deserve
That name, with following any course you take ;
Yet, for your own sake, I could wish your spirit
Would let you spare all broad terms of the King ;
Or, on my life, you will at last repent it.

 By. What can he do?

 D'A. All that you cannot fear.

 By. You fear too much ; be by, when next I see him,
And see how I will urge him in this suit ;
He comes : mark you, that think he will not grant it.

   Enter HENRY, EPERNON, SOISSONS, JANIN.

I am become a suitor to your highness.

 He. For what, my lord, 'tis like you shall obtain.

 By. I do not much doubt that ; my services,
I hope, have more strength in your good conceit [1]
Than to receive repulse in such requests.

 He. What is it?

 By. That you would bestow on one whom I shall
   name
The keeping of the Citadel of Bourg.

 He. Excuse me, sir, I must not grant you that.

 By. Not grant me that?

 He. It is not fit I should :
You are my governor in Burgundy,
And province governors, that command in chief,
Ought not to have the charge of fortresses ;
Besides, it is the chief key of my kingdom.
That opens towards Italy, and must therefore
Be given to one that hath immediately
Dependence on us.

 By. These are wondrous reasons :
Is not a man depending on his merits

     [1] Opinion.

As fit to have the charge of such a key
As one that merely hangs upon your humours?

He. Do not enforce your merits so yourself ;
It takes away their lustre and reward.

By. But you will grant my suit ?

He. I swear I cannot,
Keeping the credit of my brain and place.

By. Will you deny me, then ?

He. I am enforced :
I have no power, more than yourself, in things
That are beyond my reason.

By. Than myself?
That's a strange slight in your comparison ;
Am I become th'example of such men
As have least power ?   Such a diminutive?
I was comparative in the better sort ;
And such a King as you would say, I cannot
Do such or such a thing, were I as great
In power as he ; even that indefinite " he "
Express'd me full : this moon is strangely changed.

He. How can I help it ?   Would you have a king
That hath a white beard have so green a brain ?

By. A plague of brain ! what doth this touch your
        brain ?
You must give me more reason, or I swear——

He. Swear ? what do you swear ?

By. I swear you wrong me,
And deal not like a king, to jest and slight
A man that you should curiously reward ;
Tell me of your grey beard ?   It is not grey
With care to recompense me, who eased your care.

He. You have been recompensed, from head to foot.

By. With a distrusted dukedom ?   Take your duke-
        dom

Bestow'd on me again; it was not given
For any love; but fear and force of shame.

He. Yet 'twas your honour; which, if you respect not,
Why seek you this addition?

By. Since this honour
Would show you loved me too, in trusting me,
Without which love and trust honour is shame;
A very pageant and a property:
Honour, with all its adjuncts, I deserve,
And you quit my deserts with your grey beard.

He. Since you expostulate the matter so,
I tell you plain, another reason is
Why I am moved to make you this denial,[1]
That I suspect you to have had intelligence
With my vow'd enemies.

By. Misery of virtue,
Ill is make good with worse! This reason pours
Poison for balm into the wound you made;
You make me mad, and rob me of my soul,
To take away my tried love and my truth.
Which of my labours, which of all my wounds,
Which overthrow, which battle won for you,
Breeds this suspicion? Can the blood of faith,
Lost in all these to find it proof and strength,
Beget disloyalty? All my rain is fall'n
Into the horse-fair,[2] springing pools and mire,
And not in thankful grounds or fields of fruit;
Fall then before us, O thou flaming crystal,
That art the uncorrupted register
Of all men's merits, and remonstrate here
The fights, the dangers, the affrights and horrors,
Whence I have rescued this unthankful King:

[1] Refusal.

[2] Place where horses were sold; naturally dirty.

2 B

And show, commix'd with them, the joys, the glories
Of his state then ; then his kind thoughts of me,
Then my deservings, now my infamy ;
But I will be mine own king ; I will see
That all your chronicles be fill'd with me,
That none but I, and my renowned sire,
Be said to win the memorable fields
Of Arques and Dieppe ; and none but we of all
Kept you from dying there in an hospital ;
None but myself, that won the day at Dreux ;
A day of holy name, and needs no night ;
Nor none but I at Fontaine Françoise burst
The heart-strings of the leaguers ; I alone
Took Amiens in these arms, and held her fast
In spite of all the pitchy fires she cast,
And clouds of bullets pour'd upon my breast,
Till she show'd yours, and took her natural form ;
Only myself (married to victory)
Did people Artois, Douay, Picardy,
Bethune and Saint Paul, Bapaûme and Courcelles,
With her triumphant issue.
 He. Ha, ha, ha !   [*Exit.*
  [BYRON *drawing, and is held by* D'AUVERGNE.
D'A. O hold, my lord ; for my sake, mighty spirit !
            [*Exeunt.*

  Enter BYRON, D'AUVERGNE *following, unseen.*

 By. Respect, revenge, slaughter, repay for aughter.
What's grave in earth, what awful, what abhorr'd,
If my rage be ridiculous ?   I will make it
The law and rule of all things serious.
So long as idle and ridiculous kings
Are suffer'd, soothed, and wrest all right to safety,
So long is mischief gathering massacres

For their cursed kingdoms, which I will prevent.
Laughter? I'll fright it from him, far as he
Hath cast irrevocable shame; which ever
Being found is lost, and lost returneth never;
Should kings cast off their bounties with their dangers?
He that can warm at fires where virtue burns,
Hunt pleasure through her torments, nothing feel
Of all his subjects suffer; but, long hid
In wants and miseries, and having past
Through all the gravest shapes of worth and honour,
For all heroic fashions to be learn'd
By those hard lessons, show an antique vizard,
Who would not wish him rather hew'd to nothing
Than left so monstrous? Slight my services?
Drown the dead noises of my sword in laughter?
My blows as but the passages of shadows,
Over the highest and most barren hills,
And use me like no man; but as he took me
Into a desert, gash'd with all my wounds,
Sustain'd for him, and buried me in flies;
Forth, vengeance, then, and open wounds in him
Shall let in Spain and Savoy.

        [*Offers to draw and* D'Au. *again holds him.*

D'A. O my lord,
This is too large a licence given your fury;
Give time to it; what reason suddenly
Cannot extend respite doth oft supply.

  By. While respite holds revenge the wrong doubles,
And so the shame of sufferance; it torments me
To think what I endure at his shrunk hands,
That scorns the gift of one poor fort to me,
That have subdued for him (O injury!)
Forts, cities, countries, ay, and yet my fury.   [*Exeunt.*[1]

       [1] As they are going out Henry reappears.

He. Byron?

D'A. My lord, the King calls.

He. Turn, I pray ;
How now ? from whence flow these distracted faces?
From what attempt return they, as disclaiming
Their late heroic bearer ? what, a pistol ?
Why, good my lord, can mirth make you so wrathful ?

By. Mirth ? 'twas a mockery, a contempt, a scandal
To my renown for ever ; a repulse
As miserably cold as Stygian water,
That from sincere earth issues, and doth break
The strongest vessels, not to be contain'd
But in the tough hoof of a patient ass.

He. My lord, your judgment is not competent ;
In this dissension I may say of you
As fame says of the ancient Eleans,
That in th'Olympian contentions,
That ever were the justest arbitrators,
If none of them contended, nor were parties.
Those that will moderate[1] disputations well,
Must not themselves affect the coronet ;
For as the air contain'd within our ears,
If it be not in quiet, nor refrains,
Troubling our hearing with offensive sounds :
But our affected instrument of hearing,
Replete with noise, and singings in itself,
It faithfully receives no other voices ;
So, of all judgments, if within themselves
They suffer spleen, and are tumultuous ;
They cannot equal differences without them ;
And this wind, that doth sing so in your ears,
I know is no disease bred in yourself,
But whisper'd in by others ; who is swelling

------
[1] Judge.

Your veins with empty hope of much, yet able
To perform nothing; are like shallow streams
That make themselves so many heavens to sight;
Since you may see in them, the moon and stars,
The blue space of the air; as far from us,
To our weak senses, in those shallow streams,
As if they were as deep as heaven is high;
Yet with your middle finger only sound them,
And you shall pierce them to the very earth;
And therefore leave them, and be true to me,
Or you'll be left by all; or be like one
That in cold nights will needs have all the fire,
And there is held by others, and embraced
Only to burn him; your fire will be inward,
Which not another deluge can put out.

                [BYRON *kneels while the* King *goes on.*

O innocence, the sacred amulet
'Gainst all the poisons of infirmity;
Of all misfortune, injury, and death,
That makes a man in tune still in himself;
Free from the hell to be his own accuser,
Ever in quiet, endless joy enjoying;
No strife nor no sedition in his powers;
No motion in his will against his reason,
No thought 'gainst thought, nor (as 'twere in the con-
      fines
Of wishing and repenting) doth possess
Only a wayward and tumultuous peace,
But (all parts in him, friendly and secure,
Fruitful of all best things in all worst seasons)
He can with every wish be in their plenty;
When the infectious guilt of one foul crime
Destroys the free content of all our time.

  By. 'Tis all acknowledged, and, though all too late,

Here the short madness of my anger ends:
If ever I did good I lock'd it safe
In you, th'impregnable defence of goodness;
If ill, I press it with my penitent knees
To that unsounded depth whence nought returneth.

He. 'Tis music to mine ears; rise then, for ever
Quit of what guilt soever till this hour,
And nothing touch'd in honour or in spirit,
Rise without flattery, rise by absolute merit.

Enter EPERNON *to the* King, BYRON, &c.
Enter SAVOY *with three* Ladies.

Ep. Sir, if it please you to be taught any courtship, take you to your stand; Savoy is at it with three mistresses at once; he loves each of them best, yet all differently.

He. For the time he hath been here, he hath talked a volume greater than the Turk's Alcaron; stand up close; his lips go still.

Sa. Excuse me, excuse me; the King has ye all.

1st. True sir, in honourable subjection.

2nd. To the which we are bound by our loyalty.

Sa. Nay, your excuse, your excuse, intend me for affection; you are all bearers of his favours, and deny him not your opposition by night.

3rd. You say rightly in that; for therein we oppose us to his command.

1st. In the which he never yet pressed us.

2nd. Such is the benediction of our peace.

Sa. You take me still in flat misconstruction, and conceive not by me.

1st. Therein we are strong in our own purposes; for it were something scandalous for us to conceive by you.

2nd. Though there might be question made of
your fruitfulness, yet dry weather in harvest does no
harm.

He. They will talk him into Savoy; he begins to
hunt down.

Sa. As the King is, and hath been, a most admired,
and most unmatchable soldier, so hath he been, and is,
a sole excellent, and unparalleled courtier.

He. Pauvre amy mercy.

1st. Your highness does the King but right, sir.

2nd. And heaven shall bless you for that justice,
with plentiful store of want in ladies' affections.

Sa. You are cruel, and will not vouchsafe me audience to any conclusion.

1st. Beseech your grace conclude, that we may present
our curtsies to you, and give you the adieu.

Sa. It is said the King will bring an army into
Savoy.

2nd. Truly we are not of his council of war.

Sa. Nay, but vouchsafe me.

3rd. Vouchsafe him, vouchsafe him, else there is no
play in't.

1st. Well, I vouchsafe your grace.

Sa. Let the King bring an army into Savoy, and
I'll find him sport for forty years.

He. Would I were sure of that, I should then have
a long age, and a merry.

1st. I think your grace would play with his army at
balloon.

2nd. My faith, and that's a martial recreation.

3rd. It is next to impious courting.

Sa. I am not he that can set my squadrons over-
night, by midnight leap my horse, curry seven miles,
and by three leap my mistress, return to mine army

again, and direct as I were infatigable ; I am no such tough soldier.

   1st. Your disparity is believed, sir.

   2nd. And 'tis a piece of virtue to tell true.

   3rd. God's me, the King !

   Sa. Well, I have said nothing that may offend.

   1st. 'Tis hoped so.

   2nd. If there be any mercy in laughter.

   Sa. I'll take my leave.

After the tedious stay my love hath made,
Most worthy to command our earthly zeal,
I come for pardon, and to take my leave ;
Affirming, though I reap no other good
By this my voyage, but t'have seen a prince
Of greatness in all grace so past report,
I nothing should repent me ; and to show
Some token of my gratitude, I have sent
Into my treasury the greatest jewels
In all my cabinet of Beatrice,
And of my late deceased wife, th'Infanta,
Which are two basins and their ewers of crystals,
Never yet valued [1] for their workmanship,
Nor the exceeding riches of their matter.
And to your stable, worthy Duke of Byron,
I have sent in two of my fairest horses.

   By. Sent me your horses ! upon what desert ?
I entertain no presents but for merits
Which I am far from at your highness' hands,
As being of all men to you the most stranger ;
There is as ample bounty in refusing
As in bestowing ; and with this I quit you.

   Sa. Then have I lost nought but my poor good-will.

---

[1] They are too costly to be priced.

He. Well, cousin, I with all thanks welcome that,
And the rich arguments with which you prove it,
Wishing I could to your wish welcome you.
Draw, for your Marquisate, the articles
Agreed on in our composition,
And it is yours; but where you have proposed
(In your advices) my design for Milan,
I will have no war with the King of Spain
Unless his hopes prove weary of our peace;
And, princely cousin, it is far from me
To think your wisdom needful of my counsel,
Yet love oft-times must offer things unneedful;
And therefore I would counsel you to hold
All good terms with his Majesty of Spain:
If any troubles should be stirr'd betwixt you,
I would not stir therein, but to appease them;
I have too much care of my royal word
To break a peace so just and consequent,
Without force of precedent injury;
Endless desires are worthless of just princes,
And only proper to the swinge of tyrants.

Sa. And all parts spoke like the Most Christian King.
I take my humblest leave, and pray your highness
To hold me as your servant and poor kinsman,
Who wisheth no supremer happiness
Than to be yours. To you, right worthy princess,
I wish for all your favours pour'd on me
The love of all these ladies mutually,
And, so they please their lords, that they may please
Themselves by all means. And be you assured,
Most lovely princesses, as if your lives,
You cannot be true women if true wives. [*Exit.*

He. Is this he, Epernon, that you would needs persuade us courted so absurdly?

Ep. This is even he, sir, howsoever he hath studied his parting courtship.

He. In what one point seemed he so ridiculous as you would present [1] him?

Ep. Behold me, sir, I beseech you behold me ; I appear to you as the great Duke of Savoy with these three ladies.

He. Well, sir, we grant your resemblance.

Ep. He stole a carriage, sir, from Count d'Auvergne here.

D'A. From me, sir?

Ep. Excuse me, sir, from you, I assure you : here, sir, he lies at the Lady Antoinette, just thus, for the world, in the true posture of Count d'Auvergne.

D'A. Y'are exceeding delightsome.

He. Why, is not that well? it came in with the organ hose.

Ep. Organ hose? a pox on't! let it pipe itself into contempt ; he hath stolen it most feloniously, and it graces him like a disease.

He. I think he stole it from D'Auvergne indeed.

Ep. Well, would he have robbed him of all his other diseases, he were then the soundest lord in France.

D'A. As I am, sir, I shall stand all weathers with you.

Ep. But, sir, he hath praised you above th'invention of rhymers.

He. Wherein? or how?

Ep. He took upon him to describe your victories in war, and where he should have said, you were the most absolute soldier in Christendom (no ass could have missed it), he delivered you for as pretty a fellow of your hands as any was in France.

---

[1] Represent.

He. Marry, God dild [1] him!

Ep. A pox on him!

He. Well, to be serious, you know him well
To be a gallant courtier : his great wit
Can turn him into any form he lists,
More fit to be avoided than deluded.
For my Lord Duke of Byron here well knows
That it infecteth, where it doth affect ;
And where it seems to counsel, it conspires.
With him go all our faults, and from us fly,
With all his counsel, all conspiracy.

[1] God yield him, *i.e.*, God reward him.

THE TRAGEDY OF CHARLES,
DUKE OF BYRON

DRAMATIS PERSONÆ [1]

HENRY IV., King of France.
DAUPHIN.
DUKE BYRON.
D'AUVERGNE.
Lord Ambassador of Spain.
EPERNON.
D'ESCURES.
JANIN.
SOISSONS.
VITRY.
PRÂLIN.
BRUN, a Captain.
MONTIGNY.
VARENNES.
VIDAME.
Chancellor.
Archbishop.
HARLEY, ⎫
POTIER, ⎬ Judges.
FLEURY, ⎭
LA FIN.
Captain of Guard.
Messenger.
Hangman.
Bishops, Ushers, Soldiers, Guards, &c.

QUEEN MARIE.
Mademoiselle D'ENTRAGUES, the King's Mistress.
Ladies.
Nurse.

Cupid, in the Mask.

[1] Now first printed.

THE TRAGEDY OF CHARLES, DUKE OF BYRON

ACT THE FIRST

SCENE I

Enter HENRY, VIDAME, D'ESCURES, EPERNON, JANIN.

E. Byron fall'n in so traitorous a relapse,
Alleged for our ingratitude; what offices,
Titles of honour, and what admiration
Could France afford him that it pour'd not
on?
When he was scarce arrived at forty years,
He ran through all chief dignities of France.
At fourteen years of age he was made Colonel
To all the Suisses serving then in Flanders;
Soon after he was Marshal of the camp,
And shortly after, Marshal General:
He was received High Admiral of France
In that our Parliament we held at Tours;
Marshal of France in that we held at Paris.

And at the siege of Amiens he acknowledged
None his superior but ourself, the King :
Though I had there the Princes of the blood,
I made him my Lieutenant-General,
Declared him jointly the prime Peer of France,
And raised his barony into a duchy.

 Ja. And yet, my lord, all this could not allay
The fatal thirst of his ambition ;
For some have heard him say he would not die
Till on the wings of valour he had reach'd
One degree higher ; and had seen his head
Set on the royal quarter of a crown :
Yea, at so unbelieved a pitch he aim'd
That he hath said his heart would still complain
Till he aspired the style of Sovereign.
And from what ground, my lord, rise all the levies
Now made in Italy ? from whence should spring
The warlike humour of the Count Fuentes ?
The restless stirrings of the Duke of Savoy ?
The discontent the Spaniard entertain'd,
With such a threatening fury, when he heard
The prejudicial conditions
Proposed him, in the treaty held at Vervins ?
And many other braveries [1] this way aiming,
But from some hope of inward aid from hence ?
And that all this directly aims at you,
Your highness hath by one intelligence [2]
Good cause to think ; which is your late advice,
That the sea army, now prepared at Naples,
Hath an intended enterprise on Provence ;
Although the cunning Spaniard gives it out
That all is for Algiers.

 He. I must believe,

----

   [1] Flourishes.   Scout.

That without treason bred in our own breasts
Spain's affairs are not in good estate,
To aim at any action against France;
And if Byron should be their instrument,
His alter'd disposition could not grow
So far wide in an instant; nor resign
His valour to these lawless resolutions
Upon the sudden; nor without some charms
Of foreign hopes and flatteries sung to him:
But far it flies my thoughts that such a spirit,
So active, valiant, and vigilant,
Can see itself transform'd with such wild furies.
And like a dream it shows to my conceits,
That he who by himself hath won such honour,
And he to whom his father left so much,
He that still daily reaps so much from me,
And knows he may increase it to more proof
From me than any other foreign king;
Should quite against the stream of all religion,
Honour, and reason, take a course so foul,
And neither keep his oath, nor save his soul.
Can the poor keeping of a citadel
Which I denied [1] to be at his disposure,
Make him forego the whole strength of his honours?
It is impossible; though the violence
Of his hot spirit made him make attempt
Upon our person for denying him,
Yet well I found his loyal judgment served
To keep it from effect; besides being offer'd
Two hundred thousand crowns in yearly pension,
And to be general of all the forces
The Spaniards had in France; they found him still
As an unmatch'd Achilles in the wars,

---

[1] Refused.

2C

So a most wise Ulysses to their words,
Stopping his ears at their enchanted sounds ;
And plain he told them that although his blood
Being moved by Nature, were a very fire
And boil'd in apprehension of a wrong ;
Yet should his mind hold such a sceptre there
As would contain it from all act and thought
Of treachery or ingratitude to his prince.
Yet do I long, methinks, to see La Fin,
Who hath his heart in keeping ; since his state
Grown to decay and he to discontent,
Comes near the ambitious plight of Duke Byron.
My Lord Vidame, when does your lordship think
Your uncle of La Fin will be arrived?

Vi. I think, my lord, he now is near arriving ;
For his particular journey and devotion
Vow'd to the holy Lady of Loretto,
Was long since past and he upon return.

He. In him, as in a crystal that is charm'd,
I shall discern by whom and what designs
My rule is threaten'd ; and that sacred power
That hath enabled this defensive arm,
When I enjoy'd but an unequal nook
Of that I now possess, to front a king
Far my superior ; and from twelve set battles
March home a victor, ten of them obtain'd
Without my personal service ; will not see
A traitorous subject foil me, and so end
What his hand hath with such success begun.

Enter a Lady, *and a* Nurse *bringing the* Dauphin.

Ep. See the young dauphin brought to cheer your
highness.

He. My royal blessing, and the King of heaven

Make thee an aged and a happy king.
Help, nurse, to put my sword into his hand.
Hold, boy, by this ; and with it may thy arm
Cut from thy tree of rule all traitorous branches
That strive to shadow and eclipse thy glories.
Have thy old father's angel for thy guide,
Redoubled be his spirit in thy breast ;
Who when this state run like a turbulent sea
In civil hates and bloody enmity,
Their wraths and envies like so many winds
Settled and burst ; and like the halcyon's [1] birth,
Be thine to bring a calm upon the shore,
In which the eyes of war may ever sleep ;
As overwatch'd with former massacres,
When guilty, made noblesse feed on noblesse ;
All the sweet plenty of the realm exhausted ;
When the naked merchant was pursued for spoil,
When the poor peasants frighted neediest thieves
With their pale leanness, nothing left on them
But meagre carcases sustain'd with air,
Wandering like ghosts affrighted from their graves ;
When with the often and incessant sounds
The very beasts knew the alarum bell,
And, hearing it, ran bellowing to their home :
From which unchristian broils and homicides
Let the religious sword of justice free
Thee and thy kingdoms govern'd after me.
O heaven ! or if th'unsettled blood of France,
With ease and wealth, renew her civil furies,
Let all my powers be emptied in my son
To curb and end them all, as I have done.
Let him by virtue, quite out of from fortune

---

[1] The kingfisher ; she was supposed to lay her eggs in calm weather.

Her feather'd shoulders and her winged shoes,
And thrust from her light feet her turning-stone,
That she may ever tarry by his throne.
And of his worth, let after ages say,
(He fighting for the land, and bringing home
Just conquests, laden with his enemies' spoils),
His father pass'd [1] all France in martial deeds,
But he his father twenty times exceeds.   [*Exeunt*.

Enter the Duke *of* BYRON, D'AUVERGNE, *and* LA FIN.

By. My dear friends, D'Auvergne and La Fin,
We need no conjurations to conceal
Our close intendments, to advance our states
Even with our merits, which are now neglected ;
Since Bretagne is reduced, and breathless war
Hath sheathed his sword and wrapt his ensigns up ;
The King hath now no more use of my valour,
And therefore I shall now no more enjoy
The credit that my service held with him ;
My service that hath driven through all extremes,
Through tempest, droughts, and through the deepest
          floods,
Winters of shot, and over rocks so high
That birds could scarce aspire their ridgy tops.
The world is quite inverted : virtue thrown
At vice's feet, and sensual peace confounds
Valour and cowardice, fame and infamy ;
The rude and terrible age is turn'd again,
When the thick air hid heaven, and all the stars
Were drown'd in humour, tough and hard to pierce ;
When the red sun held not his fixed place,
Kept not his certain course, his rise and set,
Nor yet distinguish'd with his definite bounds,
          [1] Surpassed.

Nor in his firm conversions were discern'd
The fruitful distances of time and place,
In the well-varied seasons of the year;
When th'incomposed incursions of floods
Wasted and eat the earth, and all things show'd
Wild and disorder'd, nought was worse than now.
We must reform and have a new creation
Of state and government, and on our chaos
Will I sit brooding up another world.
I who, through all the dangers that can siege
The life of man, have forced my glorious way
To the repairing of my country's ruins,
Will ruin it again, to re-advance it.
Roman Camillus saved the state of Rome
With far less merit than Byron hath France,
And how short of this is my recompense.
The King shall know I will have better price
Set on my services, in spite of whom
I will proclaim and ring my discontents
Into the farthest ear of all the world.

   La. How great a spirit he breathes! how learn'd!
      how wise!
But, worthy prince, you must give temperate air
To your unmatch'd and more than humane wind,
Else will our plots be frost-bit in the flower.

   D'A. Betwixt ourselves we may give liberal vent
To all our fiery and displeased impressions;
Which nature could not entertain with life
Without some exhalation; a wrong'd thought
Will break a rib of steel.

   By. My princely friend,
Enough of these eruptions; our grave counsellor
Well knows that great affairs will not be forged
But upon anvils that are lined with wool;

We must ascend to our intentions' top
Like clouds, that be not seen till they be up.
   La. Oh, you do too much ravish, and my soul
Offer to music in your numerous breath,
Sententious, and so high, it wakens death :
It is for these parts that the Spanish King
Hath sworn to win them to his side
At any price or peril ; that great Savoy
Offers his princely daughter, and a dowry
Amounting to five hundred thousand crowns,
With full transport of all the sovereign rights
Belonging to the State of Burgundy ;
Which marriage will be made the only cement
T'effect and strengthen all our secret treaties.
Instruct me therefore, my assured prince,
Now I am going to resolve the King
Of his suspicions, how I shall behave me.
   By. Go, my most trusted friend, with happy feet ;
Make me a sound man with him ; go to Court
But with a little train, and be prepared
To hear, at first, terms of contempt and choler,
Which you may easily calm, and turn to grace,
If you beseech his highness to believe
That your whole drift and course for Italy
(Where he hath heard you were) was only made
Out of your long well-known devotion
To our right holy Lady of Loretto,
As you have told some of your friends in Court ;
And that in passing Milan and Turin,
They charged you to propound my marriage
With the third daughter of the Duke of Savoy ;
Which you have done, and I rejected it,
Resolved to build upon his royal care
For my bestowing, which he lately vow'd.

La. Oh, you direct, as if the god of light
Sat in each nook of you, and pointed out
The path of empire, charming all the dangers
On both sides, arm'd with his harmonious finger.

By. Besides, let me entreat you to dismiss
All that have made the voyage with your lordship,
But specially the curate ; and to lock
Your papers in some place of doubtless safety,
Or sacrifice them to the god of fire ;
Considering worthily that in your hands
I put my fortunes, honour, and my life.

La. Therein the bounty that your grace hath shown
    me,
I prize past life, and all things that are mine,
And will undoubtedly preserve and tender
The merit of it, as my hope of heaven.

By. I make no question ; farewell, worthy friend.

                                        [*Exit.*

HENRY, CHANCELLOR, LA FIN, D'ESCURES, JANIN ;
    HENRY *having many papers in his hand.*

He. Are these proofs of that purely Catholic zeal
That made him wish no other glorious title,
Than to be call'd the scourge of Huguenots ?

Ch. No question, sir, he was of no religion ;
But, upon false grounds, by some courtiers laid,
Hath oft been heard to mock and jest at all.

He. Are not his treasons heinous ?

All. Most abhorr'd.

Ch. All is confirm'd that you have heard before,
And amplified with many horrors more.

He. Good de La Fin, you were our golden plummet,
To sound this gulf of all ingratitude ;
In which you have with excellent desert

Of loyalty and policy express'd
Your name in action ; and with such appearance
Have proved the part of his ingrateful treasons,
That I must credit more than I desired.

 La. I must confess, my lord, my voyages
Made to the Duke of Savoy and to Milan
Were with endeavour that the wars return'd
Might breeed some trouble to your Majesty,
And profit those by whom they were procured ;
But since, in their designs, your sacred person
Was not excepted, which I since have seen,
It so abhorr'd me, that I was resolved
To give you full intelligence thereof ;
And rather choosed to fail in promises
Made to the servant, than infringe my fealty
Sworn to my royal sovereign and master.

 He. I am extremely discontent to see
This most unnatural conspiracy ;
And would not have the marshal of Byron
The first example of my forced justice ;
Nor that his death should be the worthy cause
That my calm reign (which hitherto hath held
A clear and cheerful sky above the heads
Of my dear subjects) should so suddenly
Be overcast with clouds of fire and thunder ;
Yet on submission, I vow still his pardon.

 Ja. And still our humble counsels, for his service,
Would so resolve you, if he will employ
His honour'd valour as effectually
To fortify the state against your foes
As he hath practised bad intendments with them.

 He. That vow shall stand, and we will now address
Some messengers to call him home to Court ;
Without the slenderest intimation

Of any ill we know ; we will restrain
(With all forgiveness, if he will confess)
His headlong course to ruin ; and his taste
From the sweet poison of his friendlike foes ;
Treason hath blister'd heels, dishonest things
Have bitter rivers, though delicious springs.
D'Escures, haste you unto him and inform,
That having heard by sure intelligence
Of the great levies made in Italy
Of arms and soldiers, I am resolute
Upon my frontiers to maintain an army,
The charge whereof I will impose on him ;
And to that end expressly have commanded
De Vic, our Lord Ambassador in Suisse,
To demand levy of six thousand men ;
Appointing them to march where Duke Byron
Shall have directions ; wherein I have follow'd
The counsel of my Constable his gossip ;
Whose liked advice, I made him know by letters,
Wishing to hear his own from his own mouth,
And by all means conjure his speediest presence ;
Do this with utmost haste.

    De. I will, my lord.   [*Exit* D'Escures.

    He. My good Lord Chancellor, of many pieces,
More than is here, of his conspiracies
Presented to us by our friend La Fin,
You only shall reserve these seven-and-twenty,
Which are not those that most conclude against him ;
But mention only him ; since I am loth
To have the rest of the conspirators known.

    Ch. My lord, my purpose is to guard all these
So safely from the sight of any other
That in my doublet I will have them sew'd ;
Without discovering them to mine own eyes,

Till need or opportunity requires.

　　He. You shall do well, my lord; they are of weight;
But I am doubtful [1] that his conscience
Will make him so suspicious of the worst
That he will hardly be induced to come.

　　Ja. I much should doubt that too, but that I hope
The strength of his conspiracy as yet
Is not so ready, that he dare presume
By his refusal to make known so much
Of his disloyalty.

　　He. I yet conceive
His practices are turned to no bad end;
And, good La Fin, I pray you write to him,
To hasten his repair; and make him sure
That you have satisfied me to the full
For all his actions, and have utter'd nought
But what might serve to banish bad impressions.

　　La. I will not fail, my lord.

　　He. Convey your letters
By some choice friend of his, or by his brother;
And for a third excitement to his presence,
Janin, yourself shall go, and with the power
That both the rest employ to make him come,
Use you the strength of your persuasions.

　　Ja. I will, my lord, and hope I shall present him.

　　　　　　　　　　　　　　　　　　[*Exit* JANIN.

Enter EPERNON, SOISSONS, VITRY, PRÂLIN, &c.

　　Ep. Will't please your Majesty to take your place?
The Mask is coming.

　　He. Room, my lords; stand close.

　　　　　　　　　　[1] Afraid

Music and a song above, and Cupid *enters with a table* [1] *written hung about his neck ; after him two torch bearers ; after them* MARIE, D'EN-TRAGUES, *and four ladies more with their torch-bearers, &c.* Cupid *speaks.*

Cu. My lord, these nymphs, part of the scatter'd train
Of friendless Virtue (living in the woods
Of shady Arden, and of late not hearing
The dreadful sounds of war, but that sweet peace
Was by your valour lifted from her grave,
Set on your royal right-hand ; and all virtues
Summon'd with honour, and with rich rewards,
To be her handmaids) : these I say, the Virtues,
Have put their heads out of their caves and coverts,
To be your true attendants in your Court ;
In which desire I must relate a tale
Of kind and worthy emulation
'Twixt these two Virtues, leaders of the train ;
This on the right hand is Sophrosyne,
Or Chastity ; this other Dapsyle,
Or Liberality ; their emulation
Begat a jar, which thus was reconciled.
I (having left my goddess mother's lap,
To hawk and shoot at birds in Arden groves,)
Beheld this princely nymph with much affection,
Left killing birds, and turn'd into a bird ;
Like which I flew betwixt her ivory breasts,
As if I had been driven by some hawk,
To sue to her for safety of my life ;
She smiled at first, and sweetly shadow'd me
With soft protection of her silver hand ;

[1] Tablet.

Sometimes she tied my legs in her rich hair,
And made me (past my nature, liberty)
Proud of my fetters.   As I pertly sat
On the white pillows of her naked breasts,
I sung for joy; she answer'd note for note,
Relish for relish, with such ease and art
In her divine division,[1] that my tunes
Show'd like the god of shepherds' to the sun's,
Compared with hers; ashamed of which disgrace,
I took my true shape, bow, and all my shafts,
And lighted all my torches at her eyes,
Which (set about her in a golden ring)
I follow'd birds again, from tree to tree,
Kill'd and presented, and she kindly took.
But when she handled my triumphant bow,
And saw the beauty of my golden shafts,
She begg'd them of me.   I, poor boy, replied
I had no other riches; yet was pleased
To hazard all and stake them 'gainst a kiss,
At an old game I used, call'd penny-prick.[2]
She, privy to her own skill in the play,
Answer'd my challenge, so I lost my arms;
And now my shafts are headed with her looks,
One of which shafts she put into my bow,
And shot at this fair nymph, with whom before,
I told your Majesty she had some jar.
The nymph did instantly repent all parts
She play'd in urging that effeminate war,
Loved and submitted; which submission
This took so well, that now they both are one;
And as for your dear love their discords grew,

[1] Modulation.

[2] An old game, in which pieces of iron were thrown at a stick, on which a penny stood.

So for your love they did their loves renew.
And now to prove them capable of your Court,
In skill of such conceits and qualities
As here are practised, they will first submit
Their grace in dancing to your highness' doom,
And play ; the prease [1] to give their measures room.

Music, dance, &c., which done, Cupid *speaks.*

If this suffice for one Court compliment,
To make them gracious and entertain'd,
Behold another parcel of their courtship,
Which is a rare dexterity in riddles,
Shown in one instance, which is here inscribed.
Here is a riddle, which if any knight
At first sight can resolve, he shall enjoy
This jewel he annex'd ; which though it show
To vulgar eyes no richer than a pebble,
And that no lapidary nor great man
Will give a sou for it, 'tis worth a kingdom ;
For 'tis an artificial stone composed
By their great mistress, Virtue, and will make
Him that shall wear it live with any little
Sufficed, and more content than any king,
If he that undertakes cannot resolve it,
And that these nymphs can have no harbour here
(It being consider'd that so many virtues
Can never live in Court), he shall resolve
To leave the Court, and live with them in Arden.

  Ep. Pronounce the riddle ; I will undertake it.
  Cu. 'Tis this, sir.
What's that a fair lady most of all likes,
Yet ever makes show she least of all seeks ?
That's ever embraced and affected [2] *by her,*

—————————
[1] Crowd.   [2] Desired.

Yet never is seen to please or come nigh her :
Most served in her night-weeds ; does her good in a corner,
But a poor man's thing, yet doth richly adorn her ;
Most cheap and most dear, above all worldly pelf,
That is hard to get in, but comes out of itself?

Ep. Let me peruse it, Cupid.

Cu. Here it is.

Ep. Your riddle is good fame.

Cu. Good fame ? how make you that good ?

Ep. Good fame is that a good lady most likes, I am
sure.

Cu. That's granted.

Ep. " Yet ever makes show she least of all seeks " :
for she likes it only for virtue, which is not glorious.

He. That holds well.

Ep. 'Tis " ever embraced and affected by her," for
she must persevere in virtue or fame vanishes ; " yet
never seen to please or come nigh her," for fame is
invisible.

Cu. Exceedingly right.

Ep. " Most served in her night-weeds," for ladies
that most wear their night-weeds come least abroad, and
they that come least abroad serve fame most, according
to this : *Non forma sed fama in publicum exire*
debet.

He. 'Tis very substantial.

Ep. " Does her good in a corner "—that is, in her
most retreat from the world, comforts her ; " but a
poor man's thing :" for every poor man may purchase
it, " yet doth richly adorn " a lady.

Cu. That all must grant.

Ep. " Most cheap," for it costs nothing, " and most
dear," for gold cannot buy it ; " above all worldly
pelf," for that's transitory, and fame eternal. " It is

hard to get in;" that is hard to get; "but comes out of itself," for when it is virtuously deserved with the most inward retreat from the world, it comes out in spite of it. And so, Cupid, your jewel is mine.

Cu. It is: and be the virtue of it yours.
We'll now turn to our dance, and then attend
Your highness' will, as touching our resort,
If virtue may be entertain'd in Court.

He. This show hath pleased me well, for that it figures
The reconcilement of my Queen and mistress:
Come, let us in and thank them, and prepare
To entertain our trusty friend Byron.   [*Exeunt.*

*[A portion of the play, and the division between
Acts I. and II. are lost.]*

ACT THE THIRD

SCENE I

Enter the Duke of BYRON, D'AUVERGNE, BRUN.

Y. Dear friend, we must not be more true
      to kings,
      Than kings are to their subjects ; there are
      schools
Now broken ope in all parts of the world,
First founded in ingenious Italy,
Where some conclusions of estate are held
That for a day preserve a prince, and ever
Destroy him after ; from thence men are taught
To glide into degrees of height by craft,
And then lock in themselves by villany.
But God, who knows kings are not made by art,
But right of nature, nor by treachery propt,
But simple virtue, once let fall from heaven
A branch of that green tree, whose root is yet
Fast fix'd above the stars, which sacred branch
We well may liken to that laurel spray
That from the heavenly eagle's golden seres
Fell in the lap of great Augustus' wife ;
Which spray once set grew up into a tree

Whereof were garlands made, and emperors
Had the estates and foreheads crown'd with them ;
And as the arms of that tree did decay,
The race of great Augustus wore away ;
Nero being last of that imperial line,
The tree and emperor together died.
Religion is a branch, first set and blest
By heaven's high finger in the hearts of kings,
Which whilom grew into a goodly tree ;
Bright angels sat and sung upon the twigs,
And royal branches, for the heads of kings,
Were twisted of them ; but since squint-eyed envy
And pale suspicion dash'd the heads of kingdoms
One 'gainst another, two abhorred twins,
With two foul tails, stern War and Liberty,
Enter'd the world. The tree that grew from heaven
Is overrun with moss ; the cheerful music
That heretofore hath sounded out of it
Begins to cease, and as she casts her leaves,
By small degrees the kingdoms of the earth
Decline and wither ; and look, whensoever
That the pure sap in her is dried-up quite,
The lamp of all authority goes out,
And all the blaze of princes is extinct.
Thus, as the poet sends a messenger
Out to the stage, to show the sum of all
That follows after ; so are kings' revolts,
And playing both ways with religion,
Fore-runners of afflictions imminent,
Which (like a chorus) subjects must lament.

D'A. My lord, I stand not on these deep discourses
To settle my course to your fortunes ; mine
Are freely and inseparably link'd,
And to your love, my life.

2D

By. Thanks, princely friend ;
And whatsoever good shall come of me,
Pursued by all the Catholic Princes' aids
With whom I join, and whose whole states proposed
To win my valour, promise me a throne,
All shall be, equal with my myself, thine own.

 Brun. My lord, here is D'Escures, sent from the
  King,
Desires access to you.

Enter D'ESCURES.

By. Attend him in.

D'E. Health to my lord the duke.

By. Welcome, D'Escures :
In what health rests our royal sovereign ?

D'E. In good health of his body, but his mind
Is something troubled with the gathering storms
Of foreign powers, that, as he is inform'd,
Address themselves into his frontier towns ;
And therefore his intent is to maintain
The body of an army on those parts,
And yield their worthy conduct to your valour.

 By. From whence hears he that any storms are
  rising ?

D'E. From Italy ; and his intelligence
No doubt is certain, that in all those parts
Levies are hotly made ; for which respect,
He sent to his ambassador, De Vic,
To make demand in Switzerland for the raising
With utmost diligence of six thousand men,
All which shall be commanded to attend
On your direction, as the Constable,
Your honour'd gossip, gave him in advice,
And he sent you by writing ; of which letters

He would have answer and advice from you
By your most speedy presence.

   By. This is strange,
That when the enemy is t'attempt his frontiers
He calls me from the frontiers; does he think
It is an action worthy of my valour
To turn my back to an approaching foe?

   D'E. The foe is not so near but you may come
And take more strict directions from his highness
Than he thinks fit his letters should contain,
Without the least attainture of your valour.
And therefore, good my lord, forbear excuse,
And bear yourself on his direction;
Who, well you know, hath never made design
For your most worthy service, where he saw
That anything but honour could succeed.

   By. I will not come, I swear.

   D'E. I know your grace
Will send no such unsavoury reply.

   By. Tell him, that I beseech his Majesty
To pardon my repair till th'end be known
Of all these levies now in Italy.

   D'E. My lord, I know that tale will never please
     him,
And wish you, as you love his love and pleasure,
To satisfy his summons speedily,
And speedily I know he will return you.

   By. By heaven, it is not fit, if all my service
Makes me know anything: beseech him, therefore,
To trust my judgment in these doubtful charges,
Since in assured assaults it hath not fail'd him.

   D'E. I would your lordship now would trust his
     judgment.

   By. God's precious, y'are importunate past measure,

And, I know, further than your charge extends.
I'll satisfy his highness ; let that serve ;
For by this flesh and blood, you shall not bear
Any reply to him but this from me.

   D'E. 'Tis nought to me, my lord ; I wish your good,
And for that cause have been importunate.

                  [*Exit* D'ESCURES.

   Brun. By no means go, my lord ; but with distrust
Of all that hath been said or can be sent,
Collect your friends, and stand upon your guard ;
The King's fair letters, and his messages
Are only golden pills, and comprehend [1]
Horrible purgatives.   [*Exit* BRUN.

   By. I will not go,
For now I see the instructions lately sent me,
That something is discover'd, are too true,
And my head rules none of those neighbour nobles
That every pursuivant [2] brings beneath the axe :
If they bring me out, they shall see I'll hatch
Like to the blackthorn, that puts forth its leaf,
Not with the golden fawnings of the sun,
But sharpest showers of hail, and blackest frosts.
Blows, batteries, breaches, showers of steel and blood,
Must be his downright messenger for me,
And not the mizzling [3] breath of policy.
He, he himself, made passage to his crown
Through no more armies, battles, massacres,
Than I will ask him to arrive at me ;
He takes on him my executions,
And on the demolitions that this arm
Hath shaken out of forts and citadels,
Hath he advanced the trophies of his valour ;
Where I, in those assumptions may scorn

     [1] Contain.   [2] King's messenger.   [3] Drizzling.

And speak contemptuously of all the world,
For any equal yet I ever found ;
And in my rising, not the Syrian star
That in the lion's mouth undaunted shines,
And makes his brave ascension with the sun,
Was of th'Egyptians with more zeal beheld,
And made a rule to know the circuit
And compass of the year, than I was held
When I appear'd from battle ; the whole sphere,
And full sustainer of the state we bear ;
I have Alcides-like gone under th'earth,
And on these shoulders borne the weight of France :
And for the fortunes of the thankless King,
My father, all know, set him in his throne,
And if he urge me, I may pluck him out.

Enter Messenger.

Me. Here is the president, Janin, my lord ;
Sent from the King, and urgeth quick access.

By. Another pursuivant ? and one so quick ?
He takes next course with me, to make him stay :
But let him in, let's hear what he importunes.

Enter JANIN.

Ja. Honour, and loyal hopes to Duke Byron !

By. No other touch me : say, how fares the King ?

Ja. Fairly, my lord ; the cloud is yet far off
That aims at his obscuring, and his will
Would gladly give the motion to your powers
That would disperse it ; but the means, himself
Would personally relate in your direction.

By. Still on that haunt ?

Ja. Upon my life, my lord,
He much desires to see you, and your sight

Is now grown necessary to suppress
(As with the glorious splendour of the sun)
The rude winds that report breathes in his ears,
Endeavouring to blast your loyalty.

By. Sir, if my loyalty stick in him no faster
But that the light breath of report may loose it,
So I rest still unmoved, let him be shaken.

Ja. But these aloof abodes, my lord, bewray
That there is rather firmness in your breath
Than in your heart. Truth is not made of glass,
That with a small touch, it should fear to break,
And therefore should not shun it ; believe me
His arm is long, and strong ; and it can fetch
Any within his will, that will not come :
Not he that surfeits in his mines of gold,
And for the pride thereof compares with God,
Calling (with almost nothing different)
His powers invincible, for omnipotent,
Can back your boldest fort 'gainst his assaults.
It is his pride, and vain ambition,
That hath but two stairs in his high designs ;
The lowest envy, and the highest blood,
That doth abuse you ; and gives minds too high,
Rather a will by giddiness to fall
Than to descend by judgment.

    By. I rely
On no man's back nor belly ; but the King
Must think that merit, by ingratitude crack'd,
Requires a firmer cementing than words.
And he shall find it a much harder work
To sodder broken hearts than shiver'd glass.

Ja. My lord, 'tis better hold a Sovereign's love
By bearing injuries, than by laying out
  ir his displeasure ; princes' discontents,

Being once incensed, are like the flames of Etna,
Not to be quench'd, nor lessen'd; and be sure,
A subject's confidence in any merit
Against his Sovereign, that makes him presume
To fly too high, approves him like a cloud
That makes a show as it did hawk at kingdoms,
And could command all raised beneath his vapour:
When suddenly, the fowl that hawk'd so fair,
Stoops in a puddle, or consumes in air.

By. I fly with no such aim, nor am opposed
Against my Sovereign; but the worthy height
I have wrought by my service I will hold.
Which if I come away, I cannot do;
For if the enemy should invade the frontier,
Whose charge to guard, is mine, with any spoil,
Although the King in placing of another
Might well excuse me, yet all foreign kings,
That can take note of no such secret quittance,
Will lay the weakness here, upon my wants;
And therefore my abode is resolute.

Ja. I sorrow for your resolution,
And fear your dissolution will succeed.

By. I must endure it.

Ja. Fare you well, my lord. [*Exit* JANIN.

Enter BRUN.

By. Farewell to you;
Captain, what other news?

Brun. La Fin salutes you.

By. Welcome, good friend; I hope your wish'd
arrival
Will give some certain end to our designs.

Brun. I k ow not that, my lord; reports are raised

So doubtful and so different, that the truth
Of any one can hardly be assured.

    By. Good news, D'Auvergne; our trusty friend La
      Fin
Hath clear'd all scruple with his Majesty,
And utter'd nothing but what served to clear
All bad suggestions.

    Brun. So he says, my lord;
But others say, La Fin's assurances
Are mere deceits; and wish you to believe
That when the Vidame, nephew to La Fin,
Met you at Autun, to assure your doubts,
His uncle had said nothing to the King
That might offend you; all the journey's charge
The King defray'd; besides, your truest friends
Will'd me to make you certain that your place
Of government is otherwise disposed :
And all advise you, for your latest hope,
To make retreat into the Franche Comte.

    By. I thank them all, but they touch not the depth
Of the affairs betwixt La Fin and me ;
Who is return'd contented to his house,
Quite freed of all displeasure or distrust ;
And therefore, worthy friends, we'll now to Court.

    D'A. My lord, I like your other friend's advices
Much better than La Fin's ; and on my life
You cannot come to Court with any safety.

    By. Who shall infringe it ?   I know all the Court
Have better apprehension of my valour
Than that they dare lay violent hands on me ;
If I have only means to draw this sword,
I shall have power enough to set me free
From seizure by my proudest enemy.   [*Exeunt.*

Enter EPERNON, VITRY, PRÂLIN.

Ep. He will not come, I dare engage my hand.

Vi. He will be fetch'd then, I'll engage my head.

Pr. Come, or be fetch'd, he quite hath lost his
    honour

In giving these suspicions of revolt
From his allegiance; that which he hath won
With sundry wounds, and peril of his life,
With wonder of his wisdom, and his valour,
He loseth with a most enchanted glory;
And admiration of his pride and folly.

Vi. Why, did you never see a fortunate man
Suddenly raised to heaps of wealth and honour?
Nor any rarely great in gifts of nature,
As valour, wit, and smooth use of the tongue,
Set strangely to the pitch of popular likings?
But with as sudden falls the rich and honour'd
Were overwhelm'd by poverty and shame,
Or had no use of both above the wretched.

Ep. Men ne'er are satisfied with that they have;
But as a man, match'd with a lovely wife,
When his most heavenly theory of her beauties
Is dull'd and quite exhausted with his practice;
He brings her forth to feasts, where he, alas!
Falls to his viands with no thought like others
That think him blest in her, and they, poor men,
Court, and make faces, offer service, sweat
With their desires' contention, break their brains
For jests and tales; sit mute, and lose their looks
(Far out of wit, and out of countenance),
So all men else do; what they have, transplant,
And place their wealth in thirst of what they want.

Enter HENRY, CHANCELLOR, VIDAME, D'ESCURES,
JANIN.

He. He will not come : I must both grieve and
    wonder
That all my care to win my subjects' love,
And in one cup of friendship to commix
Our lives and fortunes, should leave out so many
As give a man (contemptuous of my love,
And of his own good, in the kingdom's peace)
Hope, in a continuance so ungrateful,
To bear out his designs in spite of me.
How should I better please all, than I do ?
When they supposed I would have given some
Insolent garrisons, others citadels,
And to all sorts, increase of miseries ;
Province by province, I did visit all
Whom those injurious rumours had dissway'd,
And show'd them how I never sought to build
More forts for me than were within their hearts ;
Nor use more stern constraints that their good wills
To succour the necessities of my crown ;
That I desired to add to their contents
By all occasions, rather that subtract ;
Nor wish'd I that my treasury should flow
With gold that swum-in in my subjects' tears ;
And then I found no man that did not bless
My few years' reign, and their triumphant peace ;
And do they now so soon complain of ease ?
He will not come ?

    Enter BYRON, D'AUVERGNE, brother, *with others*.

    Ep. O madness, he is come !
    Ch. The Duke is come, my lord.
    He. Oh, sir, y'are welcome,

And fitly, to conduct me to my house.

By. I must beseech your Majesty's excuse,
That, jealous of mine honour, I have used
Some of mine own commandment in my stay,
And came not with your highness' soonest summons.

He. The faithful servant right in Holy Writ,
That said he would not come and yet he came.
But come you hither, I must tell you now
Not the contempt you stood to in your stay,
But the bad ground that bore up your contempt,
Makes you arrive at no port but repentance,
Despair, and ruin.

By. Be what port it will,
At which your will will make me be arrived,
I am not come to justify myself,
To ask you pardon, nor accuse my friends.

He. If you conceal my enemies you are one,
And then my pardon shall be worth your asking,
Or else your head be worth my cutting off.

By. Being friend and worthy fautor of myself,
I am no foe of yours, nor no impairer,
Since he can no way worthily maintain
His prince's honour that neglects his own;
And if your will have been to my true reason
(Maintaining still the truth of loyalty)
A check to my free nature and mine honour,
And that on your free justice I presumed
To cross your will a little, I conceive
You will not think this forfeit worth my head.

He. Have you maintain'd your truth of loyalty?
When since I pardon'd foul intentions,
Resolving to forget eternally
What they appear'd in, and had welcomed you
As the kind father doth his riotous son,

I can approve facts fouler than th'intents
Of deep disloyalty and highest treason.

By. May this right hand be thunder to my breast,
If I stand guilty of the slenderest fact,
Wherein the least of those two can be proved ;
For could my tender conscience but have touch'd
At any such unnatural relapse ;
I would not with this confidence have run
Thus headlong in the furnace of a wrath,
Blown, and thrice kindled ; having way enough
In my election [1] both to shun and slight it.

He. Y'are grossly and vaingloriously abused : [2]
There is no way in Savoy nor in Spain,
To give a fool that hope of your escape ;
And had you not, even when you did, arrived,
With horror to the proudest hope you had,
I would have fetch'd you.

By. You must then have used
A power beyond my knowledge, and a will
Beyond your justice. For a little stay
More than I used would hardly have been worthy
Of such an open expedition ;
In which to all the censures [3] of the world
My faith and innocence had been foully soil'd ;
Which I protest by heaven's bright witnesses
That shine far, far, from mixture with our fears,
Retain as perfect roundness as their spheres.

He. 'Tis well, my lord ; I thought I could have
frighted
Your firmest confidence : some other time,
We will, as now in private, sift your actions,
And pour more than you think into the sieve ;
Always reserving clemency and pardon

---

[1] Choice.   [2] Deceived.   [3] Opinions.

Upon confession, be you ne'er so foul.
Come. let's clear up our brows : shall we to tennis?

By. Ay, my lord, if I may make the match.
The Duke Epernon and myself will play
With you and Count Soissons.

Ep. I know, my lord,
You play well, but you make your matches ill.

He. Come, 'tis a match.   [*Exit.*

By. How like you my arrival?

Ep. I'll tell you as a friend in your ear.
You have given more perferment to your courage
Than to the provident counsels of your friends.

D'A. I told him so, my lord, and much was grieved
To see his bold approach, so full of will.

By. Well, I must bear it now, though but with th'
head,
The shoulders bearing nothing.

Ep. By Saint John,
'Tis a good headless resolution.   [*Exeunt.*

ACT THE FOURTH

SCENE I

Enter the Duke of Byron, D'Auvergne.

Y. O the most base fruits of a settled peace!
　　In men I mean; worse than their dirty
　　　fields,
　　Which they manure much better than
　　　themselves:
For them they plant and sow, and ere they grow
Weedy and choked with thorns, they grub and proin,[1]
And make them better than when cruel war
Frighted from thence the sweaty labourer;
But men themselves, instead of bearing fruits,
Grow rude and foggy, overgrown with weeds,
Their spirits and freedoms smother'd in their ease;
And as their tyrants and their ministers
Grow wild in prosecution of their lusts,
So they grow prostitute, and lie, like whores,
Down, and take up, to their abhorr'd dishonours;
The friendless may be injured and oppress'd,
The guiltless led to slaughter, the deserver

[1] Prune.

430

Given to the beggar; right be wholly wrong'd,
And wrong be only honour'd till the strings
Of every man's heart crack, and who will stir
To tell authority that it doth err?
All men cling to it, though they see their bloods
In their most dear associates and allies,
Pour'd into kennels by it, and who dares
But look well in the breast whom that impairs?
How all the Court now looks askew on me!
Go by without saluting, shun my sight,
Which, like a March sun, agues breeds in them,
From whence of late 'twas health to have a beam.

D'A. Now none will speak to us; we thrust ourselves
Into men's companies, and offer speech
As if not made for their diverted ears,
Their backs turn'd to us, and their words to others.
And we must, like obsequious parasites,
Follow their faces, wind about their persons
For looks and answers, or be cast behind,
No more view'd than the wallet of their faults.

Enter SOISSONS.

By. Yet here's one views me, and I think will speak.
So. My lord, if you respect your name and race,
The preservation of your former honours,
Merits, and virtues, humbly cast them all
At the King's mercy; for beyond all doubt
Your acts have thither driven them; he hath proofs
So pregnant[1] and so horrid, that to hear them
Would make your valour in your very looks
Give up your forces, miserably guilty;
But he is most loth (for his ancient love
To your rare virtues); and in their impair,

[1] Evident.

The full discouragement of all that live
To trust or favour any gifts in nature,
T'expose them to the light, when darkness may
Cover her own brood, and keep still in day
Nothing of you but that may brook her brightness.
You know what horrors these high strokes do bring,
Raised in the arm of an incensed king.

By. My lord, be sure the King cannot complain
Of anything in me but my true service,
Which in so many dangers of my death
May so approve my spotless loyalty,
That those quite opposite horrors you assure,
Must look out of his own ingratitude,
Or the malignant envies of my foes,
Who pour me out in such a Stygian flood,
To drown me in myself, since their deserts
Are far from such a deluge, and in me
Hid like so many rivers in the sea.

So. You think I come to sound you : fare you well.
[*Exit.*

Enter CHANCELLOR, EPERNON, JANIN, VIDAME, VITRY,
    PRÂLIN, *whipering by couples, &c.*

D'A. See, see, not one of them will cast a glance
At our eclipsed faces.

By. They keep all
To cast in admiration on the King ;
For from his face are all their faces moulded.

D'A. But when a change comes we shall see them
    all
Changed into water, that will instantly
Give look for look, as if it watch'd to greet us ;
Or else for one they'll give us twenty faces,
Like to the little specks on sides of glasses.

By. Is't not an easy loss to lose their looks
Whose hearts so soon are melted?

D'A. But methinks,
Being courtiers, they should cast best looks on men
When they thought worst of them.

By. Oh no, my lord,
They ne'er dissemble but for some advantage;
They sell their looks and shadows, which they rate
After their markets, kept beneath the State;
Lord, what foul weather their aspects do threaten!
See in how grave a brake [1] he sets his vizard:
Passion of nothing, see, and excellent gesture!
Now courtship goes a ditching in their foreheads,
And we are fall'n into those dismal ditches.
Why even thus dreadfully would they be rapt,
If the King's butter'd eggs were only spilt.

Enter HENRY.

He. Lord Chancellor.

Ch. Ay, my lord.

He. And Lord Vidame.

[Exit, with CHANCELLOR, *&c.*

By. And not Byron? here's a prodigious change!

D'A. He cast no beam on you.

By. Why, now you see
From whence their countenances were copied.

Enter the Captain *of* BYRON'S Guard, *with a letter.*

D'A. See, here comes some news, I believe, my lord.

By. What says the honest captain of my guard?

Ca. I bring a letter from a friend of yours.

By. 'Tis welcome, then.

D'A. Have we yet any friends?

[1] Expression.

Ca. More than ye would, I think : I never saw
Men in their right minds so unrighteous
In their own causes.

By. See what thou hast brought.
He will us to retire ourselves, my lord,
And makes as if it were almost too late.
What says my captain ? shall we go or no ?

Ca. I would your dagger's point had kiss'd my heart,
When you resolved to come.

By. I pray thee, why ?

Ca. Yet doth that senseless apoplexy dull you ?
The devil or your wicked angel blinds you,
Bereaving all your reason of a man,
And leaves you but the spirit of a horse
In your brute nostrils, only power to dare.

By. Why, dost thou think my coming here hath
　　brought me
To such an unrecoverable danger ?

Ca. Judge by the strange ostents [1] that have suc-
　　ceeded
Since your arrival ; the kind fowl, the wild duck
That came into your cabinet, so beyond
The sight of all your servants, or yourself ;
That flew about, and on your shoulder sat,
And which you had so fed and so attended
For that dumb love she show'd you ; just as soon
As you were parted, on the sudden died.
And to make this no less than an ostent,
Another that hath fortuned [2] since confirms it :
Your goodly horse, Pastrana, which the Archduke
Gave you at Brussels, in the very hour
You left your strength, fell mad, and kill'd himself ;
The like chanced to the horse the great Duke sent you,

---

[1] Portents.　　　　　　　　[2] Chanced.

And, with both these, the horse the Duke of Lorraine
Sent you at Vimie, made a third presage
Of some inevitable fate that touch'd you,
Who, like the other, pined away and died.

By. All these together are indeed ostentful,
Which, by another like, I can confirm :
The matchless Earl of Essex, whom some make
(In their most sure divinings of my death)
A parallel with me in life and fortune,
Had one horse likewise that the very hour
He suffer'd death (being well the night before)
Died in his pasture.   Noble, happy beasts,
That die, not having to their wills to live ;
They use no deprecations nor complaints,
Nor suit for mercy ; amongst them, the lion
Serves not the lion, nor the horse the horse,
As man serves man : when men show most their spirits
In valour, and their utmost dares to do
They are compared to lions, wolves, and boars ;
But by conversion, none will say a lion
Fights as he had the spirit of a man.
Let me then in my danger now give cause
For all men to begin that simile.
For all my huge engagement I provide me
This short sword only, which, if I have time
To show my apprehender, he shall use
Power of ten lions if I get not loose.   [*Exeunt.*

Enter HENRY, CHANCELLOR, VIDAME, JANIN, VITRY,
PRÂLIN.

He. What shall we do with this unthankful man ?
Would he of one thing but reveal the truth
Which I have proof of underneath his hand,
He should not taste my justice.   I would give
Two hundred thousand crowns that he would yield

But such means for my pardon as he should ;
I never loved man like him ; would have trusted
My son in his protection, and my realm ;
He hath deserved my love with worthy service,
Yet can he not deny but I have thrice
Saved him from death ; I drew him off the foe
At Fontoine Françoise, where he was engaged,
So wounded, and so much amazed [1] with blows,
That, as I play'd the soldier in his rescue,
I was enforced to play the Marechal,
To order the retreat, because he said
He was not fit to do it, nor to serve me.

Ch. Your Majesty hath used your utmost means
Both by your own persuasions, and his friends,
To bring him to submission, and confess
(With some sign of repentance) his foul fault :
Yet still he stands prefract [2] and insolent.
You have in love and care of his recovery
Been half in labour to produce a course
And resolution what were fit for him.
And since so amply it concerns your crown,
You must by law cut off, what by your grace
You cannot bring into the state of safety.

Ja. Begin at th'end, my lord, and execute,
Like Alexander with Parmenio.
Princes, you know, are masters of their laws,
And may resolve them to what forms they please,
So all conclude in justice ; in whose stroke
There is one sort of manage [3] for the great ;
Another for inferior : the great mother
Of all productions, grave Necessity,
Commands the variation ; and the profit,
So certainly foreseen, commends the example.

　　　[1] Bewildered.　　　　[2] Obstinate.　　　[3] Treatment.

He. I like not executions so informal,
For which my predecessors have been blamed :
My subjects and the world shall know my power,
And my authority by law's usual course
Dares punish ; not the devilish heads of treason,
But their confederates, be they ne'er so dreadful.
The decent ceremonies of my laws,
And their solemnities, shall be observed
With all their sternness and severity.

Vi. Where will your highness have him apprehended ?

He. Not in the Castle, as some have advised,
But in his chamber.

Pr. Rather in your own,
Or coming out of it ; for 'tis assured
That any other place of apprehension,
Will make the hard performance end in blood.

Vi. To shun this likelihood, my lord, 'tis best
To make the apprehension near your chamber ;
For all respect and reverence given the place,
More than is needful, to chastise the person,
And save the opening of too many veins,
Is vain and dangerous.

He. Gather you your guard,
And I will find fit time to give the word
When you shall seize on him and on D'Auvergne.

Vi. We will be ready to the death, my lord.

[*Exeunt.*

He. O Thou that govern'st the keen swords of kings,
Direct my arm in this important stroke,
Or hold it being advanced [1] ; the weight of blood,
Even in the basest subject, doth exact
Deep consultation, in the highest king ;
For in one subject, death's unjust affrights,

[1] Uplifted.

Passions,[1] and pains, though he be ne'er so poor,
Ask more remorse [2] than the voluptuous spleens
Of all kings in the world deserve respect ;
He should be born grey-headed that will bear
The sword of empire ; judgment of the life,
Free state, and reputation of a man,
If it be just and worthy, dwells so dark
That it denies access to sun and moon ;
The soul's eye sharpen'd with that sacred light
Of whom the sun itself is but a beam,
Must only give that judgment ; O how much
Err those kings then, that play with life and death,
And nothing put into their serious states
But humour and their lusts ; for which alone
Men long for kingdoms ; whose huge counterpoise
In cares and dangers, could a fool comprise,
He would not be a king, but would be wise.

Enter BYRON, *talking with the* Queen ; EPERNON *with*
   D'ENTRAGUES ; D'AUVERGNE *with another lady ;*
   MONTIGNY ; *others attending.*

He. Here comes the man, with whose ambitious head
(Cast in the way of treason) we must stay
His full chase of our ruin and our realm ;
This hour shall take upon her shady wing
His latest liberty and life to hell.
   D'A. We are undone.   [*Exit* D'AUVERGNE.
   Qu. What's that ?
   By. I heard him not.
   He. Madam, y'are honour'd much that Duke Byron
Is so observant : some, to cards with him ;
You four, as now you come, sit to Primero [3] ;
And I will fight a battle at the chess.

   [1] Sorrows.   [2] Pity.   [3] An old game at cards.

By. A good safe fight, believe me ; other war
Thirsts blood and wounds, and his thirst quench'd is
    thankless.

Ep. Lift, and then cut.

By. 'Tis right the end of lifting ;
When men are lifted to their highest pitch,
They cut off those that lifted them so high.

Qu. Apply you all these sports so seriously ?

By. They first were from our serious acts devised,
The best of which are to the best but sports,
(I mean by best the greatest) for their ends
In men that serve them best, are their own pleasures.

Qu. So in those best men's services, their ends
Are their own pleasures ; pass.

By. I vie't.[1]

He. I see't,
And wonder at his frontless [2] impudence.

                             [*Exit* HENRY.

Ch. How speeds your majesty ?

Qu. Well ; the Duke instructs me
With such grave lessons of morality
Forced out of our light sport, that if I lose,
I cannot but speed well.

By. Some idle talk,
For courtship's sake, you know, does not amiss.

Ch. Would we might hear some of it.

By. That you shall ;
I cast away a card now, makes me think
Of the deceased worthy King of Spain.

Ch. What card was that ?

By. The king of hearts, my lord ;
Whose name yields well the memory of that king,
Who was indeed the worthy king of hearts,

           [1] Stake it.   [2] Shameless.

And had, both of his subjects' hearts and strangers',
Much more than all the kings of Christendom.

   Ch. He won them with his gold.

   By. He won them chiefly
With his so general piety and justice ;
And as the little, yet great Macedon,
Was said, with his humane philosophy
To teach the rapeful Hyrcans marriage,
And bring the barbarous Sogdians to nourish,
Not kill, their aged parents as before ;
Th'incestuous Persians to reverence
Their mothers, not to use them as their wives ;
The Indians to adore the Grecian gods ;
The Scythians to inter, not eat their parents ;
So he, with his divine philosophy
(Which I may call it, since he chiefly used it),
In Turkey, India, and through all the world,
Expell'd profane idolatry, and from earth
Raised temples to the highest : whom with the word
He could not win, he justly put to sword.

   Ch. He sought for gold and empire.

   By. 'Twas religion,
And her full propagation that he sought ;
If gold had been his end, it had been hoarded,
When he had fetch'd it in so many fleets,
Which he spent not on Median luxury,
Banquets, and women, Calidonian wine,
Nor dear Hyrcanian fishes, but employ'd it
To propagate his empire ; and his empire
Desired t'extend so, that he might withal
Extend Religion through it, and all nations
Reduce to one firm constitution
Of piety, justice, and one public weal ;
To which end he made all his matchless subjects

Make tents their castles and their garrisons;
True Catholics countrymen; and their allies,
Heretics, strangers, and their enemies.
There was in him the magnanimity.

Mon. To temper your extreme applause, my lord,
Shorten and answer all things in a word,
The greatest commendation we can give
To the remembrance of that king deceased,
Is that he spared not his own eldest son,
But put him justly to a violent death,
Because he sought to trouble his estates.

By. Is't so?

Ch. That bit, my lord; upon my life,
'Twas bitterly replied, and doth amaze him.

The King *suddenly enters, having determined what
to do.*

He. It is resolved; a work shall now be done,
Which, while learn'd Atlas shall with stars be crown'd,
While th'ocean walks in storms his wavy round,
While moons at full repair their broken rings;
While Lucifer foreshows Aurora's springs,
And Arctos sticks above the earth unmoved,
Shall make my realm be blest, and me beloved.
Call in the Count D'Auvergne.

Enter D'AUVERGNE.

A word, my lord.
Will you become as wilful as your friend,
And draw a mortal justice on your heads,
That hangs so black and is so loth to strike?
If you would utter what I know you know
Of his inhumane treason, one strong bar
Betwixt his will and duty were dissolved,
For then I know he would submit himself.

Think you it not as strong a point of faith
To rectify your loyalties to me,
As to be trusty in each other's wrong?
Trust that deceives ourselves is treachery,
And truth that truth conceals an open lie.

 D'A. My lord, if I could utter any thought
Instructed with disloyalty to you,
And might light any safety to my friend,
Though mine own heart came after, it should out.

 He. I know you may, and that your faiths affected
To one another are so vain and false
That your own strengths will ruin you : ye contend
To cast up rampires [1] to you in the sea,
And strive to stop the waves that run before you.

 D'A. All this, my lord, to me is mystery.

 He. It is?   I'll make it plain enough, believe me :
Come, my Lord Chancellor, let us end our mate.

   Enter VARENNES, *whispering to* BYRON.

 Va. You are undone, my lord.

 By. Is it possible?

 Qu. Play, good my lord : whom look you for?

 Ep. Your mind
Is not upon your game.

 By. Play, pray you play.

 He. Enough, 'tis late, and time to leave our play,
On all hands ; all forbear the room.   My lord,
Stay you with me ; yet is your will resolved
To duty and the main bond of your life?
I swear, of all th'intrusions I have made
Upon your own good and continued fortunes,
This is the last ; inform me yet the truth,
And here I vow to you (by all my love,

     [1] Ramparts.

By all means shown you, even to this extreme,
When all men else forsake you), you are safe.
What passages have slipt 'twixt Count Fuentes,
You, and the Duke of Savoy?

   By. Good my lord,
This nail is driven already past the head;
You much have overcharged an honest man;
And I beseech you yield my innocence justice,
(But with my single valour) 'gainst them all
That thus have poison'd your opinion of me,
And let me take my vengeance by my sword:
For I protest I never thought an action
More than my tongue hath utter'd.

   He. Would 'twere true;
And that your thoughts and deeds had fell no fouler.
But you disdain submission, not remembering
That (in intents urged for the common good)
He that shall hold his peace being charged to speak
Doth all the peace and nerves of empire break,
Which on your conscience lie; adieu, good night.

                        [Exit.

   By. Kings hate to hear what they command men
      speak;
Ask life, and to desert of death ye yield.
Where medicines loathe, it irks men to be heal'd.

Enter VITRY, *with two or three of the* Guard, EPERNON,
   VIDAME, *following.* VITRY *lays hand on* BYRON'S
   sword.

   Vi. Resign your sword, my lord; the King com-
      mands it.
   By. Me to resign my sword? what King is he
Hath used it better for the realm than I?
My sword! that all the wars within the length,

Breadth, and the whole dimensions of great France
Hath sheathed betwixt his hilt and horrid point,
And fix'd ye all in such a flourishing peace?
My sword, that never enemy could enforce,
Bereft me by my friends!   Now, good my lord,
Beseech the King, I may resign my sword
To his hand only.

Enter JANIN.

Ja. You must do your office,
The King commands you.
Vi. 'Tis in vain to strive,
For I must force it.
By. Have I ne'er a friend,
That bears another for me?   All the guard?
What, will you kill me? will you smother here
His life that can command and save in field
A hundred thousand lives?   For manhood sake,
Lend something to this poor forsaken hand;
For all my service, let me have the honour
To die defending of my innocent self,
And have some little space to pray to God.

Enter HENRY.

He. Come, you are an atheist, Byron, and a traitor
Both foul and damnable.   Thy innocent self?
No leper is so buried quick in ulcers
As thy corrupted soul.   Thou end the war,
And settle peace in France?   What war hath raged
Into whose fury I have not exposed
My person, which is as free a spirit as thine?
Thy worthy father and thyself combined
And arm'd in all the merits of your valours,
Your bodies thrust amidst the thickest fights,

Never were bristled with so many battles,
Nor on the foe have broke such woods of lances
As grew upon my thigh, and I have marshall'd.
I am ashamed to brag thus; where envy
And arrogance their opposite bulwark raise,
Men are allow'd to use their proper praise:
Away with him.   [*Exit* HENRY.

  By. Away with him! live I,
And hear my life thus slighted?   Cursed man,
That ever the intelligencing lights   .
Betray'd me to men's whorish fellowships,
To princes' Moorish slaveries; to be made
The anvil on which only blows and wounds
Were made the seed and wombs of other honours;
A property for a tyrant to set up,
And puff down with the vapour of his breath.
Will you not kill me?

  Vi. No, we will not hurt you;
We are commanded only to conduct you
Into your lodging.

  By. To my lodging? where?

  Vi. Within the Cabinet of Arms, my lord.

  By. What! to a prison?   Death! I will not go.

  Vi. We'll force you then.

  By. And take away my sword;
A proper point of force; ye had as good
Have robb'd me of my soul; slaves of my stars,
Partial and bloody; O that in mine eyes
Were all the sorcerous poison of my woes,
That I might witch ye headlong from your height,
So trample out your execrable light.

  Vi. Come, will you go, my lord?   This rage is
    vain.

  By. And so is all your grave authority;

And that all France shall feel before I die.
Ye see all how they use good Catholics.

Ep. Farewell for ever! so have I discern'd
An exhalation that would be a star
Fall when the sun forsook it, in a sink.
Shoes ever overthrow that are too large,
And hugest cannons burst with overcharge.

Enter D'AUVERGNE, PRÂLIN, *following with a*
Guard.

Pr. My lord, I have commandment from the King
To charge you go with me, and ask your sword.

D'Au. My sword! who fears it? it was ne'er the
death
Of any but wild boars; I prithee take it;
Hadst thou advertised this when last we met,
I had been in my bed, and fast asleep
Two hours ago.   Lead; I'll go where thou wilt.

                                        [*Exit.*

Vi. See how he bears his cross, with his small
strength
On easier shoulders than the other Atlas.

Ep. Strength to aspire is still [1] accompanied
With weakness to endure; all popular gifts
Are colours, it will bear no vinegar;
And rather to adverse affairs betray
Thine arm against them; his state still is best
That hath most inward worth; and that's best tried
That neither glories, nor is glorified.   [*Exeunt.*

[1] Always.

ACT THE FIFTH

SCENE I

Henry, Soissons, Janin, D'Escures, *cum aliis.*

HE. What shall we think, my lords, of these
          new forces
        That, from the King of Spain, hath past
          the Alps?
For which, I think, his Lord Ambassador
Is come to Court, to get their pass for Flanders?
  Ja. I think, my lord, they have no end for Flanders;
Count Maurice being already enter'd Brabant
To pass to Flanders, to relieve Ostend,
And th'Archduke full prepared to hinder him;
For sure it is that they must measure forces,
Which (ere this new force could have past the Alps)
Of force must be encounter'd.
  So. 'Tis unlikely
That their march hath so large an aim as Flanders.
  D'E. As these times sort, they may have shorter
          reaches,
That would pierce further.
  He. I have been advertised
How Count Fuentes (by whose means this army
Was lately levied; and whose hand was strong

447

In thrusting on Byron's conspiracy)
Hath caused these cunning forces to advance,
With colour only to set down in Flanders;
But hath intentional respect to favour
And countenance his false partisans in Bresse,
And friends in Burgundy; to give them heart
For the full taking of their hearts from me.
Be as it will; we shall prevent their worst;
And therefore call in Spain's Ambassador.

Enter Ambassador *with others.*

What would the Lord Ambassador of Spain?

Am. First, in my master's name, I would beseech
Your highness' hearty thought that his true hand,
Held in your vowed amities, hath not touch'd
At any least point in Byron's offence,
Nor once had notice of a crime so foul;
Whereof, since he doubts not you stand resolved,
He prays your league's countinuance in this favour,
That the army he hath raised to march for Flanders
May have safe passage by your frontier towns,
And find the river free that runs by Rhone.

He. My lord, my frontiers shall not be disarm'd,
Till, by arraignment of the Duke of Byron
My scruples are resolved, and I may know
In what account to hold your master's faith,
For his observance of the league betwixt us.
You wish me to believe that he is clear
From all the projects caused by Count Fuentes,
His special agent; but where deeds pull down,
Words may repair no faith.   I scarce can think
That his gold was so bounteously employ'd
Without his special counsel and command:
These faint proceedings in our royal faiths

Make subjects prove so faithless ; if because
We sit above the danger of the laws,
We likewise lift our arms above their justice,
And that our heavenly Sovereign bounds not us
In those religious confines out of which
Our justice and our true laws are inform'd ;
In vain have we expectance that our subjects
Should not as well presume to offend their earthly,
As we our heavenly Sovereign ; and this breach
Made in the forts of all society,
Of all celestial, and humane respects,
Makes no strengths of our bounties, counsels, arms,
Hold out against their treasons ; and the rapes
Made of humanity and religion,
In all men's more than Pagan liberties,
Atheisms, and slaveries, will derive their springs
From their base precedents, copied out of kings.
But all this shall not make me break the commerce
Authorised by our treaties.   Let your army
Have the directest pass ; it shall go safe.

Am. So rest your highness ever, and assured
That my true Sovereign hates all opposite thoughts.

He. Are our despatches made to all the kings,
Princes, and potentates of Christendom,
Ambassadors and province governors,
T'inform the truth of this conspiracy ?

Ja. They all are made, my lord, and some give out
That 'tis a blow given to religion,
To weaken it, in ruining of him
That said he never wish'd more glorious title
Than to be call'd the scourge of Huguenots.

So. Others that are like favourers of the fault,
Said 'tis a politic advice from England
To break the sacred javelins both together.

2F

He. Such shut their eyes to truth ; we can but set
His lights before them, and his trumpet sound
Close to their ears ; their partial wilfulness,
In resting blind and deaf, or in perverting
What their most certain senses apprehend,
Shall not discomfort our imperial justice,
Nor clear the desperate fault that doth enforce it.

Enter VITRY.

Vi. The peers of France, my lord, refuse t'appear
At the arraignment of the Duke of Byron.

He. The Court may yet proceed ; and so command it.
'Tis not their slackness to appear shall serve
To let my will t'appear in any fact
Wherein the boldest of them tempts my justice.
I am resolved, and will no more endure
To have my subjects make what I command
The subject of their oppositions ;
Who evermore make slack their allegiance,
As kings forbear their penance.   How sustain
Your prisoners their strange durance ?

Vi. One of them,
Which is the Count d'Auvergne, hath merry spirits,
Eats well and sleeps : and never can imagine
That any place where he is, is a prison ;
Where on the other part, the Duke Byron,
Enter'd his prison as into his grave,
Rejects all food, sleeps not, nor once lies down ;
Fury hath arm'd his thoughts so thick with thorns
That rest can have no entry : he disdains
To grace the prison with the slenderest show
Of any patience, lest men should conceive
He thought his sufferance in the best sort fit ;
And holds his bands so worthless of his worth,

That he impairs it, to vouchsafe to them
The best part of the peace that freedom owes it :
That patience therein is a willing slavery,
And like the camel stoops to take the load,
So still he walks ; or rather as a bird,
Enter'd a closet, which unawares is made
His desperate prison, being pursued, amazed
And wrathful beats his breast from wall to wall,
Assaults the light, strikes down himself, not out,
And being taken, struggles, gasps, and bites,
Takes all his taker's strokings to be strokes,
Abborreth food, and with a savage will
Frets, pines, and dies for former liberty :
So fares the wrathful Duke ; and when the strength
Of these dumb rages break out into sounds,
He breathes defiance to the world, and bids us
Make ourselves drunk with the remaining blood
Of five and thirty wounds received in fight
For us and ours ; for we shall never brag
That we have made his spirits check at death.
This rage in walks and words ; but in his looks
He comments all, and prints a world of books.

 He. Let others learn by him to curb their spleens,
Before they be curb'd ; and to cease their grudges.
Now I am settled in my sun of height,
The circular splendour and full sphere of state,
Take all place up from envy : as the sun,
At height, and passive o'er the crowns of men,
His beams diffused, and down-right pour'd on them,
Cast but a little or no shade at all :
So he that is advanced above the heads
Of all his emulators, with high light,
Prevents their envies, and deprives them quite.

          [Exeunt.

Enter the CHANCELLOR, HARLEY, POTIER, FLEURY, *in
scarlet gowns;* LA FIN, D'ESCURES, *with other
officers of state.*

Ch. I wonder at the prisoner's so long stay.

Ha. I think it may be made a question
If his impatience will let him come.

Po. Yes, he is now well staid: time and his judgment
Have cast his passion and his fever off.

Fl. His fever may be past, but for his passions,
I fear me we shall find it spiced too hotly,
With his old powder.

D'E. He is sure come forth;
The carosse [1] of the Marquis of Rosny
Conducted him along to th'arsenal,
Close to the river-side: and there I saw him
Enter a barge cover'd with tapestry,
In which the King's guards waited and received him.
Stand by there, clear the place.

Ch. The prisoner comes:
My Lord La Fin, forbear your sight awhile;
It may incense the prisoner: who will know,
By your attendance near us, that your hand
Was chief in his discovery; which as yet,
I think he doth not doubt. [2]

La. I will forbear
Till your good pleasures call me.   [*Exit* LA FIN.

Ha. When he knows
And sees La Fin accuse him to his face,
The Court I think will shake with his distemper.

Enter VITRY, BYRON, *with others and a* Guard.

Vi. You see, my lord, 'tis in the golden chamber.

---
[1] Coach.   [2] Fear.

By. The golden chamber? where the greatest kings
Have thought them honour'd to receive a place,
And I have had it: am I come to stand
In rank and habit here of men arraign'd,
Where I have sat assistant, and been honour'd
With glorious title of the chiefest virtuous,
Where the King's chief solicitor hath said
There was in France no man that ever lived
Whose parts were worth my imitation;
That but mine own worth I could imitate none:
And that I made myself inimitable
To all that could come after; whom this Court
Hath seen to sit upon the flower-de-luce
In recompense of my renowned service.
Must I be sat on now by petty judges?
These scarlet robes, that come to sit and fight
Against my life dismay my valour more,
Than all the bloody cassocks Spain hath brought
To field against it.

    Vi. To the bar, my lord.

                         [*He salutes and stands to the bar.*

    Ha. Read the indictment.

    Ch. Stay, I will invert,
For shortness' sake, the form of our proceedings,
And out of all the points the process holds,
Collect five principal, with which we charge you.

    1. First you conferr'd with one, called Picoté
At Orleans born, and into Flanders fled,
To hold intelligence by him with the Archduke,
And for two voyages to that effect,
Bestow'd on him five hundred fifty crowns.

    2. Next you held treaty with the Duke of Savoy,
Without the King's permission; offering him
    service and assistance 'gainst all men,

In hope to have in marriage his third daughter.

   3. Thirdly, you held intelligence with the Duke,
At taking in of Bourg, and other forts ;
Advising him, with all your prejudice,
'Gainst the King's army and his royal person.

   4. The fourth is, that you would have brought the
       King
Before Saint Katherine's fort, to be there slain ;
And to that end writ to the governor,
In which you gave him notes to know his highness.

   5. Fifthly, You sent La Fin to treat with Savoy,
And with the Count Fuentes, of more plots,
Touching the ruin of the King and realm.

   By. All this, my lord, I answer, and deny.
And first for Picoté : he was my prisoner,
And therefore I might well confer with him ;
But that our conference tended to the Archduke
Is nothing so : I only did employ him
To Captain La Fortune, for the reduction
Of Severre to the service of the King,
Who used such speedy diligence therein,
That shortly 'twas assured his Majesty.

   2. Next, For my treaty with the Duke of Savoy ;
Roncas, his secretary, having made
A motion to me for the Duke's third daughter,
I told it to the King, who having since
Given me the understanding by La Force
Of his dislike, I never dream'd of it.

   3. Thirdly, For my intelligence with the Duke,
Advising him against his highness' army :
Had this been true I had not undertaken
Th'assault of Bourg, against the King's opinion,
Having assistance but by them about me ;
And, having won it for him, had not been

Put out of such a government so easily.

    4. Fourthly, For my advice to kill the King;
I would beseech his highness' memory
Not to let slip that I alone dissuaded
His viewing of that fort; informing him
It had good mark-men, and he could not go
But in exceeding danger, which advice
Diverted him; the rather since I said
That if he had desire to see the place
He should receive from me a plot of it;
Offering to take it with five hundred men,
And I myself would go to the assault.

    5. And lastly, For intelligences held
With Savoy and Fuentes; I confess
That being denied to keep the citadel,
Which with incredible peril I had got,
And seeing another honour'd with my spoils,
I grew so desperate that I found my spirit
Enraged to any act, and wish'd myself
Cover'd with blood.

    Ch. With whose blood?

    By. With mine own;
Wishing to live no longer, being denied,
With such suspicion of me, and set will
To rack my furious humour into blood.
And for two months' space I did speak and write
More than I ought, but have done ever well,
And therefore your informers have been false,
And, with intent to tyrannize, suborn'd.

    Fl. What if our witnesses come face to face,
And justify much more than we allege?

    By. They must be hirelings, then, and men corrupted.

    Po. What think you of La Fin?

    By. I hold La Fin

An honour'd gentleman, my friend and kinsman.

   Ha. If he then aggravate what we affirm
With greater accusations to your face,
What will you say?

   By. I know it cannot be.

   Ch. Call in my Lord La Fin.

   By. Is he so near,
And kept so close from me? Can all the world
Make him a treacher?

Enter LA FIN.

   Ch. I suppose, my lord,
You have not stood within, without the ear
Of what hath here been urged against the Duke;
If you have heard it, and upon your knowledge
Can witness all is true, upon your soul,
Utter your knowledge.

   La. I have heard, my lord,
All that hath pass'd here, and upon by soul,
(Being charged so urgently in such a Court)
Upon my knowledge I affirm all true;
And so much more as, had the prisoner lives
As many as his years, would make all forfeit.

   By. O all ye virtuous powers, in earth and heaven,
That have not put on hellish flesh and blood,
From whence these monstrous issues are produced,
That cannot bear in execrable concord,
And one prodigious subject, contraries;
Nor (as the isle that of the world admired,
Is sever'd from the world) can cut yourselves
From the consent and sacred harmony
Of life, yet live; of honour, yet be honour'd;
As this extravagant and errant rogue,
From all your fair decorums and just laws

Finds power to do, and like a loathsome wen
Sticks to the face of nature and this Court;
Thicken this air, and turn your plaguy rage
Into a shape as dismal as his sin;
And with some equal horror tear him off
From sight and memory. Let not such a Court,
To whose fame all the kings of Christendom
Now laid their ears, so crack her royal trump,
As to sound through it, that her vaunted justice
Was got in such an incest. Is it justice
To tempt and witch a man to break the law,
And by that witch condemn him? Let me draw
Poison into me with this cursed air
If he bewitch'd me and transform'd me not;
He bit me by the ear, and made me drink
Enchanted waters; let me see an image
That utter'd these distinct words: *Thou shalt die,
O wicked king;* and if the devil gave him
Such power upon an image, upon me
How might he tyrannize? that by his vows
And oaths so Stygian had my nerves and will
In more awe than his own. What man is he
That is so high but he would higher be?
So roundly sighted, but he may be found
To have a blind side, which by craft pursued,
Confederacy, and simply trusted treason,
May wrest him past his angel and his reason?

 Ch. Witchcraft can never taint an honest mind.

 Ha. True gold will any trial stand untouch'd.

 Po. For colours that will stain when they are
  tried,
The cloth itself is ever cast aside.

 By. Sometimes the very gloss in anything
Will seem a stain; the fault not in the light,

Nor in the guilty object, but our sight.
My gloss, raised from the richness of my stuff,
Had too much splendour for the owly eye
Of politic and thankless royalty ;
I did deserve too much ; a pleurisy
Of that blood in me is the cause I die.
Virtue in great men must be small and slight,
For poor stars rule where she is exquisite.
'Tis tyrannous and impious policy
To put to death by fraud and treachery ;
Sleight is then royal when it makes men live,
And if it urges faults, urgeth to forgive.
He must be guiltless that condemns the guilty.
Like things do nourish like and not destroy them ;
Minds must be found that judge affairs of weight,
And seeing hands, cut corrosives from your sight.
A lord intelligencer ? hangman-like,
Thrust him from human fellowship to the desert,
Blow him with curses ; shall your justice call
Treachery her father ? would you wish her weigh
My valour with the hiss of such a viper ?
What have I done to shun the mortal shame
Of so unjust an opposition ?
My envious stars cannot deny me this,
That I may make my judges witnesses ;
And that my wretched fortunes have reserved
For my last comfort ; ye all know, my lords,
This body, gash'd with five and thirty wounds,
Whose life and death you have in your award,
Holds not a vein that hath not open'd been,
And which I would not open yet again
For you and yours ; this hand that writ the lines
Alleged against me hath enacted still
More good than there it only talk'd of ill.

I must confess my choler hath transferr'd
My tender spleen to all intemperate speech,
But reason ever did my deeds attend.
In worth of praise, and imitation,
Had I borne any will to let them loose,
I could have flesh'd them with bad services
In England lately, and in Switzerland ;
There are a hundred gentlemen by name
Can witness my demeanour in the first,
And in the last ambassage I adjure
No other testimonies than the Seigneurs
De Vic and Sillery, who amply know
In what sort and with what fidelity
I bore myself, to reconcile and knit
In one desire so many wills disjoin'd
And from the King's allegiance quite withdrawn.
My acts ask'd many men, though done by one ;
And I were but one I stood for thousands,
And still I hold my worth, though not my place :
Nor slight me, judges, though I be but one.
One man, in one sole expedition,
Reduced into th'imperial power of Rome,
Armenia, Pontus, and Arabia,
Syria, Albania, and Iberia,
Conquer'd th'Hyrcanians, and to Caucasus
His arm extended ; the Numidians
And Afric to the shores meridional
His power subjected ; and that part of Spain
Which stood from those parts that Sertorius ruled,
Even to the Atlantic sea he conquered.
Th'Albanian kings he from the kingdoms chased,
And at the Caspian sea their dwellings placed ;
Of all the earth's globe, by power and his advice,
The round-eyed ocean saw him victor thrice.

And what shall let [1] me, but your cruel doom,
To add as much to France as he to Rome,
And to leave justice neither sword nor word
To use against my life ; this senate knows
That what with one victorious hand I took
I gave to all your uses with another ;
With this I took and propt the falling kingdom,
And gave it to the King ; I have kept
Your laws of state from fire, and you yourselves
Fix'd in this high tribunal, from whose height
The vengeful Saturnals of the League
Had hurl'd ye headlong ; do ye then return
This retribution ? can the cruel King
The kingdom, laws, and you, all saved by me,
Destroy their saver ? what, ay me ! I did
Adverse to this, this damn'd enchanter did,
That took into his will my motion ;
And being bank-rout both of wealth and worth,
Pursued with quarrels and with suits in law,
Fear'd by the kingdom, threaten'd by the King,
Would raise the loathed dunghill of his ruins
Upon the monumental heap of mine ;
Torn with possessed whirlwinds may he die,
And dogs bark at his murderous memory.

    Ch. My lord, our liberal sufferance of your speech
Hath made it late, and for this session
We will dismiss you ; take him back, my lord.

               [*Exit* VIT. *and* BYRON.

    Ha. You likewise may depart.   [*Exit* LA FIN.

    Ch. What resteth now
To be decreed 'gainst this great prisoner ?
A mighty merit and a monstrous crime
Are here concurrent ; what by witnesses,

          [1] Prevent.

His letters, and instructions we have proved,
Himself confesseth, and excuseth all
With witchcraft and the only act of thought.
For witchcraft, I esteem it a mere strength
Of rage in him, conceived 'gainst his accuser,
Who being examined hath denied it all.
Suppose it true, it made him false ; but wills
And worthy minds witchcraft can never force.
And for his thoughts that brake not into deeds,
Time was the cause, not will ; the mind's free act
In treason still is judged as th'outward fact.
If his deserts have had a wealthy share
In saving of our land from civil furies,
Manlius had so that saved the Capitol ;
Yet for his after traitorous factions
They threw him headlong from the place he saved.
My definite sentence, then, doth this import :
That we must quench the wild-fire with his blood
In which it was so traitorously inflamed ;
Unless with it we seek to incense the land.
The King can have no refuge for his life,
If his be quitted ; this was it that made
Louis th'Eleventh renounce his countrymen,
And call the valiant Scots out of their kingdom
To use their greater virtues and their faiths
Than his own subjects, in his royal guard.
What then conclude your censures ?

    Omnes. He must die.

    Ch. Draw then his sentence formally, and send him ;
And so all treasons in his death attend him. [*Exeunt.*

Enter BYRON, EPERNON, SOISSONS, JANIN, VIDAME,
             D'ESCURES.

    Vid. I joy you had so good a day, my lord.

By. I won it from them all; the Chancellor
I answer'd to his uttermost improvements;
I moved my other judges to lament
My insolent misfortunes, and to loathe
The pocky soul and state-bawd, my accuser.
I made reply to all that could be said
So eloquently, and with such a charm
Of grave enforcements, that methought I sat,
Like Orpheus, casting reins on savage beasts;
At the arm's end, as 'twere, I took my bar
And set it far above the high tribunal,
Where, like a cedar on Mount Lebanon,
I grew, and made my judges show like box-trees;
And box-trees right their wishes would have made
    them,
Whence boxes should have grown, till they had strook
My head into the budget; but, alas!
I held their bloody arms with such strong reasons,
And, by your leave, with such a jerk of wit,
That I fetch'd blood upon the Chancellor's cheeks.
Methinks I see his countenance as he sat,
And the most lawyerly delivery
Of his set speeches; shall I play his part?
    Ep. For heaven's sake, good my lord.
    By. I will, i'faith.
"Behold a wicked man, a man debauch'd;
A man contesting with his King; a man
On whom, my lord, we are not to connive,
Though we may condole; a man
That *Læsa Majestate* sought a lease
Of *plus quam satis.* A man that *vi et armis*
Assail'd the King, and would *per fas et nefas*
Aspire the kingdom;" here was lawyer's learning.
    Ep. He said not this, my lord, that I have heard.

By. This, or the like, I swear. I pen no speeches.

So. Then there is good hope of your wish'd acquittal.

By. Acquittal? they have reason ; were I dead
I know they cannot all supply my place.
Is't possible the King should be so vain
To think he can shake me with fear of death ?
Or make me apprehend that he intends it ?
Thinks he to make his firmest men his clouds ?
The clouds, observing their aërial natures,
Are borne aloft, and then to moisture changed,
Fall to the earth ; where being made thick, and cold,
They lose both all their heat and levity ;
Yet then again recovering heat and lightness,
Again they are advanced : and by the sun
Made fresh and glorious : and since clouds are rapt
With these uncertainties, now up, now down,
Am I to flit so with his smile or frown ?

Ep. I wish your comforts and encouragements
May spring out of your safety ; but I hear
The King hath reason'd so against your life,
And made your most friends yield so to his reasons
That your estate is fearful.

By. Yield t'his reasons ?
Oh, how friends' reasons and their freedoms stretch
When power sets his wide tenters [1] to their sides !
How like a cure, by mere opinion,
It works upon our blood ! like th'ancient gods
Are modern kings, that lived past bounds themselves,
Yet set a measure down to wretched men ;
By many sophisms they made good deceit ;
And, since they pass'd in power, surpass'd in right :
When kings' wills pass, the stars wink, and the sun
Suffers eclipse : rude thunder yields to them

---

[1] Machines for stretching cloth.

His horrid wings : sits smooth as glass engazed ;
And lightning sticks 'twixt heaven and earth amazed :
Men's faiths are shaken, and the pit of truth
O'erflows with darkness, in which Justice sits,
And keeps her vengeance tied to make it fierce ;
And when it comes, th'increased horrors show
Heaven's plague is sure, though full of state, and slow.

             [*Within.*

 Sister. O my dear lord and brother ! O the Duke !

 By. What sounds are these, my lord ? hark, hark,
  methinks
I hear the cries of people.

 Ep. 'Tis for one,
Wounded in fight here at Saint Anthony's gate.

 By. 'Sfoot, one cried the Duke : I pray hearken
Again, or burst yourselves with silence, no :
What countryman's the common headsman here ?

 So. He's a Burgonian.

 By. The great devil he is !
The bitter wizard told me, a Burgonian
Should be my headsman ; strange concurrences :
'Sdeath ! who's here ?

  Enter four Ushers, *bare ;* CHANCELLOR, HARLEY,
   POTIER, FLEURY, VITRY, PRÁLIN, *with others.*

Oh, then I am but dead,
Now, now ye come all to pronounce my sentence.
I am condemn'd unjustly : tell my kinsfolks
I die an innocent : if any friend
Pity the ruin of the State's sustainer,
Proclaim my innocence ; ah, Lord Chancellor,
Is there no pardon ? will there come no mercy ?
Ay, put your hat on, and let me stand bare.
Show yourself a right lawyer.

Ch. I am bare :
What would you have me do?

By. You have not done
Like a good Justice, and one that knew
He sat upon the precious blood of virtue ;
Y'ave pleased the cruel King, and have not borne
As great regard to save as to condemn ;
You have condemn'd me, my Lord Chancellor,
But God acquits me. He will open lay
All your close treasons against him, to colour
Treasons laid to his truest images ;
And you, my lord, shall answer this injustice,
Before his judgment-seat : to which I summon
In one year and a day your hot appearance.
I go before, by men's corrupted dooms,
But they that caused my death shall after come
By the immaculate justice of the Highest.

Ch. Well, good my lord, commend your soul to him
And to his mercy ; think of that, I pray.

By. Sir, I have thought of it, and every hour
Since my affliction, ask'd on naked knees
Patience to bear your unbelieved injustice :
But you, nor none of you, have thought of him
In my eviction : y'are come to your benches
With plotted judgments ; your link'd ears so loud
Sing with prejudicate winds, that nought is heard
Of all poor prisoners urge 'gainst your award.

Ha. Passion, my lord, transports your bitterness
Beyond all colour and your proper judgment ;
No man hath known your merits more than I,
And would to God your great misdeeds had been
As much undone as they have been conceal'd ;
The cries of them for justice, in desert,
Have been so loud and piercing that they deafen'd

2G

The ears of mercy ; and have labour'd more
Your judges to compress than to enforce them.

   Po. We bring you here your sentence ; will you read
      it ?

   By. For heaven's sake, shame to use me with such
      rigour ;

I know what it imports, and will not have
Mine ear blown into flames with hearing it.
Have you been one of them that have condemn'd me ?

   Fl. My lord, I am your orator : God comfort you !

   By. Good sir, my father loved you so entirely
That if you have been one, my soul forgives you.
It is the King (most childish that he is,
That takes what he hath given) that injures me :
He gave grace in the first draught of my fault,
And now restrains it : grace again I ask ;
Let him again vouchsafe it. Send to him,
A post will soon return : the Queen of England
Told me that if the wilful Earl of Essex
Had used submission, and but ask'd her mercy,
She would have given it, past resumption.
She, like a gracious princess, did desire
To pardon him : even as she pray'd to God,
He would let down a pardon unto her ;
He yet was guilty, I am innocent :
He still refused grace, I importune it.

   Ch. This ask'd in time, my lord, while he besought it,
And ere he had made his severity known,
Had, with much joy to him, I know been granted.

   By. No, no, his bounty then was misery,
To offer when he knew 'twould be refused ;
He treads the vulgar path of all advantage,
And loves men for their vices, not for their virtues.
My service would have quicken'd gratitude

In his own death, had he been truly royal ;
It would have stirr'd the image of a king
Into perpetual motion ; to have stood
Near the conspiracy restrain'd at Mantes ;
And in a danger, that had then the wolf
To fly upon his bosom, had I only held
Intelligence with the conspirators,
Who stuck at no check but my loyalty,
Nor kept life in their hopes but in my death.
The siege of Amiens would have soften'd rocks,
Where cover'd all in showers of shot and fire,
I seem'd to all men's eyes a fighting flame
With bullets cut, in fashion of a man ;
A sacrifice to valour, impious king !
Which he will needs extinguish with my blood.
Let him beware : justice will fall from heaven.
In the same form I served in that siege,
And by the light of that, he shall discern
What good my ill hath brought him ; it will nothing
Assure his state : the same quench he hath cast
Upon my life, shall quite put out his fame.
This day he loseth what he shall not find
By all days he survives ; so good a servant,
Nor Spain so great a foe ; with whom, alas !
Because I treated, am I put to death ?
'Tis but a politic glose [1] ; my courage raised me,
For the dear price of five and thirty scars,
And that hath ruin'd me, I thank my stars :
Come, I'll go where ye will, ye shall not lead me.

   Ch. I fear his frenzy ; never saw I man
Of such a spirit so amazed at death.

   Ha. He alters every minute : what a vapour
The strongest mind is to a storm of crosses.   [*Exeunt.*

                [1] Pretence.

Manet EPERNON, SOISSONS, JANIN, VIDAME,
               D'ESCURES.

Ep. Oh of what contraries consists a man !
Of what impossible mixtures ! vice and virtue,
Corruption, and eternnesse, at one time,
And in one subject, let together, loose !
We have not any strength but weakens us,
No greatness but doth crush us into air.
Our knowledges do light us but to err,
Our ornaments are burthens : our delights
Are our tormentors ; fiends that, raised in fears,
At parting shake our roofs about our ears.

So. O Virtue, thou art now far worse than Fortune :
Her gifts stuck by the Duke when thine are vanish'd ;
Thou bravest thy friend in need : necessity,
That used to keep thy wealth, contempt, thy love,
Have both abandon'd thee in his extremes ;
Thy powers are shadows, and thy comfort, dreams.

Vid. O real Goodness, if thou be a power,
And not a word alone, in humane uses,
Appear out of this angry conflagration,
Where this great captain, thy late temple, burns,
And turn his vicious fury to thy flame :
From all earth's hopes mere gilded with thy fame :
Let piety enter with her willing cross,
And take him on it ; ope his breast and arms,
To all the storms necessity can breathe,
And burst them all with his embraced death.

Ja. Yet are the civil tumults of his spirits
Hot and outrageous : not resolved, alas !
(Being but one man) render the kingdom's doom ;
He doubts, storms, threatens, rues, complains, im-
     plores ;

Grief hath brought all his forces to his looks,
And nought is left to strengthen him within,
Nor lasts one habit of those grieved aspects ;
Blood expels paleness, paleness blood doth chase,
And sorrow errs [1] through all forms in his face.

D'E. So furious is he, that the politic law
Is much to seek, how to enact her sentence :
Authority back'd with arms, though he unarm'd,
Abhors his fury, and with doubtful eyes
Views on what ground it should sustain his ruins,
And as a savage boar that (hunted long,
Assail'd and set up) with his only eyes
Swimming in fire, keeps off the baying hounds,
Though sunk himself, yet holds his anger up,
And snows it forth in foam ; holds firm his stand,
Of battalous [2] bristles ; feeds his hate to die,
And whets his tusks with wrathful majesty :
So fares the furious Duke, and with his looks
Doth teach death horrors ; makes the hangman learn
New habits for his bloody impudence,
Which now habitual horror from him drives,
Who for his life shuns death, by which he lives.

Enter CHANCELLOR, HARLEY, POTIER, FLEURY,
VITRY, PRÂLIN.

Vi. Will not your lordship have the Duke dis-
tinguish'd
From other prisoners ? where the order is
To give up men condemn'd into the hands
Of th'executioner ; he would be the death
Of him that he should die by, ere he suffer'd
Such an abjection.

[1] Wanders.   [2] Angry.

Ch. But to bind his hands,
I hold it passing needful.

Ha. 'Tis my lord,
And very dangerous to bring him loose.

Pr. You will in all despair and fury plunge him,
If you but offer it.

Po. My lord, by this
The prisoner's spirit is something pacified,
And 'tis a fear that th'offer of those bands
Would breed fresh furies in him, and disturb
The entry of his soul into her peace.

Ch. I would not that for any possible danger,
That can be wrought by his unarmed hands ;
And therefore in his own form bring him in.

Enter BYRON, *a Bishop or two, with all the* Guards ;
Soldiers *with muskets.*

By. Where shall this weight fall? on what region
Must this declining prominent pour his load?
I'll break my blood's high billows 'gainst my stars.
Before this hill be shook into a flat,
All France shall feel an earthquake; with what
    murmur,
This world shrinks into chaos!

Archbishop. Good my lord,
Forego it willingly ; and now resign
Your sensual powers entirely to your soul.

By. Horror of death, let me alone in peace,
And leave my soul to me, whom it concerns ;
You have no charge of it ; I feel her free :
How she doth rouse, and like a falcon stretch
Her silver wings ; as threatening death with death ;
At whom I joyfully will cast her off.
I know this body but a sink of folly,

The ground-work and raised frame of woe and frailty;
The bond and bundle of corruption;
A quick corse, only sensible of grief,
A walking sepulchre, or household thief:
A glass of air, broken with less than breath,
A slave bound face to face to death, till death.
And what said all you more? I know, besides,
That life is but a dark and stormy night
Of senseless dreams, terrors, and broken sleeps:
A tyranny, devising pains to plague
And make man long in dying, racks his death;
And death is nothing; what can you say more?
I bring a long globe and a little earth,
Am seated like earth, betwixt both the heavens,
That if I rise, to heaven I rise; if fall,
I likewise fall to heaven; what stronger faith
Hath any of your souls? what say you more?
Why lose I time in these things? Talk of knowledge,
It serves for inward use. I will not die
Like to a clergyman; but like the captain
That pray'd on horseback, and with sword in hand,
Threaten'd the sun, commanding it to stand;
These are but ropes of sand.

    Ch. Desire you then
To speak with any man?

    By. I would speak with La Force and Saint Blancart.
Do they fly me?
Where is Prevost, controller of my house?

    Pr. Gone to his house i'th' country three days since.

    By. He should have stay'd here, he keeps all my
      blanks.[1]

Oh, all the world forsakes me! wretched world,
Consisting most of parts that fly each other;

                [1] Papers.

A firmness, breeding all inconstancy,
A bond of all disjunction ; like a man
Long buried, is a man that long hath lived ;
Touch him, he falls to ashes ; for one fault,
I forfeit all the fashion of a man ;
Why should I keep my soul in this dark light,
Whose black beams lighted me to lose my self ?
When I have lost my arms, my fame, my wind,
Friends, brother, hopes, fortunes, and even my fury ?
O happy were the man could live alone,
To know no man, nor be of any known !

Ha. My lord, it is the manner once again
To read the sentence.

By. Yet more sentences ?
How often will you make me suffer death,
As ye were proud to hear your powerful dooms ?
I know and feel you were the men that gave it,
And die most cruelly to hear so often
My crimes and bitter condemnation urged.
Suffice it I am brought here, and obey,
And that all here are privy to the crimes.

Ch. It must be read, my lord, no remedy.

By. Read, if it must be, then, and I must talk.

Ha. The process being extraordinarily made and
examined by the Court, and chambers assembled——

By. Condemn'd for depositions of a witch ?
The common deposition, and her whore
To all whorish perjuries and treacheries.
Sure he call'd up the devil in my spirits,
And made him to usurp my faculties :
Shall I be cast away now he's cast out ?
What justice is in this ? dear countrymen,
Take this true evidence, betwixt heaven and you,
And quit me in your hearts.

Ch. Go on.

Ha. Against Charles Gontaut of Byron, Knight of both the Orders, Duke of Byron, Peer and Marshal of France, Governor of Burgundy, accused of treason, in a sentence was given the twenty-second of this month, condemning the said Duke of Byron of high treason, for his direct conspiracies against the King's person, enterprises against his state——

By. That is most false; let me for ever be
Deprived of heaven, as I shall be of earth,
If it be true; know, worthy countrymen,
These two and twenty months I have been clear
Of all attempts against the king and state.

Ha. Treaties and treacheries with his enemies, being Marshal of the King's army, for reparation of which crimes they deprived him of all his estates, honours, and dignities, and condemned him to lose his head upon a scaffold at the Greave.[1]

By. The Greave? had that place stood for my dispatch
I had not yielded; all your forces should not
Stir me one foot; wild horses should have drawn
My body piecemeal ere you all had brought me.

Ha. Declaring all his goods, moveable and immoveable, whatsoever, to be confiscate to the King; the Seigneury of Byron to lose the title of Duchy and Peer for ever.

By. Now is your form contented?

Ch. Ay, my lord,
And I must now entreat you to deliver
Your order up; the King demands it of you.

By. And I restore it, with my vow of safety
In that world where both he and I are one,

[1] Public place of execution; *la place de Grève.*

I never brake the oath I took to take it.   •

Ch. Well, now, my lord, we'll take our latest leaves,
Beseeching heaven to take as clear from you
All sense of torment in your willing death,
All love and thought of what you must leave here
As when you shall aspire heaven's highest sphere.

By. Thanks to your lordship, and let me pray too
That you will hold good censure of my life
By the clear witness of my soul in death
That I have never pass'd act 'gainst the King,
Which, if my faith had let me undertake,
They had been three years since amongst the dead.

Ha. Your soul shall find his safety in her own.
Call the executioner.

By. Good sir, I pray
Go after and beseech the Chancellor
That he will let my body be interr'd
Amongst my predecessors at Byron.

D'E. I go, my lord.   [*Exit.*

By. Go, go! can all go thus,
And no man come with comfort? Farewell, world!
He is at no end of his actions blest
Whose ends will make him greatest, and not best;
They tread no ground, but ride in air on storms
That follow state, and hunt their empty forms;
Who see not that the valleys of the world
Make even right with mountains, that they grow
Green and lie warmer, and ever peaceful are,
When clouds spit fire at hills and burn them bare;
Not valleys' part, but we should imitate streams,
That run below the valleys and do yield
To every molehill; every bank embrace
That checks their currents; and when torrents come,
That swell and raise them past their natural height,

How mad they are, and troubled ; like low streams
With torrents crown'd, are men with diadems.

    Vi. My lord, 'tis late ; will't please you to go up ?

    By. Up ? 'tis a fair preferment—ha, ha, ha !
There should go shouts to upshots ; not a breath
Of any mercy, yet ? Come, since we must ;
Who's this ?   [*The* HANGMAN *enters.*

    Pr. The executioner, my lord.

    By. Death ! slave, down ! or by the blood that moves
      me
I'll pluck thy throat out; go, I'll call you straight,
Hold, boy ; and this—

    Hang. Soft, boy, I'll bar you that.   [*Blindfolds him.*

    By. Take this then, yet, I pray thee, that again
I do not joy in sight of such a pageant
As presents death ; though this life have a curse,
'Tis better than another that is worse.

    Arch. My lord, now you are blind to this world's
      sight,
Look upward to a world of endless light.

    By. Ay, ay, you talk of upward still to others,
And downwards look, with headlong eyes, yourselves.
Now come you up, sir ; but not touch me yet ;
Where shall I be now ?

    Hang. Here, my lord.

    By. Where's that ?

    Hang. There, there, my lord.

    By. And where, slave, is that there ?
Thou seest I see not ? yet I speak as I saw ;
Well, now, is't fit ?

    Hang. Kneel, I beseech your grace,
That I may do mine office with most order.

    By. Do it, and if at one blow thou art short,
Give one and thirty, I'll endure them all.

Hold ; stay a little. Comes there yet no mercy ?
High heaven curse these exemplary proceedings ;
When justice fails, they sacrifice our example.

Hang. Let me beseech you I may cut your hair.

By. Out, ugly image of my cruel justice !
Yet wilt thou be before me ? stay my will,
Or by the will of heaven I'll strangle thee.

Vi. My lord, you make too much of this your body,
Which is no more your own.

By. Nor is it yours ;
I'll take my death with all the horrid rites
And representments of the dread it merits ;
Let tame nobility and numbed fools
That apprehend not what they undergo,
Be such exemplary and formal sheep ;
I will not have him touch me till I will ;
If you will needs rack me beyond my reason,
Hell take me but I'll strangle half that's here,
And force the rest to kill me. I'll leap down
If but once more they tempt me to despair ;
You wish my quiet, yet give cause of fury :
Think you to set rude winds upon the sea,
Yet keep it calm ? or cast me in a sleep
With shaking of my chains about mine ears ?
O honest soldiers, you have seen me free
From any care of many thousand deaths ;
Yet of this one the manner doth amaze me.
View, view this wounded bosom, how much bound
Should that man make me that would shoot it through.
Is it not pity I should lose my life
By such a bloody and infamous stroke ?

Soldier. Now by thy spirit, and thy better angel,
If thou wert clear, the continent of France
Would shrink beneath the burden of thy death

Ere it would bear it.

   Vi. Who's that?

   Sol. I say well,

And clear your justice, here is no ground shrinks;

If he were clear it would; and I say more,

Clear, or not clear, if he with all his foulness,

Stood here in one scale, and the King's chief minion

Stood in another, here, put here a pardon,

Here lay a royal gift, this, this in merit,

Should hoise the other minion into air.

   Vi. Hence with that frantic.

   By. This is some poor witness

That my desert might have outweigh'd my forfeit:

But danger haunts desert when he is greatest;

His hearty ills are proved out of his glances,

And kings' suspicions needs no balances;

So here's a most decretal end of me:

Which I desire, in me may end my wrongs.

Commend my love, I charge you, to my brothers,

And by my love and misery command them

To keep their faiths that bind them to the King,

And prove no stomachers of my misfortunes;

Nor come to Court till time hath eaten out

The blots and scars of my opprobrious death.

And tell the Earl, my dear friend of D'Auvergne,

That my death utterly were free from grief

But for the sad loss of his worthy friendship;

And if I had been made for longer life

I would have more deserved him in my service;

Beseeching him to know I have not used

One word in my arraignment that might touch him,

Had I no other want than so ill meaning.

And so farewell for ever. Never more

Shall any hope of my revival see me.

Such is the endless exile of dead men.
Summer succeeds the spring; autumn the summer;
The frosts of winter, the fall'n leaves of autumn:
All these, and all fruits in them yearly fade,
And every year return: but cursed man
Shall never more renew his vanish'd face.
Fall on your knees then, statists,[1] ere ye fall,
That you may rise again: knees bent too late,
Stick you in earth like statues: see in me
How you are pour'd down from your clearest heavens;
Fall lower yet, mix'd with th'unmoved centre,
That your own shadows may no longer mock ye.
Strike, strike, O strike; fly, fly, commanding soul,
And on thy wings for this thy body's breath,
Bear the eternal victory of death.

[1] Statesmen.

EDINBURGH
COLSTON AND COY LIMITED
PRINTERS